CONTEMPORARY LATIN AMERICAN CLASSICS

J. Cary Davis, *General Editor*

TWO PLAYS

Crown of Light

One of These Days . . .

RODOLFO USIGLI

Translated by Thomas Bledsoe
Introduction by Willis Knapp Jones
Foreword by J. Cary Davis

Southern Illinois University Press   *Carbondale and Edwardsville*
Feffer & Simons, Inc., *London and Amsterdam*

CONTENTS

Foreword   J. CARY DAVIS

Suave patria: te amo no cual mito, sino por
tu verdad de pan bendito . . .
—Ramón López Velarde, *La Suave Patria*

When I first read these two plays by Rodolfo Usigli, in the
excellent translations by Mr. Thomas Bledsoe, I was immediately struck not by how different they are in time and
space, but by how similar they are in theme and spirit—the
Making of a Nation, and how both bring out the essential
spirit of the Mexican people at widely separated points in
history. In both we have groups of men, who have it in
their power to shape and mold events about them: in
Crown of Light the Emperor Charles V, scheming to trick
the conquered Indians of Mexico into loyalty and obedi-
ence to the Crown through a fake miracle, and in *One of
These Days*, the politicians and "king makers" whose plans
to rule Indoland with a puppet president backfire. In the
one, we are led inevitably to believe in the occurrence of a
true miracle, in the other we see the puppet, Mr. Nobody,
transformed almost overnight into a masterful statesman
who dares to defy the Colossus of the North (Demoland,
or the USA) and sets his country on the road of inde-
pendent progress. In the first, the miracle welds the Mexican people into one nation, and in the second the heroic
"little man" dies at the height of his achievement, leaving
his backers and associates again facing the problem of a
successor. In either case, one is sorely tempted to repeat

Robert Burns's oft-quoted aphorism, "The best laid plans
o' mice an' men gang aft a-gley."

In *Crown of Light*, Usigli departs from tradition in having not one Juan Diego who meets the Virgin on successive days, but a series of Juans, each bringing his private
testimony of the celestial visitation. The audience never
sees the mad nun who was to have impersonated the Virgin, but is introduced to all the key figures among the
friars and missionaries in Mexico at this time. In *One of
These Days*, the playwright conveys the impression of a
foreign tongue by the device of reversing the spelling of all
the words used by the ambassador from Demoland. It
would be interesting to hear how this is handled in an
actual stage presentation.

Ambassador Usigli would be the first to disclaim for
himself any intensely religious quality, yet the reader cannot
fail to sense the deep moral tone that runs through both
plays, from the conscientious Bishop Zumárraga of the first
play to José Gómez Urbina, the patriotic Mr. Nobody of
the second.

For an insight into the dramatist's purposes and personal philosophy in general, one can do no better than to
quote herewith a letter to this editor, from Oslo dated May
21, 1969, which can serve as the author's preface.

Dear Professor Davis,

You are entirely right and there are indeed a contrast *and*
a tie between *Crown of Shadows* and *One of These Days* . . .
even though they are neither intimate enemies nor inimical
brothers.

Two of the master lines in my dramatic production are the
historical and the political, which I have dubbed *impolítica* and
antihistórica. This is not just a juvenile obeisance to the literary majesty of paradox. Impolitic because, while dealing
strictly with political material, I take a non-, or anti-, political
standing. The Spanish adjective not only means rash or im-
prudent but is also the equivalent of impolite, and I have
always upheld the theory that drama, and the theatre at large,

if it is an art, is an art in shirt-sleeves. Antihistorical not because of an arrogant, impetuous pretension of changing the
occurrence of the historical events or the events themselves, but
out of an aim of interpreting them from a different angle, of
refocusing them more in harmony with my own time or with
the future, or simply with my temperament than the approach
of professional historians. And here we have a first reference of
kinship: where Crown of Light is an antihistorical comedy,
One of These Days . . . is a phantasy impolitic.

In the latter line I have written a certain number of plays:
Tres comedias impolíticas (the ovum of the general approach),
La última puerta, El gesticulador, Los fugitivos, Un día de
éstos . . . and, quite recently, El gran circo del mundo, concerned with the nuclear crossroads of our day, in all of which
the treatment is not only impolitic and disrespectful and bad-
mannered, but also fights the political trend toward making
myths out of ordinary happenings by turning them into works
Ad Majorem Politicam Gloriam.

Crown of Light is part of a trilogy, with Crown of Shadows
and Crown of Fire—a trilogy devoted to what I consider the
three fundamental Mexican Myths—inditing the word myth in
its loftiest connotation of supernaturalness, superiority, or
superreality as contrasted with the political micro- or mini-
myths begotten by assembly line, by political mythomania. (I
have come to believe that politicians, everywhere in the world,
are under the impression that they can exist only by becoming
myths.) The myths I advocate and revere are those of political
sovereignty (Crown of Shadows: Juárez vs. Maximilian); territorial or national sovereignty (Crown of Fire: Cuauhtémoc vs.
Cortez), and spiritual sovereignty (Crown of Light: the synthe-
sis of paganism and Catholicism).

Here we face again a contrast, which is also a tie, between
the two plays included in this volume. The awesome, everlasting myths and the day-to-day mythomania which I consider
stupid, destructive, and ludicrous.

About One of These Days . . . I think it pertinent to
transcribe here the opinion of Elmer Rice in a letter dated
October 23, 1964.

"*Dear Mr. U:*

I read your play with great interest. It is well conceived and well written and I enjoyed the sly political and philosophical commentary.

Whether or not a play of this sort would be accepted by an American Audience, I cannot predict. There is a theory among Broadway professionals that political plays, satirical plays, and plays without romantic interest are "poison at the box-office." When you roll all three in one, you really pose a problem. But before the play is even put to the test of audience approval, some bold manager must be able to convince his backers to gamble a minimum of $100,000 on the production. In today's theatre, that is not a simple matter.

May I mention something that troubles me a little? While I am aware that your play was written some years ago, it happens that the theme of presidential assassination is, at the moment, a very sensitive one—particularly when the treatment is semisatirical. I may be entirely wrong about this, and in any case I hope you'll understand that no criticism of your play or your intention is meant."

I have of course the greatest admiration for Mr. Rice's personality and works—and "minority"—but I must point out that *One of These Days* . . . is really a love story, a romance between the haphazard President Gómez Urbina (*presidente por arte de birlibirloque,* as they say in Spain) and his underdeveloped but fascinating Indoland. And, on the other hand, I feel certain that there is no satirical element implied in the death of my President proper.

There is an old literary game, invented, I think, by the old Parisian magazine *Les Annales Littéraires:* Which are the so-many books that you would like to have on a deserted island? We have never been more conscious of living in an anguishing wilderness or deserted island than today, under the infernal cramming of overpopulation and the more hellish remedy of decimating it by wars to survive. Since we must live in loneliness—in what I have come to call "oslitude" in Norway, which

are the myths that we would take to our deserted island, to our
final castle? Certainly not the petty ones elaborated around the
chiefs of state, or governors, or senators but those that are
likely to nurture us and our hope in humanity and help us to
nurture our children. I am not trying, however, to put forward
a thesis. I don't believe in theses. Not one of my plays, antihistorical, impolitic or of any other description has started
from a thesis. It is my considered and profound conviction
that all the great literary works are apt to have a hind-thesis: a
look at *Don Quixote, Oedipus,* and *Hamlet* is enough to prove
it. But every book or play emanating from a previous thesis has
only an artificial life, and, happily, a short duration. The literary or artistic creation must be a work of love to fully exist.
It is the dialogue between Pygmalion and Galatea. The rest,
thesis, narcissism as in Dali, defense of fleeting political doc-
trines, or ambitions, imperialism, colonialism, overnationalism,
or even Marxism or religious creeds, like a good deal of pop
and op art, is only masturbation.

It has often been told about *Un día de éstos* . . . that it
anticipated the Cuban events by several years. All I can say is
that when I wrote it I did not bear in mind any country other
than Indoland. What I believe I can affirm is that it is one of
the first plays, if not the first, written about the right to
sovereignty and self-determination that belongs to all peoples
and that has become a matter of general concern in our time.
It was written in 1955 and certain real events seem to have
vouched for its validity in later years: the Cuban *status quo* and
the assassination of President John F. Kennedy, which shook
the world and grieved me deeply personally. But I cannot be
held responsible for the imitation of art by nature.

A great friend of mine, most unfortunately departed from
our world, José María González de Mendoza . . . used to amuse
himself by prophesying that I would inevitably become a member of the Mexican Academy of the Language, which I haven't
and won't, and that I was doomed to be burnt at the stake in
the main square of Mexico City for having written *Crown of
Light.* So far—and I touch wood and keep my fingers crossed—

I have not had to call the firemen. In my lifelong struggle to demolish taboos and to recapture and project certain basic elements of faith, I have always thought that if my plays do not serve their purpose they can just as well be burnt. But also if they have served it.

It is indeed a privilege to see these two plays included in your most important collection, and I take advantage of this opportunity to thank through you the Southern Illinois University and its Press.

Cordially yours,
Rodolfo Usigli

In an interview in Mexico City on July 9, 1970, which appeared the following day in the newspaper *Excelsior*, Ambassador Usigli maintained that the Mexican theatre of today suffers from a cultural colonialism. According to him, the younger dramatists flee from form, just as men and women avoid, or try to avoid, reality. They imitate Europeans and flee from Mexico, at a time when Mexican literature is becoming more and more appreciated in Europe. This he attributes to word tension today.

Usigli continues, saying "I believe that each writer who does his job [well] devotes himself [completely] to his country. Although no writer is free from politics, I feel that the first position of the writer is not to have any political party." Thus, in spite of shortening distances, and the development of better communications, the world—for Mexicans—is Mexico, and by focusing on Mexico's problems, these become universal. With few exceptions (he says), America has no classics in the theatre.

The playwright concludes: "For me the theatre is the living voice of the peoples, and the people that have no theatre have not truth . . . I try to present [in my plays] *persons*, because it seems to me that the Human Being is the fundamental element of the theatre." He insists that his plays are not poetic—he does not write hymns, nor poems patriotic or antipatriotic—he simply tells, or confesses, what he feels.

Certainly the two plays in this volume are essentially Mexican, in heart and soul; and yet they strike a chord that rings with universal appeal. The author's own feelings are also very evident. No one could accuse him of anti-patriotism—quite the contrary. As for whether or not he is a poet, let the reader decide.

THOMAS BLEDSOE was born in Abilene, Texas, June 22, 1907, but part of his childhood was spent in Guatemala, Central America, and the following early years in New Orleans. Later, he worked as a writer in New York and the Southwest where he was rewrite editor of *New Mexico, a Guide to the Colorful State*, New Mexico Federal Writers' Project (Hastings House, New York, 1940), to which he also contributed original essays.

As a professor of English, he has taught for more than twelve years in Mexico, Colombia, South America, and Spain. He has also lectured on literature and history at various universities and institutes in the United States, Latin America, and Europe.

His writings abroad have been widely acclaimed, having been published in Argentina, Colombia, Mexico, Spain, Italy, Greece, and Germany. Among them are: 1] *Lluvia y fuego: leyenda de nuestro tiempo* (Ediciones Cuadernos Americanos, Mexico, D.F., 1952) and 2] *The Story of Two Heroic Monasteries—Arkadi and Préveli—Crete* (House of the Double Axe, Athens, 1966). His latest book is the trilingual anthology *Poems in Praise of Fray Junípero Serra and the Missions He Founded in California*, in Catalan, Spanish, and English (Imprenta Mossèn Alcover, Palma de Mallorca, Baleares, 1969).

In addition to the two plays included in this volume, Thomas Bledsoe has translated Usigli's latest play *El gran circo del mundo* (*Magnus Circus Mundi*). He is now living in southern Spain where he is writing and also teaching Spanish and English.

WILLIS KNAPP JONES, who kindly consented to do the biographical and critical Introduction for this volume, is Professor Emeritus of Miami University, Oxford, Ohio, and twice Visiting Professor of Spanish at Southern Illinois University (1968, 1969). He is an internationally known authority on the Latin American Theater, and two of his many publications, *Manuela* (an English translation of Demetrio Aguilera Malta's *La caballeresa del sol*) and *Men and Angels* (Three Spanish American Plays in English), are part of this series of Contemporary Latin American Classics.

Carbondale, Illinois
February 1971

Introduction   WILLIS KNAPP JONES

In the early twentieth century, the only Spanish American dramatist whose name became known beyond the frontiers of his country was the Uruguayan Florencio Sánchez who flourished between 1902 and 1910. Then he died, leaving no disciples and having established neither school nor movement.

Since then, however, so many playwrights have been exercising their craft south of the Río Grande that it is becoming difficult to decide on the outstanding ones. But up to now, three of them seem most likely to earn a permanent place: Samuel Eichelbaum (1894–) of Argentina, René Marqués (1919–) of Puerto Rico, and Rodolfo Usigli (1905–) of Mexico.

In 1968 the Latin American Institute of Southern Illinois University held a Spring Drama Festival devoted to Usigli. Visiting specialists discussed his plays, their psychological background, and their production, and five enthusiastic audiences witnessed productions of his *Crown of Shadows* in translation.

Rodolfo Usigli was born in Mexico City in 1905. He once sent me a note of protest when I mistakenly put down his birth a year earlier. "When people reach my age," he wrote, "they can't afford to lose a year."

Early in life this product of Italian, Austrian, and Polish ancestry revealed his interest in the theatre. At the age of eleven he was earning fifty centavos a performance as an extra in the Castillo-Taboada troupe at Mexico's Teatro Colón.

There were no schools of drama in Mexico in those days, but ambitious to learn all he could about the stage, the youth set up his own course of study. He assigned himself the daily task of reading and analyzing half a dozen plays by well-known dramatists. Then, in the phrase of Stevenson, he "played the sedulous ape" and tried to imitate them. He also attended local performances which he checked against the drama he had studied, setting down his evaluations in essays that Mexican newspapers were glad to publish. So by the age of twenty he had become a respected theatre critic. The reviews, collected into *México en el teatro* (1932) and "Caminos del teatro en México," used as preface for Francisco Monterde's 1933 *Bibliography of the Mexican Drama*, gave him added theatrical stature.

Usigli had already tried his hand at original plays, but with no success in finding producers for them. His first comedy *El apóstol* (The Apostle, 1931) found no takers, not because he was trying to introduce psychiatry to the Mexican stage, but because the earthquake in act 2 presented problems for any stage crew. His second effort *4 Chemins 4* (Four Roads) had no appeal in a Spanish-speaking nation. Only one of his first eight plays which he now calls *Teatro a Tientas* (Fumbling Theatre) found a producer. That was *Estado de secreto* (Secret State, 1935) performed by a provincial experimental group in Guadalajara.

Perhaps the coolness of possible theatrical managers to his other plays was due to the dramatist's rambunctious—some have even said "cantankerous"—qualities. As a knowledgeable psychologist, Usigli may now be able to blame that characteristic on his unhappy boyhood. He had been born with eyes slightly crossed, a person the Spanish call "bizco." His teasing schoolmates punned on the word, and nicknamed him "Visconde" (Viscount), which also hinted at his conviction of his own superiority over most of them.

His eyes were later remedied by surgery, but his need to
defend himself against persecution by his playmates could
by then have produced that self-assertiveness that later involved him in difficulties with managers and critics.

However, Usigli was contributing in other ways to the
encouragement of his nation's drama. In answer to a question from the publisher of this present volume, Usigli has
listed his many associations with the world of the theatre.
He was professor of the History of the Mexican Theatre at
the National University Summer School in 1932, and director of the Radiophonic Theatre, 1932–34, that broadcast
plays under the Ministry of Education. He was associated
with the Orientación Theatre that came into being in 1932
to acquaint Mexico with "works characteristic of the universal theatre of every period," by performing translated
plays from German, French, Russian, Italian, and English
dramatists, and toward the end of its existence, before it
was smothered by the movies, Usigli was one of those
preparing Spanish versions for its stage.

Usigli's efforts toward the development of a Mexican
national theatre were recognized in 1935 by the award to
him of a scholarship to Professor Baker's Drama Work-
shop at Yale University. Another budding Mexican playwright, Xavier Villaurrutia (1903–50), a translator for
Orientación, was also invited to attend.

Besides gaining a better knowledge of stagecraft, Usigli
here completed at a sitting the final act of his play *El niño
y la niebla* (The Child and the Mist), based on a situation
told him by a girl he met in New Haven. His roommate
Villaurrutia wrote about keeping their cleaning woman out
of the dormitory till Usigli got up from his desk with the
completed act. Not until 1936 did he complete the first
two acts of this psychological drama. Then for fifteen years
it was turned down by one director after another in Mexico
before, finally accepted, it broke records with a run of 450
performances and won for its author the title of outstanding dramatist of the 1951 season.

This theatrical play involves a neurotic woman with a lover, trying to condition her son, a somnambulist, to kill his father while unconscious. The overwrought adolescent shoots himself instead, leaving his mother bound to her husband and unwilling to flee with her lover for fear of producing more abnormal children.

Of more importance, indeed one of his greatest plays, was another product of Usigli's studies at Yale—*El gesticulador, a Play for Demagogues*, completed in 1938. Its title might be translated as "The Blowhard" or "The Pretender." It is the story of a university professor, César Rubio, who took on the identity of a Mexican general of the same name. Realizing he had been a lifelong failure, and afraid of his example on his children, Rubio neither affirmed nor denied the belief of a historian from the United States that he was the revolutionary leader whose fate had been a mystery. He used his acquired identity to run for provincial governor then died a martyr but famous, preferring death to the revelation of his pretense. The author dedicated the tragedy to his "hypocritical fellow countrymen."

The production of this masterpiece was delayed for ten years by influential people who declared it an insult to the whole Mexican nation in its implication that they were fourflushers. Just as good a case can be made, however, using this play and others, that Usigli so loved his country that he tried to chide his countrymen out of their weaknesses as Greek dramatists attacked the vices of Athenians in hopes of correcting them.

Later after returning to Mexico from Yale, Usigli was appointed director of the National University's School of Drama and for the next two years theatre director of its Department of Fine Arts. In 1940, he founded his little theatre, The Medianoche, for the production of Mexican plays, but it was short-lived.

He had already seen a production in 1937 of his *Medio tono* (Middle Class) the first naturalistic play in Mexico since *La venganza de la gleba* (The Vengeance of the Furrows) by Federico Gamboa (1864–1939), a realistic rural drama performed in 1910. Usigli's three act tragedy was the first original play by him to be presented. An epilogue declared that the only solution for the ills of Mexico's theatres lies in realism. Not the mediocrity of the middle class, but the mediocrity and misery of Mexico's realistic theatre drove him to write it. Its author later disavowed any great interest in this sort of play.

It was followed in 1938 by *Otra primavera* (Another Springtime), about an old man considered insane. Despite the breakup of the family through its loss of property, the wife struggles to get her children settled in life, then she pretends to be insane and shuts herself up with her husband, determined to cure him or become insane herself. At all events, the couple will share life together till Spring comes again. The author reports that an English translation of it won second place in the 1959 UNESCO competition for translations. Since *Another Springtime* ruffled no one's feelings, it got an immediate production.

His next play, *La mujer no hace milagros* (Woman Accomplishes No Miracles, 1938) continues his saga of the middle class, though its Rosas family had a higher financial status than the Sierras of *Medio tono*. However, critics accused the dramatist of caricaturing some of his enemies in it. His answer in 1939 was the one act *La crítica de "La mujer no hace milagros,"* declaring that his only purpose was to serve the one enemy he recognized, the theatre. However, among the characters in the short skit were six critics, trying to understand and evaluate the play, and the public had no trouble in recognizing them. Usigli's move so enraged the critics that when he founded his Medianoche Theatre the next year, they put it out of business in six months.

A third play about the middle class, *La familia cena en casa* (The Family Dines at Home, pub. 1952) followed in 1942. With a sort of Pygmalion theme, the dramatist shows changes in the cabaret dancer whom the oldest son of the Torres Mendoza family brings home calling her his wife. The young man believes his father to be a thief and wants to shame his newly-rich family. His mother shames Carlos by her kindness to the girl. When he discovers how wrong he has been about his father, Carlos apologizes to the girl and offers to marry her, but she prefers a more down-to-earth suitor. This satirical play demonstrates how an expert technician can turn coincidences into a convincing play.

By then, the dramatist had left Mexico to become cultural attaché at the Mexican Embassy in Paris where he remained until 1946. It was during this period that he completed what is generally considered Usigli's greatest play. *Corona de sombra* (Crown of Shadows), intended to be the final part of a trilogy about what he believed were the three fundamental Mexican myths of sovereignty. Their actual chronological order is *Corona de fuego* (Crown of Fire) set in 1518 with its struggle over national sovereignty between Cortés and Cuauhtémoc; *Corona de luz* (Crown of Light) of the period 1529–31, where Christianity and paganism are in conflict; and *Corona de sombra*, embodying political struggle in 1864–67 between Juárez and Maximilian.

While in Europe, Usigli visited George Bernard Shaw, his idol, taking with him an English translation of his *Crown of Shadows*. Upon his return to Mexico, he published a second Spanish edition accompanied by a letter from the Irish dramatist declaring his willingness to certify to Usigli's dramatic proficiency, and adding: "Mexico may kill you with hunger, but it can never deny your genius."

Back in Mexico, Rodolfo Usigli offered courses at the National University in the History of the Theatre and in playwriting. Among his students were a half dozen who later numbered among the nation's leading dramatists: Emilio Carballido, Jorge Ibargüengoitia, Sergio Magaña, Héctor Mendoza, Ignacio Retes, and Luisa Josefina Hernández, who took over his classes when diplomatic duties called.

Meanwhile Usigli continued his own playwriting, including the "Corona" series that he termed "antihistórico," as he gave the name "impolítico" to his other series that included: *El gesticulador*, the farce and ballet *La última puerta* (1934–36), the three act *Los fugitivos* (pub. 1951), *Un día de éstos* (here translated), and his most recent, *El gran circo del mundo*. Though these last deal with political situations, he treats them in a non- or antipolitical manner and with an attitude in conformity with another meaning of the adjective, "impolite" or "informal."

In his comment in the Foreword of the present volume, Usigli explains his use of the other subtitle, "antihistorical." He handles his myths, he says, according to his own temperament rather than that of a professional historian. There is another possible explanation, more logical when associated with the Maximilian-Carlota play than with the Virgin of Guadalupe story. After all, history has worked strange transformations on the Austrian couple. Mexicans had seen a translation of Franz Werfel's *Juárez and Maximilian* in 1932, in which the Austrian was a puppet figure designed to enhance the glory of the Mexican. That same year *Miramar*, the dramatic poem about him by Julio Jiménez Rueda, had been performed. Even while Usigli worked on his version, *Carlota de México* by Miguel Lira was staged, and before the publication of the complete 1947 version came out, the curtain rose on Agustín Lazo's *Segundo imperio*.

To all these attempts to put history onto the stage, Usigli took exception. "Only the imagination permits an historical fact to be handled theatrically." So in his play he invented a Mexican historian whose name, Erasmo Ramírez, suggests the Dutch scholar who sought reforms from within, and gave him the task of seeking in the present the roots of the past. To present the results of that investigation, the actual present and the recalled past alternate as the action passes back and forth between Old World and New. By his term "antihistorical," Usigli implies his treat-

ment of the characters as human beings rather than historical figures. In Maximilian's death, the dramatist points
out, the emperor who never won acceptance as a Mexican
created Mexican nationality.

Interspersed among his outstanding dramas were other
Usigli plays, listed by the dramatist in a letter to the publisher of this volume. In 1936, for Teatro Orientación, he
made an adaptation of *Le Misanthrope* which he called
Alcestes. The comedy *Medio tono*, already mentioned, was
performed in 1937, then made into a movie for the Mexican star Dolores Del Río. Other plays appear in his two
volume *Teatro completo*, published by Mexico's Fondo de
Cultura Económica, the first in 1963, the second in 1966.

The 916 pages of volume 1 contain sixteen plays in the
order in which they were written. They include *Mientras
amemos* (While We Love, 1937–38), about the redemption of a man through love, who as a husband unable to
hold his wife's affection, hires an actor to play his part. It
is an intense psychological drama of possessive Martina and
her repressed "child," Bernardo of thirty-eight. Also showing the dramatist's interest in abnormal psychology came
Aguas estancadas (Stagnant Water, written 1938; performed 1952), a melodrama about a poor girl who prefers
her poor suitor to a wealthy lunatic who sees in her his dead
wife. A one act radio drama, *Sueño de día* (Day Dreams,
1940), the three scene farce, *Dios, Batidillo y la mujer*
(God, Batidillo and the Woman, 1943), and *La función
de despedida* (1949), telling with surrealistic touches of the
farewell appearance of an aging actress, are among his other
plays. One that raised a storm of protests was *Jano es una
muchacha* (Janus Is a Girl, 1952), about an amateur pros-
titute and her righteous father who owns the brothel where
she operates.

Some of Usigli's plays have also appeared in translation into other languages. *Corona de sombra* was early and
excellently translated by the Englishman W. F. Sterling
(London: Wingate, 1940). Scene 3 of act 3 also appears in

Willis K. Jones, *Latin American Literature in English*, vol.
2, "Since 1888" (New York: Frederick Ungar, 1963).
Other translations of it exist in French and Flemish.

Corona de luz and *Un día de éstos* appear in English
in this book. *Otra primavera* in a translation by Wayne
Wolfe won second prize in a UNESCO competition for
translations in 1959 and was published by Samuel French
(1961). Prof. Edna Lue Furness published *Medio tono* as
"The Great Middle Class," in *Poet Lore*, vol. 63 (Summer
1968), pp. 156–232.

Also according to their author, *La mujer hace milagros*
and his latest play, *El gran circo del mundo*, set in the
nuclear age and published in *Cuadernos Americanos*,
(Jan.–May 1968) have English versions, though he does
not indicate whether they have been published in book form.

In the preparation of the present volume, Dr. Usigli
has been extremely cordial and cooperative. Perhaps with
the passing years as ambassador of his country in Beirut,
Lebanon (1956–62) and in Oslo, Norway since then, he
has mellowed. More likely, he is no longer compelled to
fight public opinion and hostile critics. His place is now
secure as the dean of Mexican dramatists and one of the
three or four outstanding playwrights of the Spanish
American world.

Oxford, Ohio
December 1970

Crown of Light

The Virgin

An Antihistorical Comedy in three acts

Cast of characters

The Doorkeeper (*a lay brother*)
The Prior
The Minister (*Francisco de los Cobos y Molina*)
The Emissary
The Cardinal
The Friar (Friar Antonio *of Act 2 and Act 3*)
Charles V *of Germany and* I *of Spain*
Queen Isabel
Friar Juan de Zumárraga (*the first bishop of New Spain*)
Martincillo (Little Martín, *an Andalusian lay brother*)
Motolinía (*as he is called by the Indians, which means*
     The Poor One: Friar Toribio de Benavente)
Friar Bartolomé de Las Casas
Friar Martín de Valencia
Friar Pedro de Gante (*Ghent*)
Don Vasco de Quiroga
Friar Bernardino de Sahagún
The Young Indian
First Juan
Second Juan
Third Juan
The Gardener, Alonso de Murcia
Fourth Juan (Juan Darío)
The Lieutenant (*a messenger from Cortés*)
The Clarisse Nun

Note: *The use of Christian names either in Spanish or English of members of the cast is left to the preference of the director.*

ACT ONE: *The vestibule of the Monastery of St. Jerome de Yuste, Cáceres, Extremadura, Spain, in 1529.*
ACT TWO: *The bishop's study in the palace of the first bishop of New Spain, Mexico City, early in 1531.*
ACT THREE: *The same as Act 2 on the morning of 12 December 1531.*

Act I POLITICAL PROLOGUE

*The action takes place in the year 1529 in the vestibule
of the Monastery of St. Jerome de Yuste, Spain, which
was founded as a hermitage and established as a chapel
in 1407 by a bull signed by Pope Benedict XIII. De-
prived of its benediction by the bishop of Palencia,
the monastery was later restored to the possession of
its properties, and reorganized as a Jeromite nucleus
under the rules of St. Augustine. It is in Cáceres, in
the region of Extremadura, halfway along the route
taken by* CHARLES V *of Germany and* I *of Spain
when on his way to be crowned emperor of the
Romans in 1530 after a war without truce or quarter.*

*It is sunset. In the distance beyond the arches is
seen a vision of sweet-smelling orange trees like the
green shadow of a grove outside the monastery. The
light, mild but at the same time dense, is similar to
that which the Flemish masters, who originated oil
painting, can, after almost five centuries, still communicate to the visitor to exhibits and museums. The
vestibule is deserted. A professional monastic peace
flows over the place like oil. Here nothing happens and
nothing moves. The air itself floats submissively, not
agitating a leaf, or stirring a desire, or quickening the
consciousness. Suddenly, all this is shattered as when
one lets a heavy hammer fall upon a very fine rock
crystal. The heavy iron knocker resounds in a series of
cannonlike blows, one quickly following another.
One—two—three—one—two—three. A tall lay brother
in the habit of the Order of St. Jerome enters second
entrance left like a huge shadow in movement and*

3

goes to the enormous door upstage center. Keeping time to the rhythm of his steps, his rosary sounds like the sword of a mercenary when striking against a boot of worn leather. He is the DOORKEEPER *of the monastery. Three more blows of the knocker sound as the* DOORKEEPER *reaches the door and opens the small aperture of the grating.*

DOORKEEPER: *Ave María* Most Pure! Who's there?

VOICE OF THE MINISTER: . . . conceived without sin. All right. All right. Open up and I'll tell you.

DOORKEEPER: First I must know who you are.

VOICE OF THE MINISTER: Open in the name of the king.

DOORKEEPER: Here there's no king but the Lord Our God. Ask in His name, and say what you're looking for.

VOICE OF THE MINISTER: I swear by . . . I'm looking for His Majesty the Emperor.

DOORKEEPER: I don't know him. Here ——.

Another friar, tall and dressed in a habit the quality, cleanliness, and good order of which indicate a superior, appears second entrance left. A rosary hangs at his waist. He is the PRIOR. *Another knock is heard.*

PRIOR: Open, Brother, open because otherwise they'll damage our door of young cedar which doesn't deserve any such treatment:

DOORKEEPER: It's no doubt some crazy man who's looking for I don't know what emperor or thing.

PRIOR: Let him in anyhow, Brother. Man must always make his way through error. So we'll tell him, when looking at him eye to eye, that other than God no one reigns here. Go on.

The DOORKEEPER *opens the heavy door. The* MINISTER *enters hastily with an air of irritation. He is followed by the* EMISSARY *who remains secluded in the shadows.*

PRIOR: And what do you want to get at, sir, with so much noise? You've disturbed the silence of this house.

MINISTER (*approaching while the* DOORKEEPER *closes the door*): Pardon, Friar. I must see the emperor. I know he's here.

PRIOR: And who, if you please, is this emperor you speak of? The only one I know is He who is crucified in the chapel of this house—He who teaches us that it's necessary to die to reign.

MINISTER: I'm speaking of His Majesty Charles who's ——.

DOORKEEPER (*irritated*): This isn't a one-night inn for anyone.

PRIOR: Quiet, Brother. (*To the* MINISTER) Here you'll find nothing but a community of monks whose only Majesty is Jesus. Calm down and say ——.

MINISTER: With twenty-two devils on horseback ——.

The knocker sounds again, this time with measured, rhythmic strokes which suggest a serene authority.

DOORKEEPER: Again? This is getting to be more like a blacksmith's shop than even an inn. (*Another knock sounds.*)

PRIOR: Remember the door of young cedar, Brother.

Still another knock sounds. The DOORKEEPER *opens. The* CARDINAL *enters as one does into his own house. He is followed by* THE FRIAR *who remains in the shadowy corner upstage opposite to that which is occupied by the* EMISSARY.

CARDINAL (*with irritation*): It displeases me to find that a minor monastery keeps the purple waiting. Where is the king?

PRIOR: I don't know you and I don't know what you're talking about.

DOORKEEPER: The only king we know here is very well fixed in his place in the chapel. The Father Prior has already said so.

MINISTER: Lord Cardinal, try to make these good monks understand that ——.

CARDINAL: I thought I'd find you here! His Majesty——?

MINISTER: I know only as much as you do. I saw the royal coach with a broken axle stopped near this place, so I questioned the nobles who knew nothing and then the coachman who told me that the king was taking a walk— and at a time like this! Then I walked about, too, but saw no house other than this. So I inquired here, but they only answer in riddles, as you yourself can judge.

CARDINAL: I'm not talking about that. You left Salamanca after I did, but reached here before me.

MINISTER: That's because I don't wear a cassock, Your Eminence. I walk with a freer step.

CARDINAL: In any event, the king——.

PRIOR: Pardon me, but after hearing about so many things that I don't understand, I've come to the conclusion that you're looking for some one. Let me tell you, though, that here you'll not find a soul other than the brethren of the order . . . (*He pauses, a sudden suspicion dawning on him.*) Brother Doorkeeper ——.

DOORKEEPER: Father Prior ——.

PRIOR: Have you again permitted a visit here in return for alms?

DOORKEEPER: Forgive me, Father Prior. I thought that the work we're doing in the garden ——.

PRIOR: You think too much for a monk, Brother. Whom have you let in this time? For whom have you forgotten again the rules of the order and the regulations of this monastery? You know that the door here is opened only to the hungry.

DOORKEEPER: Forgive me, I beg of you. It was only a good burgher with his wife. They both seemed to need bread—for their souls.

PRIOR: How much did they give you? (*With evident reluctance, the* DOORKEEPER *hands him several pieces of gold.*) Aha. This must be returned. We aren't Franciscans here. (*He pockets the money, then turns to the* CARDINAL *and* MINISTER.) As you've heard, you gentlemen who are looking for I don't know what king, only some burgher and his wife have entered here. Will you, then, leave off disturbing the peace of this monastery and go? That is, of course, unless you're hungry and thirsty.

MINISTER: It's that ——.

CARDINAL: Monk, whoever you may be, don't you recognize a Prince of the Church?

PRIOR (*haughtily*): I recognize such a one only by the nails, and I see the prints of none in your hands. Those rings of gold aren't what I'm talking about.

CARDINAL: What impertinence! Don't you understand . . . ? Open that door at once and await the penalties that the Holy Church will impose upon you.

As the DOORKEEPER, *after a sign from the* PRIOR, *opens the door,* CHARLES V *appears downstage right. He is leading his wife,* ISABEL *of Portugal, by the hand. Unseen by the others, both are absorbed, contemplative, and smiling easily, their smiles being born of the peace and harmony of the surroundings. On seeing the* CARDINAL *exit followed by* THE FRIAR, CHARLES *pauses, thus also stopping his wife, to wait a moment while the door is being shut again.*

CHARLES V *of Germany and* I *of Spain is dressed in a brown traveling costume and resembles very much the best portraits of him. He is now the Father of Christianity over and above Pope Clement* VII, *and Lord of the World over and above Francis* I *of France and Henry* VIII *of England. He is a clear-minded, precise, and pacifist warrior. Without these traits of his, perhaps Protestantism would not have been able to establish itself in Europe. He is, moreover, the Father of New Spain, but also because of his birth, the Father*

*of the Spanish Inquisition, and, above all, the son of
Joanna the Mad. Already he is—while a host of dawns
now is breaking throughout the world—the man whom
an excess of power will, thirty years later, lead to abdi-
cate so as also to enjoy the last possession possible on
earth: that of renunciation. His mind has already been
formed to move and function in a constant play of
light and shadow, in a continual duality: Flemish-
German and Spanish; war and peace; religion, and
conflict with Rome; war against, and tolerance of
Luther; military heroism and mysticism: a duality as it
were of day and night, as shown by the dial of a time-
piece, of which Philip II will inherit nothing but the
dial of night or shadow, and the hands of suspicion
and doubt. He has just won another victory over
Francis I, now that he is preparing to receive the
crown of the Romans; but his spirit and thoughts are
away in some other mysterious realm.*

When the door is closed after the CARDINAL *and* THE
FRIAR, *the king smiles and advances a few steps, but
his smile vanishes before the* MINISTER'S *profound
salutation.*

CHARLES: Ay, Jesus!

ISABEL: Why do you say that so often, my lord?

CHARLES: I don't know. Perhaps because they're the
first words I learned in Spanish. Perhaps because they'll be
the last I'll say in my life.

ISABEL: My lord!

MINISTER (*advancing toward* CHARLES): Sire ——.

CHARLES: Admit, my lady, that this is ironic.
Thanks to our coach accident, I discover the most extraordinary landscape I've ever seen—the landscape which
unites my desire of life and my hope of death. I also discover here in Spain this incredible monastery—all so
Flemish, and for that reason already so deeply seated in my
flesh. And then . . . I see the cardinal leave but the min-

ister stay and salute me. I have the bad luck of any monarch, my lady, if not worse.

PRIOR (*advancing*): Here is your gold which can buy nothing in this place.

CHARLES: Now, another complication.

PRIOR: And go on somewhere else. It doesn't matter whether you're a king or a burgher. Here the only coin in circulation is the love of God.

CHARLES: I'll talk with you later, Father. To the people I am the king and to God I'm but a speck of dust. Leave us now, I beg of you, because even here the world pursues me. But let me hope that I be not unworthy to tread these tiles—nor to kiss them.

PRIOR (*to the* DOORKEEPER): Come, Brother.

Both exit slowly, second entrance left. CHARLES *then turns to the* MINISTER. *The* EMISSARY *conceals himself beneath an arch at upper left.*

CHARLES (*to the* MINISTER): You won't let me enjoy this place either, Here, too, I must be on horseback and fight and judge and destroy and build, instead of enjoying the evening air just as any of my peasants would.

MINISTER: Is it my fault that you're the Lord of of the World?

CHARLES: Is it my fault that the world is my lord? A lord that gives me not a moment of rest. But just let me doze for a while in this setting sun, and I'll give you whatever you ask of me.

MINISTER: All I ask of you, sire, is that you let me sleep, too—even though it be only at night.

CHARLES: So that's it. You complain. The subject's complaint always drowns out the monarch's. But I'm tired and, for you, I'm in Rome, not here. Let's sleep at the same time and that'll solve everything. Let everyone sleep at the same time—the servant and the minister, the cardinal and the king. Issue a royal decree to that effect.

MINISTER: Let's not deceive ourselves, sire, about that. As soon as the people of Spain know that they must sleep by royal decree, they'll give themselves over ferociously to insomnia.

CHARLES: I'd do the same. But what's happening now that you follow me even to this place? Let's see— Flanders? Brabant? Germany? The Palatinate? Luther? Francis of France? Clement who's going to crown me in Rome? My family? What?

MINISTER: If it were any one of those problems I'd have taken care of it in Valladolid and have saved myself this ignoble shaking up of my bones which coach trips invariably cause me. But the problem isn't any of those.

CHARLES: At last, something new under the sun?

MINISTER: My lord king, it's about America.

CHARLES (taking a step forward): About what?

MINISTER: About America, sire.

CHARLES: And what could that be? What is America? It doesn't exist.

MINISTER: Better say that it didn't exist, sire. It didn't exist even when it was discovered. But now, thanks to the German and Dutch cosmographers, your own subjects, not only does America exist, as baptized with the name of Amerigo Vespucci, but there also exist Septentrional America and Meridional America in place of what we used to call the New World.

CHARLES: America! Nonsense. There exists only the New World which is no more than New Spain, despite that charlatan of a Vespucci whom God confound as much as Vespucci has mixed up cosmography itself! I'm tempted at times to listen to my flattering cosmographers and call that land Caroland, Carolia, or Carólica. After all, it's my own creation.

MINISTER: We mustn't forget Ferdinand and Isabel, sire, who put up the money.

CHARLES: Isabel put it up. Queens always manage to have more money than kings. (He turns to ISABEL.) My lady, spare yourself this tiresome business they've brought us, and walk a while in the garden. Will you?

ISABEL: I'll return soon, my lord. (*She exits lower entrance right while the* MINISTER *bows low.*)

MINISTER (*continuing*): Nor must Columbus be forgotten who thought he was following Marco Polo but followed a different pole.

CHARLES: Columbus? To discover a continent is a small matter. To administer it is the difficulty. What would the New Continent be without my Captains Cortés and Pizarro and Alvarado, and without my magistrates and governors and bishops?

MINISTER: But the perplexing thing now, sire, is to try to understand what the New Continent is going to become because of them. In any event, America ——.

CHARLES: Again?

MINISTER: It's futile to struggle against man's self-deception and laziness, sire. For this reason, I accept the name invented in the *Introductio Cosmographicae* of Waldsemueller—or however his name's pronounced.

CHARLES: This is just the policy of my enemies. I like maps, but true ones.

MINISTER: It all comes down to the same thing. We can shout ourselves hoarse about New Spain or the West Indies or the New World—which is certainly much older than ours—but America is shorter, more deceptive, and vaguer. For that reason, it's more liable to generalizations. Perhaps some day even Spanish America—to differentiate it from the French or Saxon—will be its name because neither France nor England is going to hold back from making explorations nor from their desire to snatch away from us some bits of territory over there, and some of our power, too——(*He stops before* CHARLES's *severe look.*)

CHARLES: Where?

MINISTER: In . . . in the Indies.

CHARLES: You mean to say in *America*? Let's leave it there. You know that I'd prefer to give in rather than have family quarrels. I'm a man of peace.

MINISTER: Your wars prove that, sire.

CHARLES: What's happening, then, to America that you detain me thus during my trip to Rome? (*He sighs and walks about looking at some invisible point in space while the* MINISTER *follows him slowly.*)

MINISTER: It'd be better for you to hear that from the lips of the messenger himself, sire. But I must warn you first that the situation is complicated, and requires special attention and deep thought.

CHARLES: Is there any task which comes to me as emperor that doesn't require those? And why, pray, am I a kind of monster or Hydra to wear the heads of all my counselors and ministers?

MINISTER: With Your Majesty's pardon, in the first place, you're an absolute monarch ——.

CHARLES: My subjects force me to be one, but it's not amusing to me.

MINISTER: ——and in the second place, this is a case in which your ministers can't assume any responsibility because the problem can't be solved by means of administrative or political ability. Perhaps the only solution is through that privilege which popular imagination attributes to kings. I refer, of course, to inspiration, the daughter of divine grace. Your ministers aren't kings or emperors or inspired beings—only simple mortal animals who analyze and work.

CHARLES: In other words, the responsibility must be entirely mine, as usual.

MINISTER: Rather the glory, sire. The glory.

CHARLES: I'd like to see, even if for just once, a spirit of initiative in my ministers.

MINISTER: When you see that, sire, they'll no longer see their own heads on their shoulders.

CHARLES: But isn't that cowardice?

MINISTER: It's no more than the wish to serve you for the longest time possible.

CHARLES: That's not flattering, especially in view

of how little I know of the New . . . of the Ind . . . in
short, of *America.*

MINISTER: As to European politics, sire, we all find
ourselves in known territory which is familiar to us in the
strictest sense of the word. The monarchs are your rela-
tives, by blood or because of alliances, to a degree never
before seen in Europe. You're the monarch who has
widened the family circle most because from experience
you know two things. The first is that the family often pro-
fesses interests that are related to ours, but are always at
odds with them. The other thing you know is that it's
necessary to live as a member of a family in order to keep
alive one's distrust of the family. One of your courtiers
who's a good Christian, but sharp and audacious, has even
asked himself why you don't form a family alliance with
Luther for the purpose of keeping him closer at hand.

CHARLES: Sacrilege and stupidity! I am the Father
of Christianity. And you want me to introduce the devil
into my house?

MINISTER: The theologians will tell you, sire, that
to have the devil in the house of God is less dangerous than
to leave him in his own. Not long ago there died in Italy
one Machiavelli who expressed similar ideas when speaking
of an artichoke. And furthermore, don't forget that although you're the Father of Christianity, Francis I is the
favorite son of Rome.

CHARLES: That plunderer of paintings and statues!
This is a matter that must be attended to very soon. Pope
Clement has given me much evidence of his ill will, and
more than once I have wondered if my mission isn't to put
an end to the temporal power of the Church. Perhaps I'd
have done so by now if it had been my own idea instead of
Martin Luther's.

MINISTER: The pope should also be a member of
your family.

CHARLES (*agreeably surprised*): Now that's a good
idea.

MINISTER: In short, the politics and environment
of Europe are familiar matters to us—although at times
what we create here does turn against its own creators. But
America is on the other side of the world, sire. The information we receive from the authorities and the very letters
of Cortés himslf aren't enough to enlighten us. We don't
know, for instance, up to what point it's possible to apply
identical laws to or impose the same conduct upon Indians
as upon Spaniards. The medicine which saves one patient
often kills another, and, what's worse, the medicine which
kills one patient often saves another. The Spaniard himself,
once he's there—in America—seems to undergo a change.
To judge from the information we receive, he acquires an
exaggerated idea of his own importance. He confers on
himself a divine rank, as it were, and so is determined to
rule over the Indian.

CHARLES: Have you said "rule"? Is there any one
other than God and I who can rule in my dominions?

MINISTER: The discovery and conquest of America
have made a king of every Spanish adventurer. Just think
of Columbus, sire, whom it was necessary to bring back in
chains. And think of Cortés of whom much has been said
and more will yet be said in the sense that he aspires to
become the emperor of the Indies.

CHARLES: Cortés is the best soldier of Spain—after
me, of course— and he's loyal. Should he not be, we well
know how to reach America.

MINISTER: It may be he's loyal because he feels he's
more than a king.

CHARLES: How's that?

MINISTER: May God forgive me, but I have information to the effect that Cortés feels he's Adam sire, and
that he got together with that Indian, the Malinche or
Doña Marina, his interpreter—whom he thinks of as a sort
of Eve of Tabasco—so as to found a new paradise. But . . .
(CHARLES *is about to speak, but the* MINISTER *hastens on.*)
But in his dealings with the Indian slaves, every Spanish
soldier, every member of the Cabildo, every recipient of a

royal land grant with Indians included, every petty func-
tionary, every merchant, every member of a guild, attributes to himself a rank that's almost divine—which is more
ridiculous than sacrilegious, sire. And it'll go on being like
this for many years to come.

CHARLES: That's neither sacrilegious nor ridiculous.
I understand the situation very well, and, as a German, I
know why it's as it is. But my missionaries don't fit into
that pattern. They take the Faith and light over there, and
conduct themselves as equals and brothers of the Indians.

MINISTER: Which makes them even more dangerous because thus they develop an intolerable sense of
equality in the Indians. And, what's more, all those missionaries, including even your own brother, are bound to
Rome.

CHARLES: But the Franciscan order depends solely
upon God and, therefore, upon me. They're the only
monks who don't play Roman politics and who represent
all that my Christian soul wants for the well-being of the
inhabitants of that world. It's natural for the soldier to use
force, it's natural for the magistrate to use the law—that
is, for them to avail themselves of the instruments without
which they'd be just like other men who'd, therefore, de-
troy them and with them good government. But against
the violence that's necessary, against the justice that's indispensable (*the doorknocker sounds with authority*), God
has given us kindness and faith which are the arms of the
missionary. (*Yet more knocks.*) Arms which, rightly, in
making all men equal, give victory to the divine cause.
(*More knocks are heard.*) Come on! See who the devil is
knocking like that.

> Meanwhile, the DOORKEEPER *has entered with quick
> steps and goes to open the door. While he does so, the*
> MINISTER *continues speaking as the* CARDINAL, *at-
> tended by* THE FRIAR, *enters. With a gesture, the* CAR-
> DINAL *dismisses the* DOORKEEPER, *and then listens with
> impatience.*

MINISTER: Unfortunately, sire, the question of America isn't a theological one. It's a political question that affects interests vital to Spain.

CARDINAL (*advancing*): There you are, as always, speaking of the material things of the world which pre-occupy you. Why didn't you send for me when you knew I was looking for His Majesty? And what, Lord Minister, have you been doing about all those other matters? And what's this I've just heard about which made me hasten here at full speed from Salamanca? (*The other two look from him to each other.*)

MINISTER: Which of so many questions does Your Eminence prefer for me to answer?

CARDINAL: You let me leave here so that you could make headway with the king, knowing that——.

CHARLES: What brought you here, Cardinal?

CARDINAL: The work of the devil, lord, which goes on unbridled in Mexico.

CHARLES (*surprised*): Mex . . . i . . . co?

MINISTER: New Spain, sire. In addition to Tenoch-títlan, apparently the native barbarians call their capital city Méshico, or Mécsico, or Méjico, or something like that.

CARDINAL: I've been told of bloody incidents in Mexico, in Tlacopan, in Tlaxcallan, in Tlatelolco, in Atzca-potzálcotl, in Coyocán itself where Cortés has established his residence, in Teotihuácan, and——.

CHARLES: Those names must be simplified.

MINISTER: Your subjects, sire, will do that on their own. The Spaniard practices a proud resistance to speaking all languages well, including his own.

CARDINAL: I've not come here to talk with the king about linguistics, Lord Minister. The information which I've just received proves to me that the unhappy natives of New Spain are in mortal peril. Our Christian duty is to save them.

MINISTER: For once, Your Majesty, His eminence

and I are in agreement—the natives of New Spain must be saved.

CARDINAL: God be praised because He is opening your eyes. (*Suddenly doubtful.*) Unless I'm mistaken about that.

MINISTER: By no means. You've just said what I was going to.

CHARLES: Let's see now. You're agreed that I must save the Indians?

MINISTER: What would we do without them? If the Indians should be exterminated ——.

CARDINAL: It would be an indelible stain on the Christian majesty of Charles V.

MINISTER: That would be the least of it.

CHARLES: How's that?

MINISTER: If the Indians should disappear, who'd dig into the bowels of the earth in search of metals? Who'd haul the stone blocks to build churches, monasteries, palaces, and houses? Who'd cultivate the land? It surely wouldn't be the Spaniards who've gone to America to conquer it but certainly not to work because they went there as heroes and adventurers. And so all our projects to increase the power and wealth of Spain would fall to pieces.

CARDINAL: I knew that we couldn't agree. I can't endure any further the light tone in which you treat these matters. I speak of the souls of those unfortunate ones and of their eternal salvation.

MINISTER: And I, Your Eminence, speak of their bodies and of the salvation of Spain.

CARDINAL: What can you do with their bodies if you lose their souls?

MINISTER: Be practical. What the devil can you do with their souls if you lose their bodies?

CARDINAL: Sacrilege! Blasphemy! Only the soul gives life to the body.

MINISTER: Feed souls, Your Eminence, fatten them, and if they haven't bodies to live in, they'll only be fit for Paradise or Purgatory or Hell, according to wherever they're bound for. But help the body to live, and you'll save the soul.

CARDINAL: This is what comes from applying the teachings of the pagan Greeks to the Christian world. Nourish and fatten bodies while neglecting their souls, and all will fall into hell fire.

MINISTER: God first created the Word, but the Church always wants to have the last one.

CARDINAL: Permit——.

CHARLES: Will you explain yourselves? A question which a quarter of an hour ago seemed so alien and far away, now all at once takes on incredible proportions—as if these very walls were going to fall upon us. You speak of perdition and salvation. One speaks of bodies and the other of souls, and I see the heads of my government divided without understanding why—a matter which certainly doesn't please me—and you both seem to forget the king's presence. An end to it! Tell me what the devil this is all about.

CARDINAL: Sire, from what I'm going to tell you in the name of the Church, Your Majesty will understand what is happening.

MINISTER: By leave of Your Eminence, I think the simplest thing would be for the king to hear an account of the facts from the lips of the emissary himself.

CARDINAL (*pleased*): I was going to propose that.

MINISTER (*looking at him distrustfully*): Yes? Perhaps it's I who am mistaken now. In any event ——.

The MINISTER *goes rapidly upstage where* THE FRIAR *is hidden in the shadows. The* CARDINAL *gathers up his robes and almost runs to the place at the stone wall where the* EMISSARY *is waiting.* MINISTER *and* CARDINAL *return downstage without looking back, both shouting at the same time.*

CARDINAL *and* MINISTER: Ho there, messenger!

CHARLES *observes the confusion and laughs to himself.*

MINISTER *and* CARDINAL *(together and without turning around)*: Come! Speak!

The EMISSARY *advances unil he reaches the* CARDINAL *who seems to be seeing things, and then, turning to* CHARLES, *the* EMISSARY *drops to one knee.*

CARDINAL: I knew that some foul business was under way, sire. They've changed my messenger. They've played a trick on me!

The MINISTER, *astonished, turns to encounter behind him* THE FRIAR *who is small, dried up, and energetic.*

MINISTER: It seems to me that the foul play is Your Eminence's.

CHARLES *(laughing)*: There's nothing like haste and violence for one to play a trick on oneself. By my faith, this is worth the queen's trouble to see. Call her, Lord Cardinal. She'll be in the garden or in the chapel. That way.

Furious, the CARDINAL *signs to* THE FRIAR *to follow him and both exit downstage right.* CHARLES *turns to the* EMISSARY *who is a soldier, a first edition of the Cervantesque soldier: Castilian, and of a noble, serene, and resolute aspect. In contrast to the Maimed One of Lepanto—Cervantes himself—whose left hand was permanently disabled by a gunshot wound, thus losing its movement, this soldier's entire left arm is missing. The presence of the king and emperor impresses him like a vivifying liquor but without upsetting him.* CHARLES *motions to him to rise.*

EMISSARY: God preserve Your Highness for many years.

CHARLES: Where did you lose your arm?

EMISSARY: At the same place where I won my

heart, sire—fighting for the colors of Spain. But what matters isn't that I lost an arm for Your Highness, but that I
won my heart to serve you.

CHARLES: Are you a man of Cortés, or Alvarado, or
Pizarro?

EMISSARY: I'm a man of Spain.

CHARLES: Tell me who sent you and give me your
message at once.

ISABEL *enters downstage right, followed by the* CARDI-
NAL *who in turn is followed by* THE FRIAR. *If he dared
to do so, the* CARDINAL *would cross directly in front of
the queen. Such is his haste, though, that he begins
speaking from the entrance.*

CARDINAL: One moment, sire, I beg of you.
(CHARLES *turns. The* CARDINAL *pushes* THE FRIAR *forward.*)
Speak, Brother. Speak.

CHARLES (*looking* THE FRIAR *slowly up and down*):
Do you know who I am, Friar?

THE FRIAR: Yes, a man.

MINISTER: Friar, bow before the Majesty of
Charles V, King of Spain and Emperor of Germany,
Prince of the Palatinate, Duke of Brabant, Lord of the
New World, Emperor of the Holy Roman Empire, and
Leader of Christianity.

THE FRIAR: The Christian has no leader but
Christ Alive, and kings have more sins than ordinary men.
If I salute Charles as a man, I pay him homage. Were I to
salute him as a powerful monarch, I'd have to be hypocritical with him, and the Law of God forbids me that.

CHARLES: You have a harsh tongue, Friar, and that
pleases me. The prince hasn't yet been able to finish with
the man in me.

EMISSARY: That's because you're Spanish.

MINISTER: A Spanish prince.

THE FRIAR: This man who uses so many adjectives
must be a minister, and if he is one, he should know that
what Charles is as a prince is only what he is as a German.

EMISSARY: And what he is as a man is what he is as a Spaniard. Agreed.

CHARLES: Now that you're both here and come from the same place—perhaps I should say from the same world—tell me who sent you to me and what your messages are.

THE FRIAR: My bishop sent me.

EMISSARY: The Army of Spain sent me.

CHARLES: You speak first, soldier.

THE FRIAR: And if I were to tell you that God sent me?

CHARLES: He (*indicating the* EMISSARY) has already said that. God manifests himself in men, not in just one man, except for the case of Christ.

CARDINAL: That's to say, Most Christian Emperor, you make my Church take second place?

CHARLES: Only the bishop of your Church who for this once isn't its rock.

MINISTER: Ay, what a king I have! Like a good Spaniard, he's something of a hero and a saint, something of a theologian and a *torero*.

CARDINAL: Adulation! Where have you left——?

CHARLES (*interrupting him*): What did you say?

CARDINAL: That they flatter you, that——.

CHARLES: No (*to the* MINISTER *who shows astonishment*), you. Is that really a word you used, or is it simply that I haven't yet learned Castilian?

MINISTER: Which one of so many words, Majesty? I'm verbose, I admit, but is there a Spaniard who's mute?

CHARLES (*trying to recall*): You said *to . . . re . . . ro.*

MINISTER: Ah! A word of my own invention, sire. When I see Your Majesty and princes and nobles give yourselves over to the dangerous and fascinating play of lancing bulls, I think of the gladiators of Rome, and I also think that some day the people will make an occupation or profession of that pastime. So then as it's about fighting bulls—to *torear*, let's say—sometimes I call them *toreadores* and sometimes *toreros,* so as to give them that unmistakable coinlike quality that words imprint upon men.

CHARLES: Words! Words!

MINISTER: But, what's more, the fight with the bull will some day become like the fight against the devil ——.

CARDINAL: You left that out while you were flattering the king. You said "saint," "hero," and "theologian," but what of the devil who lives in all men, even more in kings because they're the much greater human edifice?

MINISTER: I included the devil in the theologian, Eminence. (*A gesture of protest from the* CARDINAL *who is about to speak.*)

CHARLES (*after taking* ISABEL's *hand and placing himself with her in the center of the stage amongst the others*): Quiet, gentlemen. This isn't the time for the old quarrels of Europe. My heart tells me that the hour of America is beginning. So, speak, soldier.

EMISSARY: Lord, your army is suffering in the New World because it has been deceived, betrayed—sold out. We were led to believe that we'd go there as heroes dedicated to titanic and glorious battle, but day by day we're changed into rapists, assasins, and hangmen. We've faced an enemy that, although greater in number; although expert in knowing their mountains, their lakes, and jungles; although equipped with obsidian pointed arrows and arms of flint and shields of skins; although masters of the serpent, the eagle, and the tiger whose names and symbols they've adopted as signs of rank; although warrior conquerors of other tribes—the subduers of princes and sacrificers of men—they were conquered at once by the fire of our harquebuses and mortars; by the wild gallop of our horses which they believe are fabulous monsters; by the treason which ever stirs in them like a sixth sense; by our dazzling steel and by their own orgies of blood and *pulque,* and by the very prophecies of their elemental gods of stone. But they received us as brothers and not as enemies, and they gave us their jewelry of precious stones and their plumes, and they perfumed us with incense, and they opened their palaces and huts to us and offered us their women and girls. Or else they received us like enemies and gave us manly battle. But the men of the Church have torn down their pyramids and temples; they've abolished their pleasures, their games, and their traditions; they've put out their stars and their moon, they've stopped their sun and their wind, they've caused their rain to dry up; they've scattered their fire—all of which they worshipped as gods. And those same men of the Church have made them go down into the mines or drag stone blocks from the quarries, while also forcing them, in punishment for their paganism, to build the churches of Christ with gold and silver and *tezontle*. And they've taken away from them their native languages and commerce together with their fiestas and pleasures. They've also taken away from them the arms which they had to fight with like men, and they've made them turn against us and attack us from ambush and by surprise, which are the arms of the weak and cowardly into which they've changed them.

And to use they've said that we must defend the Church of God against these idolaters who sacrifice human beings and turn them into slaves—those men who're warriors like us and who could have fought on the battlefield, giving us the exercise of battle and the glory of triumph which we must have to breathe and live. And because we've been attacked from behind, we've become tyrants instead of warriors, gang bosses instead of soldiers with no enemies to fight face to face except those which we can't defeat—the climate and the elements, sickness and drunkenness. We take plunder without pleasure and blood without victory. They've turned us into beasts more savage than the Indians themselves.

CHARLES: But you yourself have said that they were idolaters and pagans, inferior to you.

EMISSARY: They were ready to worship us like gods, but the Church wouldn't allow it; or they were ready to fight us to the death, but the Church forbade that, too.

And we wanted to live and die like what we are, like soldiers, but the Church has stopped us forever from doing that.

CARDINAL: Anathema! Anathema! What poison is there in that country that can inspire such sacrilegious thoughts in a soldier of Spain, in a creature of God? Are you, Lord King, going to tolerate that such things be said about the Faith and the Church of Christ?

CHARLES: Friar, you speak.

THE FRIAR: Charles, your Franciscan order has been betrayed and your Church sold out. We were told that we had to save the Indian, but not the Spaniard who sins more than the Indian and who, day after day, hampers us in our work of mercy. It's hard to cultivate the seed of God in man, not because he's evil, but because he's made without windows to permit the divine light to enter him. Only the fear and sorrow which come to him in life bring him to religion which promises him another life. Life must lacerate and burn him so that each wound or sore binds him to the love and fear of God, which are His blood that washes man's body instead of being consumed and drowned within him. But when I speak of wounds I don't speak of swords. When I speak of fire I don't speak of cannons or of burning buildings. And when I speak of fear I don't speak of destruction and terror.

CHARLES: You speak, but you don't speak like a missionary. Instead, you speak like an inquisitor. By my faith, you'd be better in the Holy Tribunal of the Faith, judging and condemning those who don't embrace our religion, than planting it in America amongst the pagans and idolaters out of Franciscan love for all beings. If I shudder while hearing you, what mustn't those Indians do? You speak like your cardinal and like Rome, Friar. You speak with more harshness than this soldier here, and you're more severe on the Indian than your king is, and you've more omnipotence over man than God has. You're arrogant. You speak——.

THE FRIAR (*interrupting him*): And you who are the legitimate heir of the Holy Inquisition of Spain which was founded by Ferdinand and Isabel—you speak to me in this way?

CHARLES: Political expediences are things of man, not of God. That's why the popes created the Inquisition, but this tribunal is giving us much ill fame, although more persons die in one month of nasal catarrh or fever than the Inquisition has killed since it was established. We've burnt three Jews in three years, but the people talk of three thousand. What won't they say later on! But one thing is the tribunal and another is the altar.

MINISTER: Let the people believe what they want to, sire. Without a little terror in their governments kings would be lost. They couldn't, by way of contrast, convince anyone that they're kind and magnanimous. Furthermore, the tribunals absorb the blame like unbleached paper does oil. They set the king apart and make him more beloved while they, the tribunals themselves, are more feared.

CHARLES: But the friars? Why must they act the same as kings? That's the pernicious influence of Rome. You, Friar, will administer justice in the Inquisition. That's all you're good for. To what order do you belong?

THE FRIAR: Doesn't my habit tell you that?

CHARLES: The one you're wearing is no more than a disguise. You've the soul of a Dominican. How could you be a Franciscan?

THE FRIAR: I'm a Franciscan in the Spanish style, not the Italian. If my order inclines me to kindness, Spain forces me on to fanaticism. And don't you know that it's not possible to be a missionary without being an inquisitor? That it's necessary to inquire into the depths of souls, and that this is the most painful of all? Don't you know that a missionary is a physician of souls who must purge them because man is afraid of being good and believes only in his own goodness when he has suffered? Don't you know that the fear of life must be cured with the fear of death?

And that man must naturally suffer in his body and soul because there's no other way of distinguishing health from illness, or good from evil? And don't you know that every one of us in Mexico suffers for himself and for the millions of those unfortunate ones who must be saved by making them live? Ask how Sahagún and Benavente, who's called by the Indians *Motolinía*—which means The Poor One— and Alonso de la Veracruz and Andrés de Olmos, and Las Casas and Gante—of whom it's said that he's your own brother and who's worth more than you—ask how all these suffer. How are we going to teach piety and the Christian faith to the poor Indians when the soldiers want to convince them that they, the Indians, are heroes, as this one here says, so that the Spaniards can look like heroes themselves; or when your administrators want to convince those same Indians that they're beasts of burden or moles in the mines? How, then, are those Indians to be persuaded that they're sons of God and our brothers? And now we must fight not only against what's evil in the upbringing of the Indians because their barbaric fathers and grandfathers taught them to ignore the true God, but we must also fight against all that there is of evil in the leaven of the Spaniards, of which there's much, and which your soldiers instill in the Indians and which they follow so readily. Then, later on, what's to become of the children which the appetites of heroes such as this one here get of the Indian women without marriage? Don't blame the Church for what's happening there. Blame this man and his like, and those who play politics and the profiteers, and those who've been given royal land grants with Indians included, and the magistrates and the soldiers of fortune, and the greedy, whether for sex or wealth. We, on the contrary, want only to give the Indian the Faith that saves, the God who is our happiness and our hope—all in exchange for his idols and his animallike profanity.

EMISSARY: Yet you want to do all that by force. You've destroyed their temples and have thrown out their gods.

THE FRIAR: There's only one God and when He comes, all those who're called gods disappear. We want God to reach the Indian and for him to build the house of God so that he'll love it as his own work. That's all. And what do you do instead? You want the Indians to go on being pagans and to worship the horse and war. You take away their flint weapons, but you teach them that there're others they should worship because they're newer and more destructive and more deadly, like your steel, like your harquebuses and cannons. You're not sons of God, nor do you serve Charles or Spain. You're the apostles and missionaries of Nuño de Guzmán.

EMISSARY: We carry out the civilizing mission of war that makes progress in the world.

THE FRIAR: Progress in the science of Cain! And what about what you do to the women?

EMISSARY: We make children with them to keep life going on earth and the earth in production.

THE FRIAR: Blind men! You beget children who'll be slaves because they'll be more Indian than Spanish, and that'll be your punishment. Don't you know that if things go on as they are, soon one of two things will happen? Either there won't be an Indian left alive or there won't be one Spaniard left to be counted. Don't tell men now that that's the law of war.

EMISSARY: I'll tell you this. We take away their primitive weapons from them and knock to pieces their art of war, but we teach them about better things. We give them something to live for. But you take away their stone gods and only give them a god of words. You take away from them the reality which they can touch and give them nothing more than a paradise which they can't see— a tomorrow which isn't coming.

CARDINAL: Heresy! Do you believe in God and if so why?

EMISSARY: I believe in God because I believe in Spain, because Spain *is*, because Spain did away with the Moorish infidel. I see God in every battle won, in every grain of wheat which waves in the fields of Castile, in every word of my tongue, in every narrow, winding street of Toledo, and in every piece of bread I eat and in every glass of wine I drink.

MINISTER: And you, Friar, do you believe in the goodness of your monarch and that he wants to make the New World a Christian world?

THE FRIAR: No. No, I don't believe that. I don't believe it because I see the devil possessed of every soldier and the pride that's mastering every Spaniard, and because I see the greed and rapacity of the men who seek the treasures only of this world.

CHARLES: Do you believe in Spain?

THE FRIAR: I believe in God.

EMISSARY: But for all that, you can't make the Indian see Him. That's why the Indian doesn't believe.

THE FRIAR: The Indian is by nature of a good disposition. He keeps the fiestas of The Magi and of Corpus Christi and of St. Hippolytus who's our Patron of New Spain. He takes pleasure in our religious processions. He's soft-mannered and soft-voiced, and he hasn't the pride of the devil. It's the soldier and the holder of land grants with their Indians who keep him from seeing God and who get him drunk.

EMISSARY: I've seen the Indian in those processions you speak of. He enjoys them because he decorates himself with feathers and dresses up like a woman and dances his ancient dances and gets drunk. I've also seen him leave in the fabrics of churches and palaces the signs of his gods and of his race. Then let those Indians be just warriors so we can put an end to them—or they to us.

THE FRIAR: Each offers to God what he has. You just let them all be Christians and tame. Perhaps they'll teach you to be the same some day.

CARDINAL: It must be, sire, that those wretched people come to see God.

EMISSARY: That, yes—but a god of their own, a Mexican god. Otherwise, they'll never be men again.

CARDINAL: God is no one's and He is everyone's.
God is universal.

CHARLES: Rubbish! Why don't you say at once that
God is Roman or French, as they of Rome want that vain
Francis to believe? God is Spanish, and He can't be anything other than Spanish. (*The* CARDINAL *crosses himself,
scandalized.*)

MINISTER: It would be well for the Aztecs to
understand this once and for all.

CARDINAL: But how are they going to if your soldiers excite them to fight only so as to kill them? How are
they going to believe in a God who only leads them to
death?

EMISSARY: How are they going to if your friars
prevent it, as always? How are they going to see God behind the Devil who is the one you talk to them about?

CHARLES: But what can I do who am no more than
the king?

THE FRIAR: Don't let the Indians perish if you
want to save your own soul.

EMISSARY: Don't let the Spaniards be wiped out if
you want to save Spain.

CARDINAL: Save the souls, sire.

MINISTER: Save the bodies, Prince.

CHARLES: Be quiet a while, all of you. (*He walks
back and forth a moment, then turns to* ISABEL *whose hand
he takes.*) Tell me, my lady, what you think about all this
and what you would advise me.

ISABEL: A woman's advice usually falls upon a man
like a stone into a well. Why, my lord, do you ask my
opinion when you'll end up, as always, by doing what you
want to and as you want to?

CHARLES: At least tell me what you're thinking.

ISABEL: All these are right. The idolaters must be
brought to see God.

CHARLES: If they should see Him, we'd all be lost
instead of them. They'd be our equals, or—something
worse. And God is Spanish, as I said.

ISABEL: You see? You don't want to listen to me.

CARDINAL: In God's name, Your Majesty, I beg you to speak.

MINISTER: The king always asks your counsel and he values it highly. In the name of Spain, speak, Your Majesty.

CHARLES: Speak, my lady, for my sake.

ISABEL: Lord, you men are all like children, and the stronger and more free you think yourselves, the more childlike you are. I've listened to each of you and not one thinks with his head or feels with his heart. You really talk like fools—to separate souls from bodies! What would it serve to save the bodies without saving the souls? Or what would it serve to save the souls without saving the bodies? Don't you perhaps know that God made them both and that they're husband and wife, or like flesh and blood? Some of you speak of bringing the Indians to see God, yet the king says that this mustn't be done because God is Spanish. It may be that He is. As the queen of Spain, I hope fervently that He is. But you all make yourselves nothing more than ridiculous with such ideas. Neither you (*indicating the group apart from* CHARLES) have the power to make God be seen, nor has Charles the power to prevent God from being seen if God wants to manifest Himself. Children!

CHARLES: Well, then?

MINISTER: Madam, you are not unaware of the fact that Spain is in danger. Politically, it would be a mistake to exterminate the Indians because then nothing would prevent the Spaniards from rebelling against the king. In that event, nothing would prevent Cortés from declaring himself emperor or from dividing the kingdom in some other way. On the other hand, neither can we allow the Indians to destroy the Spaniards because then nothing would prevent France or England—or all Europe, for that matter—from finishing us off and scattering to the four winds Charles V's power which the world needs to keep it in order. But you're right. It isn't in our power either to hide or to reveal God. Our duty, though, is to save the New World—and for Spain. To do this, we need both Spaniards and Indians, and we need them equally. This is a complicated case of high policy.

CARDINAL: Madam, I'll not speak to you of politics. It's imperative that the Christian faith not perish. It's also imperative now to save the souls of both Spaniards and infidels. We're experiencing a turbulent and difficult time that's propitious for the play of the infernal powers. If the New World should be lost to the Faith, the devil and Luther would take possession of it and of Europe, too. Should these things come to pass, we'll see times of disaster and affliction for all, and we'll be plunged back into the darkness of infidelity and pagan barbarity.

CHARLES: But what can I do?

ISABEL: Can you, without the will of God, move even the leaf of a tree?

CARDINAL: What can the Church do?

ISABEL: Can you reveal God?

MINISTER: What can the government do?

ISABEL: Can you take the place of God?

CARDINAL: The Church can convey the word of God.

ISABEL: Let this friar tell you if that's enough.

MINISTER: The monarch can impose his law.

ISABEL: Has the soldier told you that force is enough?

CHARLES: Well, then?

ISABEL: You can do nothing. That's clear. This is work for God. Just wait.

CARDINAL: Meanwhile, the souls of the Indians will be lost.

ISABEL: Then pray for them.

MINISTER: While we're praying, the kingdom will be lost.

CHARLES: By St. James, what a situation! All my relations envy me the possession of the New World, but, upon my faith, I'd cede it gladly to get rid of the problem.

Yet there's something in all this that I still don't understand. I've sent those infidels captains and magistrates, and a Catholic mission composed of the best men in the world. What more do they want? Why all this discontent? Why this instability which leads always to more bloodshed and destruction?

ISABEL: My lord, have you thought about how it'd be with us if those infidels were our conquerors? They, too, would have sent us their best men, but you wouldn't be content and neither would any Spanaird. There'd only be more blood and destruction.

CHARLES: How can you compare Spaniards to Indians? We finished off the Moor who was of a finer race than ours and probably superior to us. Why, then, shouldn't we exterminate the Indian? That's the true solution. Let's just finish off the Indian, and let it be by blood and destruction!

MINISTER: Did we really finish off the Moor, sire? When I say the words *alcázar, almohadón, alhóndiga,* and *alcuza, alfarería* and *albarda, almohaza, almidón,* and *almendra* and *almirez* and *albedrío,* and *alharaca* and *aceite* and *aceituna* and *barullo,* I think *Ojalá!* and have we really finished off the Moor? And then I note that I've just said *Ojalá!* And when I see how we Spaniards treat our wives, veiling not their faces but their souls and keeping them prisoners in their homes and in their ignorance, I think that rather it's the Moor who's put an end to us after so much bloodshed and destruction.

CHARLES: Poppycock! The alliances of words and languages are like the alliances of princes and monarchs. The strongest survives and, thank God Almighty, we've survived as a kingdom and a Faith, and as a power, thanks to the bloodshed and destruction.

CARDINAL: Do you know, sire—and this is what the missionaries who compose the lexicons tell me—that the Indian pronounces Castilian more in the Andalusian manner, and that our tongue is being corrupted by new words and that the Andalusian has already begun to imitate the

Mexican? And do you know that Indians who have the feeling for the grace of colors and form are now painting and sculpturing angels and holy images that already aren't really Spanish any more? Now how is this to be put an end to by bloodshed and destruction?

ISABEL: No. No more blood! No more destruction!

CHARLES: Then give me the means to prevent the one and to impede the other.

ISABEL: I've no arms nor strength other than my woman's faith. I'm going now to pray to my favorite Virgin, the Guadalupe, that she intercede for you.

CARDINAL: Perhaps, sire, if some one—a Prince of the Church, let's say—were to go there for you, we could put an end to the conflict. I think that I——.

EMISSARY: It's not friars who're needed. No Prince of the Church would be better than the missionaries, and they can't do anything.

MINISTER: Not a bad idea, though. In fact, it's an old custom. When God can't come down to earth, he sends his vicar: his Son or his Archangel, or some saint. Now, if you were to send a skillful statesman, one of your ministers, let's say, perhaps ——.

THE FRIAR: And what more could a statesman do than Cortés who's all astuteness, subtlety, and malice, and to whom the Indians attribute a rank that's superior to his? You don't know, King, that in their own entertainments the Indians dress themselves up like Cortés or Alvarado and mimic them when they want the audience to think of a great chief or a god. No. It's not that way, no.

CHARLES: Well, then?

ISABEL: There's but one way, my lord, but it's not a way for the feet of man. The only road is that of a miracle.

CARDINAL: The queen is right. Only a miracle of God can save the Indians.

MINISTER: Only a miracle can save the Spaniards.

CHARLES: A miracle? Aren't you aware of all those we have to perform to keep the wellspring of our treasury flowing? It's through that that we maintain in the people

of Spain—who're really farmers—the costly illusion that
they're a race of warriors. No. No miracles, please.

EMISSARY: What is a miracle, Friar?

THE FRIAR: You couldn't understand because you
don't believe.

ISABEL: You speak truly, Friar. There's but one
miracle and that's faith.

CHARLES: For the first time I, who've fought against
Luther and Rome, against Francis and Flanders—against
the world—feel myself lost. You all give me contradictory
advice: wait, pray, destroy. Send a cardinal, send a minister.
Say that the Church is right or that the army is. Perform a
miracle. I can't bear any more. Go away, all of you, and
leave me alone, I want to think about all this, in this
silence here, in this peace. (*To the* MINISTER.) See if that
axle has been repaired and let me know. You, Cardinal,
and you, soldier, escort the queen. You, Friar, call the
prior.

All obey, using the various exits. When ISABEL *is about
to cross the threshold,* CHARLES *speaks to her.*

CHARLES: Isabel——.

ISABEL (*pausing on the threshold*): Speak, lord and
husband.

CHARLES: What did you say is the name of your
favorite Virgin?

ISABEL: You can't have forgotten that because I've
venerated her since childhood and have her image in my
private chapel. She's the Virgin of Guadalupe of Extremadura.

CHARLES: That's it, of course. And she's a warrior
Virgin. Thank you, my lady.

ISABEL and the CARDINAL *exit upstage center followed
by the* EMISSARY. THE FRIAR *exits through the second
door left to go in search of the* PRIOR. CHARLES, *somewhat tense, walks back and forth with his hands
clasped before him while his eyes are fixed on the last*

glow of the setting sun. The center door remains open. In a moment the PRIOR *appears.* THE FRIAR *enters left and exits upstage center after casting a last, canny glance at the king.*

PRIOR: You sent for me, Brother?

CHARLES: I don't know why, but I'm certain that I'll return to this place some day. You have the monastery that has made me think the most and the landscape that has made me feel the most. Perhaps that's because it reminds me of Hieronymus Bosch who understood the shades of the landscape and painted them so well. Yes, I'll return. I wanted to tell you this. Perhaps I'll come back here some day to die.

PRIOR: God appoints the place of our death, and His finger turns it into a place full of light.

CHARLES: Until another day, Father. (*He kisses the* PRIOR'S *hand.*)

PRIOR: I'll attend you.

CHARLES: Proceed.

They exit. CHARLES *reenters a moment later as if he had forgotten something. He takes a last look around, then looks up at the sky. A familiar smile spreads across his lips. He murmurs as if savoring the words.*

CHARLES: The Virgin of Guadalupe.

MINISTER (*appearing upstage center*): Sire ——.

CHARLES: I'm coming. (*A last smile, then a last look about.*) That would be a miracle. (*He exits quickly.*)

CURTAIN

Act 2 THE SEVEN FOR MEXICO

*The action takes place in Mexico City in 1531 in the
study in the bishop's palace of the recently appointed
first bishop of New Spain,* FRIAR JUAN DE ZUMÁRRAGA.
*He is a Basque, energetic and stubborn; a man of
harsh speech but of few words. As the curtain rises,*
FRIAR JUAN, *seated at his desk, pushes away the tray
in front of him and then rises and exits left with decision, while shaking his head in negation and banging
the door after him.*

*A moment later a small lay brother of undeter-
mined age who wears the habit of the Franciscans*
Propaganda Fide *enters. He is* MARTINCILLO (LITTLE
MARTIN), *a kind of private secretary* a latere, *or servant
of the bishop, whose duty is to perform the function
of blotting paper whenever the temper of His Lordship spills over or drips the black ink of bad humor.*

On seeing that the room is empty, MARTINCILLO
*goes to the window upstage center which opens onto
a large archway that is in the process of construction.
It is afternoon. The rays of a voluptuous sun enter the
whitewashed room, tinting the whiteness of the walls
with brilliant strokes of light.* MARTINCILLO *goes to the
bishop's desk. With an evident expression of disap-
proval, he looks at the tray with its cup of chocolate
and piece of bread which are still untouched. Without
much deliberation, he takes up the cup and drinks its
contents in a single big gulp. He then picks up the
slice of bread which he conceals in the sleeve of his
habit. No sooner does he move away from the desk
than the door on the left opens and the bishop enters,*

apparently in a worse humor than when he left.
MARTINCILLO *assumes an attitude of devout immobility, like a soldier of Christ who awaits orders.*

MARTINCILLO: You haven't takcn your chocolate today either, Friar Juan.

FRIAR JUAN: You may drink it.

MARTINCILLO: I wouldn't permit myself that.

FRIAR JUAN: I know this song of old. I'll bet you've already drunk it—as usual.

MARTINCILLO: A bishop bet? Lord God, what times!

FRIAR JUAN (*without looking*): And what have you done with the bread?

MARTINCILLO: I'm saving it for my Indians.

FRIAR JUAN: *Your* Indians! What effrontery. Do you take God for a fool? Do you think He'll pardon you the theft of my chocolate because at the same time you steal my bread for an Indian?

MARTINCILLO: I don't believe He has time for such matters, but He does charge us to save and be charitable, and St. Francis recommends the *usus pauper et tenuis* of possessions.

FRIAR JUAN: You're a shyster, not a friar, Brother Martín.

MARTINCILLO: You've told me that before, but you yourself don't believe it, Brother Juan.

FRIAR JUAN: Are you forgetting that I'm the bishop of New Spain for you to speak to me so?

MARTINCILLO: You're in a bad humor today, Lord Bishop, since that's how you must be addressed.

FRIAR JUAN: I'm a Spaniard, not a saint.

MARTINCILLO (*under his breath*): If it were only that— but you're a Basque.

FRIAR JUAN: What are you saying?

MARTINCILLO: I haven't said a word.

FRIAR JUAN: Also a liar. Of course, I'm a Basque. What of it?

MARTINCILLO: That explains all, Your Lordship.

FRIAR JUAN *is about to reply, but thinks better of it and sits down at his desk.*

MARTINCILLO: You've been in a bad humor for several days and I don't understand why. You haven't confidence in me as before. You're still hard, but you mistreat me less than you're used to. Something's the matter with you, Friar Juan.

FRIAR JUAN: Forgive me if I've been hard, Brother Martín.

MARTINCILLO: It so happens that I can't forgive you . . . (FRIAR JUAN *draws himself up*) because you've done nothing for me to forgive. What's tormenting you, Friar Juan? The memory of that Indian you had burnt alive?

FRIAR JUAN: If you don't shut up, I'll forget that I'm a Franciscan and a bishop to boot, and——.

MARTINCILLO: Remember that you're a Basque. Now you're more like yourself. But if I were in your shoes I wouldn't mope. In burning that poor Indian you purified his soul and he went straight to the Lord's own Paradise. Now as all the converted Indians will follow the same straight road, when you arrive in Paradise you won't be able to recognize the charred one because it's impossible to tell one Indian from another.

FRIAR JUAN (*smiling a bit in spite of himself*): The memory of that Indian doesn't torment me, Brother. What his body suffered his soul is enjoying. He has been saved, I'm certain. But his salvation was mine also because I'll never allow another Indian to be burnt alive, and I'll not rest until I succeed in having them all considered as human beings. Las Casas and Gante and Sahagún will help me in this.

MARTINCILLO: Then what is the matter with you?

FRIAR JUAN: The king's the matter with me. That's what! (*He breaks off, angry again.*) How dare you question me? Go away and leave me in peace.

MARTINCILLO (*passing from contentment to dis-*

comfort): So you won't tell me any more. Well, then, another time. (*He starts to exit but returns.*) Oh! I forgot. There's a committee from the tailors' guild outside that wants to speak to Your Lordship.

FRIAR JUAN: What about?

MARTINCILLO: Now I'm not to blame, I assure you, Lord Bishop.

FRIAR JUAN: Speak up!

MARTINCILLO: It's about . . . about the Corpus Christi procession.

FRIAR JUAN: Go out there and tell them——.

MARTINCILLO: They'd never believe me, my lord. I've already told them everything, but they insist upon seeing Your Lordship in person.

FRIAR JUAN (*after a pause*): Very well. Let them come in. (MARTINCILLO *goes to the door.*) No. Wait. I'll go myself.

> FRIAR JUAN *rises and walks slowly to the door on the right which remains open.* MARTINCILLO *crosses himself and makes ready to listen. A moment later the energetic voice of the bishop is clearly heard.*

VOICE OF FRIAR JUAN: I've already told you no, gentlemen. When will you understand me? I know why I prohibited the procession and I know I'm right. It is a matter of extreme profanation and shame that masked men who are dressed as women appear before the Most Holy Sacrament, dancing and jumping about in impure and lascivious wiggling.

A VOICE: Your Lordship forgets that the Cabildo has permitted——.

> *While these words are being spoken,* FRIAR TORIBIO DE BENAVENTE, *whom the Indians call* MOTOLINÍA *which means* THE POOR ONE, *enters left. Although he should be dressed in a brown habit, he is wearing a blue one, as all his brethren of the order do, because, so it seems, of the absence of brown cloth in New Spain. He is*

*thin and ascetic with an expression that denotes kind-
ness and also fatigue. He goes to* MARTINCILLO *who
signs to him to stop and also to listen.*

VOICE OF FRIAR JUAN: Those who do so and
those who order it, and even those who consent to it,
although they could stop it but do not, must find someone
other than Friar Juan de Zumárraga to pardon them.

THE NEWLY-ARRIVED: What's the matter? Is the
bishop in a bad humor today?

MARTINCILLO *raises his eyes to heaven.*

VOICE OF FRIAR JUAN: And it will work no
little harm to their souls and to the doctrine which is
being taught to these Indians . . .

ANOTHER VOICE: But in Spain, Your Lordship, in
Italy——.

MARTINCILLO: Alas, Friar Toribio, Friar Toribio!

VOICE OF FRIAR JUAN: And because of this
alone, although in other countries and amongst other peoples this vain and profane and pagan custom may be
tolerated, by no means should it be permitted or consented
to amongst the Indians of this new Church.

A pause. MOTOLINÍA *smiles, then goes to a leather
chair in which he sits down with a sigh of relief.*

VOICES: We promise you to put an end to——.
          ——these doings of the Indians, Your Lord-
ship——.
          ——but let us have the procession this
year——.
          ——all the guilds——.
          ——besides those of the tailors and the
gold- and silversmiths——.
          ——allow us, Lord Bishop——.

Another pause. MARTINCILLO *makes a gesture signify-
ing doubt.*

VOICE OF FRIAR JUAN: Remember that if you don't conduct this one as God commands, on the word of a bishop, I'll prohibit the processions forever.

VOICES: Thanks, a thousand thanks, Your Lordship——.

——Your Blessing, Lord Bishop——.

——By Leave of Your Lordship——.

MARTINCILLO *gives a sigh of relief and goes to* MOTO-LINÍA.

MARTINCILLO: You seem tired, Friar Toribio.

MOTOLINÍA: The road from Tlaxcallan is long, Brother, but the Indians are charitable and gave me hospitality and food. They who are poorer than I!

While MOTOLINÍA *is speaking, a Dominican friar whose countenance shows authority, courage, grace, and briskness, and also a Spanish temper which is always at the boiling point, appears, unseen by the others, at the threshold where he remains. In this man kindness itself, which is the key to his character, assumes an extraordinary vigor and force. He is* PRIOR BARTOLOMÉ DE LAS CASAS.

LAS CASAS: Ah, Friar Toribio! Even though I don't see you often, you're not improving. Always the same.

MARTINCILLO: Welcome, Father Las Casas.

MOTOLINÍA: What do you mean by that, Brother Bartolomé?

LAS CASAS (*going to a chair with deliberate slowness while raising his index finger with firmness*): Vain as a . . . a Dominican, let's say.

MOTOLINÍA (*pained*): I? Vain?

LAS CASAS (*while sitting down*): God be with you, Brother Martín. (*To* MOTOLINÍA.) You, Brother, have the greatest of all vanities—that of poverty. And you boast of it! I've always believed that you're a Franciscan by mistake—a false Franciscan.

MOTOLINÍA (*turning red*): And you, in turn, are a true Dominican.

LAS CASAS: You were born to be a bishop—but you'll end up a friar.

MOTOLINÍA: And I'm happy about that. You, in turn, will end up a bishop.

LAS CASAS: Peace, Brother Toribio, peace. We're all just miserable missionaries.

MOTOLINÍA: Ah, but I——.

LAS CASAS (*interrupting him*): Agreed. You're the most miserable of all, Motolinía. Brother Martín, inform——.

MARTINCILLO: And since when have I stopped being Martincillo to you?

LAS CASAS: Pardon. Martincillo, let Friar Juan know that we're here. Or isn't he at home?

MARTINCILLO: Just a moment ago he was on the point of excommunicating the tailors' guild. Now he must be praying.

LAS CASAS (*good-naturedly*): Quiet, mischievous-tongued. Go and see.

MARTINCILLO *exits right.* MOTOLINÍA *shuts himself off in an unfriendly silence.* LAS CASAS *smiles.*

LAS CASAS: Come now, my Brother Motolinía, don't be angry with me. We see each other too seldom to waste time in quarreling.

MOTOLINÍA: First you attack me, and then you forget it.

LAS CASAS: That's because I've a good stomach. I digest immediately the offenses I commit. That's not easy to do, but it proves that I speak without venom and for your own good. Forgive me. (MOTOLINÍA *does not reply, although he nods his head in agreement.*) They tell me you're writing a book. Is that truly a fact?

MOTOLINÍA: In truth, it's just vanity. But what does this matter to you?

LAS CASAS (*patiently, as with a child*): I'm afraid you'll write ill of me in it, if you detest me as much as it's whispered that you do.

MOTOLINÍA: I? I detest anyone? Not even the toad itself, nor the frog in its puddle, nor the——.

LAS CASAS: I'll never believe that you're poor in your feelings. Detest me, but do tell me what you'll call your chronicle.

MOTOLINÍA (*vanquished*): Just *History of the Indians of New Spain*. I plan to relate in it all the marvels we've discovered here, but I'll not think of it as finished till we've converted and saved the last Indian of this generation. I'm learning the languages and making up lexicons with my friars and students. It's a long work, but it's most satisfying.

LAS CASAS: The capacity to learn is the clearest proof of the existence of God in man. If anyone had told me that I'd learn some of these Indian languages enough to pray in them——.

FRIAR MARTÍN DE VALENCIA, *the original head of the twelve Franciscan missionaries and who wears the habit of the Observants of the Order, enters left. He is older than the others and has been consumed by penances, vigils, and the sacrifice of himself. All that remains of him is pure fire which is very near to becoming nothing more than light.*

FRIAR MARTÍN DE VALENCIA: It pleases me to see you thus, Brothers. You don't quarrel as you used to?

LAS CASAS (*rising*): Martín de Valencia! I thought you were on your way to Spain.

MOTOLINÍA (*also rising*): Friar Martín!

LAS CASAS *embraces* FRIAR MARTÍN DE VALENCIA, *and then* MOTOLINÍA *does so.*

FRIAR MARTÍN DE VALENCIA: And I thought you were in Puerto de Plata. I am on my way to Spain, although it's possible that I'll reach another shore first.

LAS CASAS: Come now! Who can think of dying with all the work we have to do in these lands?

FRIAR MARTÍN DE VALENCIA: No one chooses his limit nor his hour. Yet the idea of not dying would be the attitude of a schismatic.

The three sit down.

LAS CASAS: Nevertheless, I've the impression that in Spain one dies when God wills, but here when one chooses to. This is like another planet. Go on to Spain, but do come back later.

FRIAR MARTÍN DE VALENCIA: Yes, I'll go to Spain so that all these horrors may be put an end to. I've sent emissaries to the king, but he doesn't reply.

LAS CASAS: I hope to hear from him soon. Nuño de Guzmán has gone too far in pillage and crime. By the Living God, I swear to you that we'll put an end to these conquistadores who've an endless lust for gold.

FRIAR MARTÍN DE VALENCIA: I've often thought that it may be a mistake to preach poverty to the Indian in so rich a country while the Spaniards take over everything.

MOTOLINÍA: First of all, the Indian, who's our son, must be educated.

LAS CASAS: Our peer, our peer! As fully rational as we.

FRIAR MARTÍN DE VALENCIA: And perhaps even more so because his reason has permitted him until now to live without worshipping God, when our own would prevent us from doing so.

MARTINCILLO *returns.*

LAS CASAS: Is the bishop praying, Martincillo?

MARTINCILLO: Friar Martín de Valencia, God preserve you! He's walking, Lord Prior Las Casas. He's walking up and down like a caged tiger. I wanted to speak to him but he sent me to the devil.

FRIAR MARTÍN DE VALENCIA: That's impossible. Friar Juan isn't capable of wanting such harm to come to you.

MARTINCILLO: He only does that to pray and ask forgiveness afterwards. He believes that if he doesn't sin he can't be redeemed. (LAS CASAS *laughs.* MOTOLINÍA *looks at him reproachfully.* FRIAR MARTÍN DE VALENCIA *shakes his head while smiling mildly.*) But what's disturbing me is that it's days since he has been himself. He doesn't sleep, he doesn't eat, and he seems to have been suffering ever since he sent his messengers to call you all here, Brothers.

FRIAR MARTÍN DE VALENCIA: What could be the matter with him? This news pains me.

MOTOLINÍA: I'm closer to him than either of you, and I know that he has some serious worries now.

LAS CASAS: What do you expect not to happen to him? The same thing that happens to us all—discouragement at times, anger with the soldiers, the magistrates, and the merchants from Spain—the slaughters, the plagues that carry off the Indians——.

MOTOLINÍA: Oh and the restoration of Tenochtítlan! The most painful sore of the indigenous family. I know what he's suffering.

MARTINCILLO: But all that's already well known, Brothers. This time it's something different. I bet you——.

FRIAR MARTÍN DE VALENCIA: Bet?

LAS CASAS: You've the soul of a soldier, Martincillo.

MARTINCILLO: The bishop calls me a shyster and the prior a soldier. We're doing well. My bishop also bets me. But I'm only speaking in a figurative sense, of course. What can a Franciscan, who'll always be a lay brother, bet but his habit and so all the better to keep the rules of the order by going practically naked? But who'd take that bet? As I'd have to bet my habit, if one should want a wager, and as I'm forbidden to bet, I'll make up for that by betting without a wager, and without betting you, I'll bet you that it's about something else.

LAS CASAS: Martincillo, you're the least religious soul I've ever come across, but you do have a certain way about you.

MARTINCILLO: The consolation of the ugly duckling.

FRIAR JUAN *enters followed by* PEDRO DE GANTE.

FRIAR JUAN: Chatterbox! I always find you talking, even if only to your shadow. When will you ever shut up?

MARTINCILLO: Whenever you order me to talk, Lord Bishop.

FRIAR JUAN: Greet Friar Pedro, then go to——.

MARTINCILLO: Again to the dev——?

FRIAR JUAN: Go to the door and when our Brothers Don Vasco and Sahagún arrive, let them come in here, and see to it that no one interrupts us. And don't you listen at the door, or for punishment you'll be put on bread and water. (MARTINCILLO *makes to protest*.) Speak, I order you to.

MARTINCILLO: I . . . I shut up. (*Exits*.)

LAS CASAS: Fell into his own trap, poor fellow.

MOTOLINÍA: Soul of God!

FRIAR JUAN: What would I do without him?

One by one FRIAR JUAN *embraces the friars*. PEDRO DE GANTE *does the same*.

FRIAR JUAN: Be seated, Brothers. I've ordered some refreshment prepared for you. And now I want to thank you all for having come at my call.

FRIAR MARTÍN DE VALENCIA: You can see that we're filled with the deepest concern for you, Friar Juan. We all have the same task, but you've more problems because they're yoked to your office of the first bishop of New Spain.

FRIAR JUAN: I swear to you that I'd prefer to be Martincillo.

LAS CASAS: Why's that? Is your stomach so bad?

MOTOLINÍA: Are you perhaps losing courage?

} *Both speaking at the same time*

PEDRO DE GANTE: He'll not lose courage because he's a Basque. But I understand him well, and for the first time in my life I'd really like to be the king so I could do in New Spain what should be done.

FRIAR JUAN: Lose courage? You ask that, Friar Toribio? We're building schools in Tlaxcallan and Tlatelolco. Every day we're converting hundreds of Indians—may God bless them! and I'm certain that our great work will meet with no obstacle from the natives of this land. But I'm beginning to believe that the devil lives in Spain and that he's a Spaniard.

LAS CASAS: Do you say that as a Basque?

FRIAR JUAN: I say it as a bishop. You've all observed how much the pagan rites of these infidels resemble those of our Church, except for the point of faith in the true God and the human sacrifices.

The door on the left opens.

MARTINCILLO (*announcing*): Don Vasco de Quiroga (FRIAR JUAN *turns with a gesture of irritation*) . . . and I . . . I'm leaving.

FRIAR JUAN (*rising and embracing* DON VASCO): Welcome.

Appropriate greetings from the others.

DON VASCO: I interrupted you. You were saying——.

FRIAR JUAN: I was going to say that more than our rites and those of the pagans resemble each other, the Spanish conquistador resembles an epidemic of smallpox and the idols of human sacrifice Camaxtle and Huitzilopoxtli.

PEDRO DE GANTE: So you can actually pronounce those names? My Flemish mixes me up entirely. I'll never be a polyglot.

DON VASCO: I heard you from the entrance, and Pedro de Gante is right. Nahuatl is difficult, but Tarascan is unpronounceable. All the words have *ts* and *zeds* combined, and it's impossible for a Spaniard to pronounce those jawbreakers. Can you say Tzintzuntzan?

PEDRO DE GANTE: Now in truth, Friar Juan, pardon my apparent impertinence. I see that you're agitated and worried, so I only wanted to calm you a little.

FRIAR JUAN: Yours wasn't levity. I know that. Well, then, although the Spaniard wasn't born to be a polyglot, I swear to you that he'll learn all the languages of the world before he'll change his character. This is what makes me despair.

DON VASCO: But you haven't called us together to talk about what we all know and suffer, Friar Juan. The tone of your message was very serious indeed.

LAS CASAS: That's why I came from so far away. Speak.

MOTOLINÍA: Unburden your bosom to us, Friar Juan.

FRIAR MARTÍN DE VALENCIA: Tell us if we can help you and in what.

PEDRO DE GANTE: You can count on me in everything. You know that.

A pause while all seat themselves, except FRIAR JUAN *who remains standing. While he is speaking, the door opens to admit* FRIAR BERNARDINO DE SAHAGÚN.

FRIAR JUAN: I've called you all together, Brothers —and especially you, Friar Pedro—to ask you who I am. (*All look at one another in astonishment.*) Who am I, I ask you? Am I the first bishop of New Spain by the grace of God and the pope? Or am I the least important flattering lackey of my king? Am I the shepherd over whom hangs the duty of saving the souls of this hemisphere? Am I, in the manner of St. Peter, the cornerstone of this Church? Or am I a mercenary? Am I a man of faith or an unbeliever?

After another pause which is filled with astonishment, all reply as in a litany which is a reflex of ecclesiastical discipline but in which there is a trace of professional distortion.

MOTOLINÍA: You are Friar Juan de Zumárraga.

FRIAR MARTÍN DE VALENCIA: You are a man of faith.

LAS CASAS: You are the bishop of New Spain.

DON VASCO: You are the cornerstone of this new Church.

PEDRO DE GANTE: You are the shepherd of souls of this hemisphere.

LAS CASAS: You are our head.

FRIAR MARTÍN DE VALENCIA: You are our support.

MOTOLINÍA: You are our hope.

PEDRO DE GANTE: You are our inspirer.

DON VASCO: You are our guide.

FRIAR BERNARDINO DE SAHAGÚN (*very softly*): You're a bishop who wants to say something to us, and we're all waiting for you to do so, Brother.

On hearing his voice, all turn to him. Rapid embraces of him by all follow in silence.

FRIAR JUAN: Thank you, Friar Bernardino. I want to tell you, Brothers, that the moment of the great test has come for me. I'm going to petition the pope, our lord, for permission to resign this diocese and retire to a reformed monastery in Italy or in France.

FRIAR MARTÍN DE VALENCIA: What are you saying, Friar Juan!

MOTOLINÍA: St. Francis help us!

DON VASCO: God be praised!

PEDRO DE GANTE: Have you lost your head!

LAS CASAS: What the deuce does this mean!

} *All together*

SAHAGÚN: You're making history, I'm certain, but

history must be narrated with clarity, simplicity, and in detail. We're listening to you.

FRIAR JUAN: I'm going to explain it all to you, Brothers, but first I must ask of you your most solemn promise, your oath, even, on your faith, that never will you say a word about what we have to deal with here, and that you'll keep silent about it to the world and to history, for all your lives and even after death. (*The astonishment of all reaches its climax. After looking at one another, they all swear, making the sign of the cross while murmuring the words* "I swear.") Thank you, Brothers. Now, come with me. (*He goes to the window.*) Stand here and tell me what you see in that patio.

LAS CASAS (*the first to go to the window*): I see a man dressed in brown.

MOTOLINÍA: A layman.

FRIAR MARTÍN DE VALENCIA: He's bending over a clump of green.

PEDRO DE GANTE: By my faith, he looks like a gardener.

FRIAR JUAN: He is a gardener who has come from Murcia. But, I tell you, look farther on, there, at the end.

DON VASCO (*after straining his sight*): I can't believe it.

LAS CASAS: A nun?

FRIAR JUAN: A nun of the Second Order. A nun of St. Clara.

MOTOLINÍA: The first to come to New Spain.

FRIAR JUAN: The first.

FRIAR MARTÍN DE VALENCIA: The Clarisse Sisters can in, fact, help us much, but——.

LAS CASAS: Ah, no! We'll be in a fine mess if women take a hand in this calvary of evangelization. Ah, no!

PEDRO DE GANTE: But I think that they can be of much service.

FRIAR JUAN: Not this one.

SAHAGÚN: Then what has she come here for? Who sent her?

FRIAR JUAN (*moving away from the window*): Be seated, Brothers. I must tell you about what is going on here.

While all are taking their seats, FRIAR JUAN *goes to the door to make certain that no one is listening. He then remains standing in an attitude of concentration before speaking. The others all wait in a silence that begins to be disturbing.*

FRIAR JUAN: I'll not remind you, Brothers, of the motives for which each of you came to the Indies. I'll not remind you either of what attracted Captain Cortés and his adventurers in the guise of soldiers, and later, the profiteers, the magistrates, the merchants, and the rest of the infectious plague of Spain and Mexico. Friar Juan de Zumárraga, the first bishop of the New World, your own poor little Brother Juan here, will neither remind you that we Franciscans, Dominicans, and members of other orders were brought to these lands by God's wind to sow His essence in them and to make His name known amongst the Indians—all for the simple reason that this is our daily work in the world. Neither shall I speak to you of the greed, nor of the eagerness for plunder and lordship of the Spaniard against whom we fight every day. Nor shall I speak of the violation of the divine Commandments nor of the miscegenation, nor of the destruction and horror. I'll say only this to you: apparently our labor has been in vain.

The Indian avoids us and the Spaniard is—I can find no other expression—incorruptible by goodness, alas. The champion of the Christian faith in the world who has confronted the pope himself—our Lord King and Emperor—seems, alas, to have taken unto himself the spiritual matters of the Church in accordance with the example and practice of Martin Luther himself. So it is, Brothers, that

extremes meet. Charles V, a Lutheran in quintessence, has
sent me by word of mouth through an emissary a command
that my most deeply rooted convictions and my sense of
what the Church should be in modern times compel me
not to obey. I believe in the Church as a fact founded on
souls and on a rock. I believe in God as an absolute reality
because God is supreme reason and common sense. And I
believe that our task in New Spain consists of making the
unfortunate Indians who're idolaters by a fatality, touch
God Himself so as to touch in Him the faith and reason
and common sense which explain to us the existence of
God, and which cry out to us the equality before God of
all the beings He has created. But what, Brothers, does
Charles V, who's not only a Lutheran but a pre-Lutheran
suckled by the wolf of the shades of past centuries—what
does he command me to do? That I perform a miracle.
(*General movement.*) He commands me to take the place
of Our Lord God and contrive the apparition of a Virgin
who's to look like a Mexican. (*Exclamations and signs of
the cross.*) And for what reason? So as at last to give definitive lordship to the Spaniard, and clearly to deprive the
Indian of all light and all hope so that he'll submit if he's
left free to worship a Virgin of his own. Yet serious as this
is, it's not all. I foresee that this scheme, if carried out,
would disrupt the Catholic Church itself, because the more
the Mexican believes in an Indian Virgin of his own, the
more he'll withdraw from the Church of Christ, and thus
the fusion of two peoples and two races will never be con-
sumated. The Indian will have his Virgin, the Spaniard
will have his Church and Christ. Thus the distance between the two will be deepened and practically endless. All
the anguish will be increased because of a new war between
two beliefs—what difference can there be between idols and
an artificial Virgin?—and because of the merciless new
slaughter that'll inevitably follow. And lest any fallibility
of the miserable bishop himself upset the imperial plan,
they've sent me a gardener from Murcia whose task is to

make rose bushes bloom in a wasteland, and also a Clarisse nun who'll pass for the supposed Virgin because she has hallucinations and visions and is as mad as if she were under the light of a full moon. This is the reason for my decision to renounce my office and retire into monastic peace. But I measure the profundity of the situation. I understand the importance of all this, its weight in the definitive salvation of the innocent Indian whom we must separate from his gods of stone and wash clean of his paganism and bring out of his darkness and error while leading him into the pious, luminous world of Jesus. Because of all this I wanted to consult you before acting because you, who work with your soul and your spirit, will tell me what I must do, not concerning my decision to retire—which was taken after a long consultation with God—but about the way to prevent the thriving of this idea which if were in another age I'd call diabolical, but which I call abominably Lutheran in ours. We must also consider the possibility that when I retire, the emperor'll send a new bishop here, perhaps a secular one, to carry out his command. Thus roses will bloom in a wasteland and the Mother of God will cease to be the Mother of humanity to become only a symbol for the Indian who's condemned to perish. My reason and my Scholasticism rebel against all this, but I want to know that I'm not alone and that I can count on your spiritual fraternity in the fight I'm preparing to undertake against the emperor. And I'll fight, Brothers, I tell you with brutal Basque frankness, more than for the Faith, because it'll also be for common sense and intelligence and reason which are like the Tarpeian rock from which faith lets itself fall so as to soar upward and enlighten the world.

SAHAGÚN: It can't be! A Tonantzin, another mother of the gods of stone, as in the Aztec mythology, alas! The regression of history.

LAS CASAS: The resurrection of all the indigenous idolatry.

FRIAR JUAN: The annihilation of all our efforts to preserve the rational human being in the Indian.

PEDRO DE GANTE: The fall back into a decayed age which was barbarous in its own way! And I've been accustomed to think of Charles as a modern monarch who's enlightened by Divine Reason.

FRIAR JUAN: Have you nothing to say, Friar Martín de Valencia?

FRIAR MARTÍN DE VALENCIA: I don't know—truly I don't know what to say. I'd prefer to hear you all first. Friar Toribio?

MOTOLINÍA (*thoughtfully*): I don't know either what to say. Coming thus suddenly the jolt is rude and shattering. I feel within me a tremendous vertigo as if the very Church were sinking. But, nevertheless, at the same time I'm beginning to think it's possible that the idea isn't so blasphemous as Friar Juan considers it to be.

FRIAR JUAN: What are you saying, Brother?

MOTOLINÍA: Forgive me. I can do no more than connect . . . I'm always thinking, as you know, about the need to organize performances of miracle and mystery plays to hurry up the evangelization of our brother Indians. Such things as, for instance, the temptation and fall of Adam and Eve, and the conquest of Rhodes and that of Jerusalem so as to show the Indian how the Cross of Christ opens up the way in heathen lands. And there could even be the representation of our own head, St. Francis, preaching his sermon to the birds. It would all help us so much to carry out our holy mission and task——.

FRIAR JUAN: You're getting away from——.

SAHAGÚN: Pardon me, but I'm afraid that our Brother hasn't yet said all he's thinking.

MOTOLINÍA: I couldn't help it, Friar Juan, but while you were speaking, it came to me that it might be about a kind of holy play that could be useful to the Faith, and——.

LAS CASAS: Absurd, like everything else about

Motolinía! (*He emphasises the Nahuatl word with sarcasm.*)

MOTOLINÍA: Oh, Brother, you're hard! But those of my order will understand what I'm thinking about—above all about the Faith and . . . I don't see it all very clearly just now—but perhaps some dramatic presentations in the style of the *Little Flowers* in action——.

LAS CASAS: Always the Poor Little One. But you're not the one of Assissi, Friar Toribio.

MOTOLINÍA (*pained*): Prior Las Casas!

FRIAR JUAN: A truce on arguments, I beg of you. Don Vasco?

DON VASCO: By my faith, Friar Juan, I'm a practical man. Perhaps I'm closer to nature than to the things of the spirit. For that reason I see this as more like an experiment in sowing and tilling the land to test its goodness. Couldn't this perhaps help us to prove whether or not the Indian can truly be fertile of spirit? The fact is we don't really know this yet. Their idols, although destroyed, still seem to cast a great shadow from under which the Indians don't seem to be willing to come out, thinking, maybe, that it'll protect them against Spain.

PEDRO DE GANTE (*who has been sunk in deep thought*): Yes. An indubitable and dark return to old profanities. Yes. But I feel something, Brothers. (*Anticipating, although unaware of it, Galileo as yet unborn.*) And yet, beneath the repellent crust, this idea lives, nevertheless. It moves . . . it moves in me in a way so as to seem that the basis itself of the idea isn't harmful.

FRIAR JUAN: Now you've heard us, Friar Martín. What are you thinking?

FRIAR MARTÍN DE VALENCIA: First of all, I think that you mustn't retire from this diocese because the destiny which the Lord has laid out for you is here. I also think that you, just as the rest of us, mustn't abandon the Indian nor turn your back on the hope of saving him. The voice of God is stronger than that of the king and emperor.

FRIAR JUAN: The voice of God is the voice of my reason and conscience, Friar Martín, and my reason and conscience order me——.

FRIAR MARTÍN DE VALENCIA: Pardon. When I came in, Friar Juan, I told our Brothers that I'm going to Spain to see the king to whom I—even as you—have sent messengers in vain, so that he'll put an end to the horrors which we see committed here every day. And you are right, Las Casas. I cannot die in this prodigious land while there remains one Indian who suffers the misery of Spanish domination. I'm old, and we old men—may God forgive me—are like that pagan god of the Latins who looked backward and forward at the same time. I, therefore, see your reasons and understand them while at the same time I see and understand those of Sahagún and Gante and Las Casas, and I listen to Brother Toribio and Don Vasco and I believe that I understand them, too. I don't know whether this is an affliction or a blessing, a blasphemy or an act of God. But I do know one thing. I know that this world of darkness and suffering in which we live must receive light and become habitable again for man, because God knows—who if not He?—that man didn't ask to be created and that he only hopes to have been for some beneficial and high and luminous purpose. I know, too, that if the human species survives, it's so as to put an end to the race of Cain so that good may reign. I ask myself, therefore, if this action of the emperor, however immoderate—I agree as to that—isn't an answer to our prayers, an effort to help the Indians in accordance with the principles of the Church.

FRIAR JUAN (*pained, distressed—and obstinate*): Do fraud, trickery, and imposture perhaps have a place in those principles? Have they a place beside Almightly God? If this is an answer to our prayers, it's certainly not what my reason led me to hope for. No. We know that, and I quote the very words, "The Redeemer of the World does not want any more miracles to be performed, because they are not necessary. Our Holy Faith is firmly founded on thousands of miracles such as we have in the Old and New Testaments." Yet Charles wants one!

FRIAR MARTÍN DE VALENCIA: What you've cited can be so, in effect and reason, for the peoples who've worshipped God for centuries. But not for these natives, alas. So let's not deny the need for miracles, Brother Bishop. You're an Erasmian, as I well know, but the very treatise writer whom you've just quoted added that "The perfect life of a Christian is a continuous miracle on earth." Do we not desire that miraculous perfection for the Indian? And do we know whether or not this mightn't be the way? Do we know, if you please, why and when and how a miracle begins? All we know is that a miracle never ends.

FRIAR JUAN: And isn't it perhaps God who gives me the reason which opposes this?

FRIAR MARTÍN DE VALENCIA: I know—we know —that you're upright and clean, inflexible in your convictions and unsubornable in your faith. But I'm not certain whether this matter shouldn't be seen more with the eyes of the soul than with those of the reason—with the heart rather than with the head. A bit, if you please, as children would see it.

FRIAR JUAN: For me, those are the same thing, Friar Martín. They can't exist separately. They're syllables of the same word. Heart means sentiment, but it also means reason. I can't renounce my criterion.

FRIAR MARTÍN DE VALENCIA: Isn't renunciation the basic, first act of a Christian?

FRIAR JUAN: Not the renunciation of God.

FRIAR MARTÍN DE VALENCIA: Wait, though. Would you perhaps renounce God or His Idea because you show a roundabout way to Him to one who cannot, who doesn't know how to follow the straight road? Do you lie to an incurably sick person who's leaving this life when you tell him that life awaits him? It's true that you don't absolutely know this, but you believe it. And all roads, whether long or short, lead to God. What can the errors of kings and of other men matter to Him? He lets them make those errors because it's a right which He conceded to them so that they can save themselves by rectifying those errors, but He ever maintains the pointer of the scales in true balance.

LAS CASAS: True. Would I perhaps stop believing in God because others come to believe in Him? But let's be honest. It would wound me deeply if God should save the conquistadores, and what's being hatched up now seems to be the means for doing so.

FRIAR MARTÍN DE VALENCIA: But aren't they also His sons?

FRIAR JUAN: That's exactly what confirms me all the more in my reason. What the emperor is counting on and also every Spanish soldier beginning with Cortés is the fathomless Franciscan meekness, the gentleness of the Poor Little One of Assisi with the wolf. But the beast that comes to us now comes from hell and pagan antiquity—from the very idolatry of the Indians which we must destroy. Ah, no! The missionary isn't made of sugar frosting, Brothers. He isn't a child who plays with sacred things! If ever a soldier needed a soul of well-tempered steel, a clear and firm voice, and a strong fist to wield the lash of Christ, it's the missionary. What do you say, Las Casas?

LAS CASAS: In Scholasticism, in the moral aspect, in political angles, I'm with you, Friar Juan. It's high time that we refused to play the conquistadores' game and bless the arms with which they kill, and to promise paradise to the Indians who die unholy deaths.

FRIAR MARTÍN DE VALENCIA: You're right about that, Brother Bartolomé. It's time for us to try to give man paradise here on earth—not just there in the beyond. And this is to be done by teaching him to do good so that we can really give him paradise.

FRIAR JUAN: Friar Toribio was speaking of miracle plays——.

LAS CASAS: A mistake and levity, I insist. Pure profanity.

FRIAR JUAN: Pardon. As if in the way of the ancient pagans it would be enough to give the Indian a little bread and a little circus and thus save our own souls.

MOTOLINÍA: I didn't speak in that sense, Friar Juan. Believe me, I beg of you. I wouldn't exchange the soul of one Indian for those of ten Spaniards. I, too, am ready to wield the sword against the soldier and the lash against the money changers, but I find that it's our duty to try every means, and that the good of the end which we are pursuing isn't contrary to the means which are being proposed to us.

FRIAR JUAN: Profane means! Irrational!

SAHAGÚN: So matters always come to be understood—Friar Juan speaks to us of the missionary's firmness and Friar Toribio demonstrates that he can be firm . . . against Friar Juan or his opinion.

FRIAR MARTÍN DE VALENCIA: I wouldn't say profane, Brother. Perhaps an imperfect means, limited and fallible—just like anything that's human. But that can't touch the Divinity, either from near or afar.

SAHAGÚN: And, furthermore, let's consider this. There're the idols which separated the Indian from God. What evil can there be in one that leads him to God? What does it matter while history and we ourselves know that it's only an idol?

PEDRO DE GANTE: Right. To believe that a tree can be God doesn't change the essence of God.

FRIAR MARTÍN DE VALENCIA: Oh, come now. God exists even for those who don't believe in Him.

MOTOLINÍA: If His entity doesn't lose with doubt, how is it going to lose with faith?

FRIAR JUAN: Ah, a moment! Our very shadow, our doubt—mine now—is the work of God.

DON VASCO: I can't dispute theology with you. For me, the representation of God is in the land which must feed man, and I feel obliged to test all fertilizers to know whether they can be productive.

PEDRO DE GANTE: Pardon, but there's another

thing. All this we're talking about gives me an idea. There's so much to think about in it! But I know, I feel that this question has a depth we've not touched upon.

FRIAR MARTÍN DE VALENCIA: I believe that we have touched upon it, Friar Pedro. It's the basic conviction that we must do whatever is for the good of our Faith, even though the means appear at times to be . . . heterodox.

PEDRO DE GANTE (*as a Fleming, with weight but not pomposity*): Have you thought of still another matter, Brothers? If that infection, that malignant and infectious plague which is the Reformation should take over all Europe, if the dark forces of Luther should triumph, what would become of our Church?

LAS CASAS: I believe that I see where you're going, Pedro, but what's more important here is——.

PEDRO DE GANTE: Please. Wouldn't it be natural that this blesséd land of New Spain should be the sanctuary or seat of our Holy Mother the Church—the New Holy Land, the New Rome?

LAS CASAS: By my habit, I thought that was it! But I think that's going too far. Not for nothing has Rome been the Eternal City of the Faith for centuries. But, above all, let's keep our feet firmly planted in *this* land.

PEDRO DE GANTE: I understand that, of course. But doesn't it seem to you that only because of the very possibility to which I referred and which perhaps may not be too far off, the emperor's idea is worthy of study?

LAS CASAS: Agreed. So let's do think about what Friar Pedro has just pointed out. The idea's worth while because all that helps the Faith in Mexico is an arm against the barbaric devil of a conquistador.

FRIAR MARTÍN DE VALENCIA (*illuminated and in an ecstasy*): True. Hasn't it been suggested that the earthly Paradise may have been situated in these very latitudes? Ah, if only this could become the New House of the Lord through the means they're proposing to us!

SAHAGÚN: I don't see the least possibility of such a thing taking place in the historical order, let's say.

FRIAR JUAN: To follow the *ab absurdo* method is rational, but to anticipate the triumph of Luther over Rome is an excess of imagination. So let's return to this land, as Las Casas has said, and to your Brother Juan here and his dilemma.

LAS CASAS: I've told you that I'm with you and that I'm with you in everything, Zumárraga. But I've been thinking that perhaps this thing can give a spiritual arm to the Indian against the Spaniard. I'm sorry that the idea didn't come from an Indian who knows the legend of the Tonantzin. But, clearly, clearly—to a poor Indian, an Indian Virgin. It isn't bad. That's why I think we mustn't be hasty because this may turn out to be a kind of Road to Damascus, you see.

FRIAR JUAN: I don't understand you.

LAS CASAS: Don't you know those ancient lands over there? If Saul had set forth from some other city on his mission of death with the letters of the High Priest for the Synagogue, perhaps he wouldn't have had time to be converted. But the road from Jerusalem to Damascus is long although Damascus may seem to be only a short distance away. In reality, however, it is far and——.

PEDRO DE GANTE: I beg of you. You're touching upon a miracle of the Faith that's not comparable to what we're dealing with now.

LAS CASAS: But didn't you touch upon the possible triumph of Luther and the other possibilities? Now that's why I believe that we must follow a long road in the examination of this matter, Brother, even when the road of the discussion stretches out equally as far as that to Damascus. I'm walking it now, as it were, and I'm beginning to see, without this influencing my convictions, that the emperor's purpose can be taken as not to be sacrilegious.

PEDRO DE GANTE: I must protest. St. Paul's conversion had nothing to do with the length of the road, and, furthermore, the Vision appeared to him when he was already near Damascus.

LAS CASAS: I'm convinced that the Vision left
Jerusalem with him and that it accompanied him all the
way. God was already in him, but Saul, like any man,
needed time to see that, so God gave him the time on that
long journey, and only when he was reaching the end of it
did the miracle work outwardly. If the journey had been
shorter——.

FRIAR MARTÍN DE VALENCIA: You're approaching dangerously near to error and blasphemy, Brother.

LAS CASAS: Pardon, but I don't believe so. God
created time, as all things, and He knows how much time
man often needs to see the light. In any event, I repeat my
proposal that we go along farther before——.

FRIAR JUAN: And don't you think that I haven't
followed a very long road of reflection, Brother? I want to
ask of you only that we not depart from the immediate
problem, from what I've decided to do, and from the counsel which I require of you. Friar Bernardino?

SAHAGÚN: In one way or another you'll make history, Friar Juan. And what is man but history? Yet be careful. There're always two ways of making history and you
might well make that of the dispersion of the Faith in
Mexico if you should retire now and leave the field to the
soldiers. When I see what the poor Indian suffers I think
that whatever thing we may give him to strengthen his
faith is good, and this is the other way of making history.
Don't retire. Are you afraid that the Indians may reproach
you——?

FRIAR JUAN: I fear only God and my conscience.
Both tell me that this is a serious crime—a fraud of faith,
of the soul, and of the reason. My own reason cannot
justify Charles's purpose.

SAHAGÚN: But, are we really dealing with reason?
Friar Martín has already spoken about that. Don't the lay
brothers and the humble friars minor who can't go to universities and who vegetate in towns and villages, change, at
times, that is, simplify the sacred texts so that their igno-

rant faithful can understand them better and even so that they, themselves as missionaries, will understand them? Don't they often Hispanize the Latin——?

FRIAR JUAN: That's the worst crime a priest can commit. God's truth ought to be difficult to come at. It should cost work, because it must be attained to as it is, not simplified, not . . . predigested.

FRIAR MARTÍN DE VALENCIA: As for that, I assure you there's a state of grace which dissipates all error.

PEDRO DE GANTE: Of course, but it emanates from heaven, not from the king. Yet in spite of everything, permit us, Friar Juan, to examine the matter from another angle, from the angle of . . . a performance, as Friar Toribio would say. Let's suppose for a moment that you carry out the king's orders. How would you go about doing so?

SAHAGÚN: A good idea that'll permit us to see the obstacles.

FRIAR JUAN: The impossibilities.

LAS CASAS: And the possibilities. This is the long road of which I was speaking. What'll we lose?

FRIAR MARTÍN DE VALENCIA: We'll even gain something. God is always a gain for man.

MOTOLINÍA: Do you agree, Friar Juan?

FRIAR JUAN (*after a long, nervous pause in which he presses his hands together while looking upward*): So be it. I know that I've already examined it all, but speak, Brothers.

MOTOLINÍA: Before anything else, we need the stage. Now, let's just suppose . . . May I ask what the instructions are, in detail, Friar Juan?

FRIAR JUAN (*with a great effort*): To make roses grow in a wasteland and have the Clarisse appear there.

PEDRO DE GANTE: Not in a church, I hope!

FRIAR JUAN: In a wasteland, I said.

MOTOLINÍA: Careful! It'll be necessary to choose a place which hasn't been given over to some idolatrous cult, and they're numerous here.

FRIAR JUAN: I've already thought about the only place where it could be, although——.

MOTOLINÍA (*softly but firmly*): Nothing escapes you. And afterward?

FRIAR JUAN (*as before, unwillingly and hard*): To cause the . . . vision, let's say, to appear on some solemn day that'll be impressive in itself, and have her speak to an Indian who has been chosen beforehand.

LAS CASAS: Wait a moment. The matter of the roses solved, will that Indian understand Castilian?

SAHAGÚN: Or will the Sister speak in Nahautl?

MOTOLINÍA: Whatever's necessary can be taught to one or the other.

FRIAR JUAN (*sarcastically*): Just so. And that's where the imposture will begin to be revealed and the secret be scattered abroad. I tell you, I've thought it all out.

MOTOLINÍA: Pardon. But I could undertake to teach whatever is necessary to the Clarisse. I suppose you have confidence in me.

FRIAR JUAN: I have. But, the Indian?

LAS CASAS: The Indian must be unaware of the whole thing. It's clear that he must receive the message, like the apparition, as a surprise if he's to believe in them.

SAHAGÚN: And how, then, is he to be chosen?

MOTOLINÍA: Perhaps a student from Tlaxcallan or Tlatelolco——.

PEDRO DE GANTE: No. A trick would be suspected at once if it were that way. Las Casas is right. If this is to be done, the Indian must be absolutely innocent.

FRIAR JUAN: And who's to find him?

FRIAR MARTÍN DE VALENCIA: Anybody can find one. For me, all Indians are innocent or simple-minded. Have you no faith, Friar Juan?

FRIAR JUAN: Only in the true, Martín de Valencia.

FRIAR MARTÍN DE VALENCIA: Does the true need faith?

FRIAR JUAN: More than anything, alas. If it were easy to believe in the truth, the world would be less absurd.

MOTOLINÍA (*as before, softly but firmly*): You're always right. But . . . may we go on? (FRIAR JUAN *nods but not without a certain repugnance.*) In that case——.

SAHAGÚN: But you spoke of a message, Friar Juan. Have they sent you the text?

DON VASCO: If they have, perhaps it would be better to reword it here. They're far away and don't know much over there about things here, but we know this land.

FRIAR MARTÍN DE VALENCIA: It's true that we know the word that's to be sown in these Indians. Like you, Don Vasco, I, too, believe in the land and I also believe that there's no better soil than the Indian for our seed.

MOTOLINÍA: Well, then, let's suppose, Brothers, that we've the stage for the action, the scenery, the cast, and the dialogue. A Virgin will appear to a simple-minded Indian and will give him a message for the salvation of his soul and the souls of all Indians. Isn't that right? What'll the Indian do then?

LAS CASAS: Allow me. Just a plain Virgin? No. The Indian's name isn't important, but that of the Virgin . . . I'd like to know——.

DON VASCO: Right. Pardon, Friar Juan, but in your instructions is a particular Virgin designated or not?

FRIAR JUAN (*after a pause which is intended to restrain his growing impatience*): I don't understand why, but it was made quite clear that the name of the Virgin of Extremadura should be used.

FRIAR MARTÍN DE VALENCIA: The Guadalupe? Ah, she's a good Virgin. This pleases me.

PEDRO DE GANTE: Guadalupe. Yes, I know. Of course. (*Evocatively.*) She's brown. Without a doubt that's why——.

LAS CASAS (*like* CHARLES V, *without knowing it*): She's a warrior Virgin and will be good for the spiritual battles of the Indian.

MOTOLINÍA: Doesn't her name have some connection with Moorish roots—the same as Guadalquivir?

SAHAGÚN: Maybe, because she helped in the battles

against the Moor. But the mountains of central Spain are
called Guadalupe, and Columbus named the two islands
he discovered in the West Indies for that Virgin.

MOTOLINÍA (*reflectively*): That's to say, a Virgin
who's Spanish is to be Mexican at the same time? But this
is more difficult for me to understand.

FRIAR JUAN (*at last breaking his silence and beginning to give free rein to his impatience*): By your leave.
It's just as I thought. I see that you're turning your eyes
away from the problem itself with this talk and are forgetting——.

MOTOLINÍA (*always with the same softness and firmness*): Only apparently so. The miracle and mystery plays
—the theatre, in a word—customarily take a man out of
himself, Friar Juan, and make him forget his personal
destiny for the collective, while also forgetting reality for
illusion, as you know. That's why——.

FRIAR JUAN: Wait a moment, Friar Toribio, I beg
of you. Brothers, because I see you setting out in the ship
of an idea which is repugnant to my reason, I request you
to postpone this discussion. I couldn't follow it now because it's only going round and round in the same circle.
Before going any further, I consider it indispensable for
you to see close up this Sister of the Order of St. Clara.
This will, I think, change your opinions about the whole
matter. But in any event we can continue our talk afterward.

FRIAR MARTÍN DE VALENCIA: That's to say you
still don't accept even the possibility?

FRIAR JUAN: I'm a Basque, Brother, if, in your
eyes, I don't have any other excuse. But just take a look at
her. Then, after having seen her, if all of you, knowing that
I believe in you as I believe in myself—or even more so—
still say that this is good and should be done, I'll do it.

LAS CASAS: This seems to me to be the most sensible course.

DON VASCO: It's always better to know who'll plow
the furrow.

PEDRO DE GANTE: I agree.

FRIAR MARTÍN DE VALENCIA: Above all, if Friar Juan asks us to, it'll be better—for every reason.

FRIAR JUAN *moves to pull the bell cord when the door right opens suddenly and a* YOUNG INDIAN, *somewhat disarrayed, enters quickly, being pushed in by a Franciscan who is* FRIAR ANTONIO, THE FRIAR *of Act 1.*

FRIAR JUAN: I was just going to have you called, Brother Antonio. How is it that you enter here without——?

FRIAR ANTONIO: I crave your forgiveness, Lord Bishop. I was coming to tell you something and there outside I found this miserable Indian listening at the door. (*He pushes* THE YOUNG INDIAN *another time, not with force but not gently either.*) Go on, explain yourself.

THE YOUNG INDIAN, *bewildered, looks about at all the missionaries as if seeking a protector, a refuge.*

FRIAR JUAN: Don't hurt him and don't mistreat him, Brother.

FRIAR ANTONIO: It's his mixture of passivity and malice that exasperates me so. He was listening at the door like a demon, and now he acts like an angel.

FRIAR JUAN: Brother Antonio! Are you forgetting what our order enjoins?

FRIAR ANTONIO: I'd never have done what I have to this one, Lord Bishop, if he hadn't exasperated me as he did. I don't know why, but it might be, as the king himself told me, that I'm an inquisitor. Anyway, I feel like one now.

FRIAR JUAN: That trip to Spain has changed you, Brother. I'll hear you in confession tomorrow.

THE YOUNG INDIAN (*at last choosing* FRIAR JUAN, *kneels at his feet and raises his bewildered eyes to him*): Tata! Tata! Father!

LAS CASAS: In Christ's name, Zumárraga, don't put your hand on his head as they're picturing us now as doing.

FRIAR JUAN: Calm yourself, son. Calm yourself. You're safe and sound here. What were you doing out there? (*He accompanies his question with a gesture that imitates listening at the door.* THE YOUNG INDIAN *smiles broadly.*) Why were you listening? What do you want? Do you understand me?

THE YOUNG INDIAN: *Tata, Tata,* Father!

FRIAR ANTONIO: He's an idiot.

FRIAR JUAN: Curb yourself, Antonio.

MOTOLINÍA: This innocent one doesn't speak Spanish yet.

LAS CASAS: And these Indians, Brother Antonio, must think we're idiots because we don't speak their language, isn't that so?

FRIAR MARTÍN DE VALENCIA: What does it matter that he doesn't speak our language? He called the bishop *Tata.* In his very conscience he recognizes the Father of his soul.

FRIAR JUAN: That's what tells me we can save them all—their instinct for the good. Friar Toribio, see if you can understand him somewhat and thus we'll know what he's looking for.

MOTOLINÍA *goes to* THE YOUNG INDIAN, *takes him gently and persuasively by the arm, draws him up, and leads him upstage left.* MARTINCILLO *enters very much upset.*

MARTINCILLO: Where has that Indian of my sins run to?

FRIAR JUAN: Ah, here you are at last! Where were you and what were you doing that you let this poor Indian get in here? Didn't I tell you I didn't want any interruptions? I haven't the words now to tell you——.

MARTINCILLO: Of course, you told me so, Lord Bishop! But . . . You haven't the words now? Then what happens is that I'm remiss, neglectful, careless, absent-minded—a dunce or crazy in the head, and so on and so on——.

FRIAR JUAN: Enough. I haven't any more names to give you. Why did you let him enter?

MARTINCILLO: Let him! I! No, indeed, my lord! What happened was that while I was giving a bit of bread to his companions and telling them a little story, he sneaked in without my seeing him.

FRIAR JUAN: Can you explain why?

MARTINCILLO: Nothing easier, my lord. You already know that all of them always want to see the bishop. Am I to blame for that?

MOTOLINÍA (*drawing near*): Martincillo speaks the truth, Friar Juan. From what I've been able to make out of that simple-minded one, he wants nothing more than to see *Tata* Bishop.

FRIAR JUAN: Then take him out, Brother Martín, and make certain that this time he really leaves but give him something before he does. And don't be again all that you've said about yourself or I'll pray to the Lord for enlightenment to find better names for you.

Somewhat embarrassed and but ill concealing his laughter, MARTINCILLO *takes* THE YOUNG INDIAN *by the arm and exits with him.*

FRIAR JUAN: Thank God!

FRIAR ANTONIO: Lord Bishop, I came to——.

FRIAR JUAN: Yes. Brothers, Friar Antonio is the latest messenger I sent to the cardinal in Spain for His Eminence to take him to the king, and he brought me the monarch's reply. Will you repeat it, Brother?

FRIAR ANTONIO (*with controlled bitterness*): His Majesty was occupied and preferred to hear Cortés' emissary first. His Majesty did me the honor of not recognizing my habit and of speaking to me harshly. His Majesty at last said that he was going to think about the matter and that I should await his summons. His Eminence advised me to wait, so I did. At last I returned with the letter which His Eminence wrote to the Lord Bishop.

FRIAR JUAN: You mustn't take things this way, Friar Antonio.

FRIAR ANTONIO: Pardon. And may St. Francis pardon me, too, because since then I've wondered if I've not mistaken my road and if it wouldn't be better for me to be a soldier of the king and not of Christ. I've been feeling so useless, Lord Bishop!

FRIAR JUAN: Enough. A Franciscan without humality isn't a Franciscan. The king replied as you all know already, Brothers. Friar Antonio, I wanted to ask you to accompany the Clarisse Sister here. I must introduce her to the Reverend Fathers.

FRIAR ANTONIO: I wanted to speak to you about her, Lord Bishop. She's . . . I don't know . . . in some sort of a trance as if something invisible possessed her.

LAS CASAS: Is she violent?

FRIAR ANTONIO: On the contrary . . . she's as if she just weren't there—or as if the others and I weren't.

FRIAR MARTÍN DE VALENCIA: In an ecstasy, perhaps?

FRIAR ANTONIO: I don't know, Father, but she doesn't give me that idea.

FRIAR JUAN: Do you think she can manage to get here?

FRIAR ANTONIO: Yes, if I can make her hear me.

FRIAR JUAN: I'm certain you can. Bring her here then at once. But gently, Brother. We'll be waiting for her.

FRIAR ANTONIO *bows slightly and exits.*

LAS CASAS: That Brother has just come back from Spain, hasn't he?

FRIAR JUAN: He made the trip with the Sister and Alonso de Murcia, the gardener.

FRIAR MARTÍN DE VALENCIA: And he knows about the instructions——?

FRIAR JUAN: I don't think so. I don't think that either the king or the cardinal considered it necessary to inform him of anything. And that makes me think he feels there's something he doesn't know about this matter and he's bitter because of it.

PEDRO DE GANTE: But you told us they'd sent you a messenger who brought you a message by word of mouth.

FRIAR JUAN: That messenger wasn't Friar Antonio who was one of our best Brothers but is so changed now that I tremble for his eternal salvation.

DON VASCO: It occurs to me that we could perhaps see the Sister one at a time so as not to alarm her.

MOTOLINÍA: Maybe she'll be disconcerted on finding us all here together . . . Don't you think that——?

FRIAR JUAN: I prefer not to think about many things now, Brother. This'll be a test for her and I want it so because it'll allow you to see into everything I've wanted to tell you. It'll also be a test for you yourselves, Brothers. I'm frank with you.

FRIAR MARTÍN DE VALENCIA: God always works His ways in us, Friar Juan, without pick or shovel.

A short, emphatic knock is heard at the door.

FRIAR JUAN: Enter.

The door opens and FRIAR ANTONIO *appears, alone.*

FRIAR JUAN (*to* FRIAR MARTÍN DE VALENCIA): May He hear you, Brother. (*To* FRIAR ANTONIO) The Sister?

FRIAR ANTONIO: She's following me, Lord Bishop. At her own pace. At the pace of the Archangel. At the pace of the Virgin who always walks with the pace of God—so it's said.

FRIAR JUAN: And she's the same?

FRIAR ANTONIO (*raising his eyes to heaven*): Trance or ecstasy? I don't know. I don't understand it. Perhaps I've lost the grace of God.

FRIAR JUAN: We'll speak of that later. When she comes in here, you'll do me the favor of closing the door and of retiring in penitence until tomorrow.

FRIAR ANTONIO: That'll do me good, Lord Bishop.

FRIAR JUAN: Thank you, Brother Antonio.

FRIAR JUAN *shuts up as though withdrawing into him-self, although he seems to check the impulse to say something more. The missionaries look at him while straightening themselves somewhat in their chairs.* FRIAR MARTIN DE VALENCIA *rises.*

FRIAR JUAN: No, no. Be seated, I beg of you.

FRIAR MARTIN DE VALENCIA *sits down again. All fix their gaze on the open door where* FRIAR ANTONIO *stands waiting beyond the threshold.* FRIAR JUAN *looks from one to another of all his colleagues. It is evident that he would like to speak, but has not everything already been said? At length, like the others, he, too, fixes his eyes on the distance beyond the door. A moment later* FRIAR ANTONIO *moves aside and steps backward.*

FRIAR ANTONIO: The Sister is arriving, Lord Bishop.

Upon the solemn, silent, expectant group of men without peers, while at the same time that the light of the full moon shines in upon them there comes down rapidly the

CURTAIN

Act 3 THE CROWN

The scene is the same as Act 2, although the construc-
tion of the bishop's palace is visibly more advanced. It
is the morning of 12 December 1531.

The morning is gloomy. The sky is filled with
large storm clouds. The darkened atmosphere in-
creases during the act, until the sky clears suddenly as
though with a flash of lightning at the end of the play
in keeping with ZUMÁRRAGA'S *revelation—so as to end*
in the brilliant light of the midday sun.

FRIAR JUAN DE ZUMÁRRAGA *is seated at his desk writing*
which he interrupts to consult one or two account
books. Something disturbs him. He gets up and goes
to the window where he looks out for a moment. The
cold air makes him shiver and slowly he shakes his
head. Our BROTHER MARTINCILLO *opens the door with-*
out knocking and enters.

FRIAR JUAN (*without turning around*): We're having bad weather this morning.

MARTINCILLO: What're you saying, Lord Bishop?
There's never bad weather in this land. Just see what beautiful morning light there is, for this is the New World,
nothing less. And what a blue sky on this December day!
It lacks only the sun and stars to be perfect.

FRIAR JUAN (*still without turning around*): Ah, im-
penitent jabberer that you are. But it's cold today.

MOTOLINÍA (*entering*): More than usually so in this
climate for these days, Friar Juan. I see that Brother Martín
forgot about me—as always.

73

MARTINCILLO (*crossing himself*): In the name of the Lord, forgive me, Friar Toribio. It seems to please Him that this one, His servant, is so absentminded.

FRIAR JUAN (*turning around with open arms*): Welcome. And doubly so for not being expected, Friar Toribio. Brother Martín, it's not God who makes chatterboxes and the absentminded. Leave us now before I scold you. Our Brother will forgive you, but not I.

MOTOLINÍA: It doesn't matter, Friar Juan. In truth, I've come to think that Brother Martín is becoming Indianized himself and thinks of me as a Poor Little One, just as the Indians do. For that I thank him.

MARTINCILLO: Heaven won't allow that, Friar Toribio. Your poverty's a true treasure and I . . . (*a look, gloomy as the morning, from* FRIAR JUAN) I'm going back to my duties which, alas, are many. (*Exits.*)

FRIAR JUAN: Well, now we can talk without having as a witness that simple-minded angel of my sins whom God has sent to punish me for them. What brings you to the city today, Friar Toribio?

MOTOLINÍA: You said you weren't expecting me, Friar Juan, but I thought that I was answering your summons.

FRIAR JUAN: What?

MOTOLINÍA: They told me yesterday in Tlatelolco that you wanted to see me.

FRIAR JUAN (*reflecting*): I don't understand this. Perhaps Brother Martín who sees that I'm preoccupied with so many matters thought your presence would help me. He's like that and at times thinks up more things than are called for.

MOTOLINÍA (*smiling*): Maybe just another proof of how much he loves you.

FRIAR JUAN: Love means concern, all right. In any event, let's not ask him if he sent for you, because he'll only talk a lot as usual. Who gave you the message?

MOTOLINÍA: An Indian from the city passed it on to one of my students.

FRIAR JUAN: It's strange, though, Toribio. Our religious training is supposed to bring us to a knowledge of God. But does it really bring us to a knowledge of men, above all if those men are these Indians who're still chained to their paganism?

MOTOLINÍA: I believe so. I believe that we all meet one another in the adoration of God.

FRIAR JUAN: You're not a simpleton, Brother Motolinía. You know well enough that our—alas—brothers the conquistadores and the receivers of land grants with Indian slaves meet and come together in adoration of the devil—of gold, as our Brother Las Casas, who loves you because he criticizes you so, would say.

MOTOLINÍA: That Dominican of my sins . . . I hope he'll become a saint, although I fear that the Spaniards will never forgive him.

FRIAR JUAN: Don't you ever turn your face to a wall just to shout out some bad words? It's good for one's health, you know. When you came in I was writing to Spain. I've the sad feeling which goes on like an ulcer, Brother Toribio, that we're not doing enough for the Indians. We're fallible and weak. And this land that's so old but so new to us has more than gold and silver and *tepuzque,* or copper, in its bowels. Sometimes it seems to me to be like an enormous, full womb which one day is going to give birth to something that Charles and his court over there don't understand and don't foresee. Something that perhaps we ourselves don't foresee or understand.

MOTOLINÍA: I agree. I often feel that the Indian whom we call our son is more likely our father or grandfather when he looks at us and gives us his smile which is humble rather than crafty.

FRIAR JUAN: Right. The Indian is closer to the origins of the world than we are. I write to Spain about these matters. We must pray and work so much because of our spiritual duties that we really haven't time nor leisure for reflection or thought. But there're times—as now just before you came in—when it occurs to me—I can't avoid the thought—that this clouded sky, this cold, hard, and lacerating air which cuts so into us all is like a protest of the very land itself against our presence here.

MOTOLINÍA: Friar Juan! How can you think that— doubt that Our Lord God Himself sent us to Mexico for the well-being and happiness of the Indians of New Spain? And you, our bishop?

FRIAR JUAN: Do you believe that perhaps we're springtime for them? Haven't you thought, even as I, that it's not we who really testify to the Indians to the presence of God because He doesn't really need us to realize His divine scheme? We're nothing more than dust which is briefly illuminated. You, the poorest of us all—haven't you sometimes thought of all this?

MOTOLINÍA (pained): I don't know what's happening to you, Friar Juan.

FRIAR JUAN: I don't shut myself up, Brother, in lexicons and works of the mind which are good and useful and noble, and which help to kill our enemy, devil time. I come face to face with live, hard and difficult work. I fight plagues. I reprimand the blasphemous ambitions in men of the sword and of quality and of men of the Audiencia. I try to unite our poor little flock of the unfaithful under the sign of the Cross. But sometimes I feel—and today more so than ever—that I can do nothing: that all of us—Indians and Spaniards alike—are on the brink of an abyss, and that if things go on as they are, some of the cautionary examples we draw from history are bound to change because Spain and Mexico will be added to Nineveh and Babylon, to Sodom and Gomorrah.

MOTOLINÍA: Allow me to protest, Brother Bishop. What matters is the idea of God.

FRIAR JUAN: God isn't an idea, Brother. He is body, blood, spirit, reason, the living air. But here the air isn't living nor is it clean, even though this is the region where our eyes become most aware of its transparency. Well, eat with me and we'll talk things over. I must let you know that I've thought much about your idea of presenting miracle plays and I can tell you . . . (*The door opens and* MARTINCILLO *appears.*) Now what's happening in this windmill?

MARTINCILLO: I'm very sorry, my Lord Bishop. I swear that I'm sorry, but he's out there again.

FRIAR JUAN: Brother Martín, you often throw it up to me that I'm a Basque, so you know the limit of my patience. Don't make me swear now. Who's out there again?

MARTINCILLO: The Indian, Lord Bishop.

FRIAR JUAN: What an extraordinary thing! Without a doubt, the only Indian in this whole land, from the way you say it.

MARTINCILLO: No. my Lord. The Indian of the visions. The one who comes here at least once a week to tell us that he talks with the saints—when not with the idols.

FRIAR JUAN: Give him something to eat and something to take to his family, and tell him to come back when he has another vision.

MARTINCILLO: It can't be done, Lord Bishop.

FRIAR JUAN: What can't be done?

MARTINCILLO: He's really determined to see you and in his lingo—which I now understand well enough although I'll never be able to speak it, God be praised—he says that he's already had it and that he's going to pitch camp in your waiting room until you see him.

FRIAR JUAN: He says that he has already had what?

MARTINCILLO: The new vision.

MOTOLINÍA: Now be patient, Friar Juan.

FRIAR JUAN: What's his name? And don't ask me whose!

MOTOLINÍA: Juan.

FRIAR JUAN: I deserve it. Well, let him come in, Brother.

MARTINCILLO: It's not my fault if they're all named after you and not after Friar Toribio or me.

MOTOLINÍA: But truly it's they who christen us, I believe. (*He smiles.*) In secret, that is.

MARTINCILLO *exits.* FRIAR JUAN *walks up and down.* MOTOLINÍA *adjusts his habit, then looks at his hands with a vague smile which spreads across his lips.* MARTINCILLO *reenters with* FIRST JUAN.

FIRST JUAN (*kisses* FRIAR JUAN's *hand*): Juan . . . Juan . . . Juan——. (*He then kisses* MOTOLINÍA's *hand.*)

FRIAR JUAN: What do you want, Juan?

FIRST JUAN *takes* MARTINCILLO *by the arm and whispers into his ear with urgency.*

FRIAR JUAN: Well, what does he say?

MARTINCILLO: I don't understand it all, Lord Bishop, but I think he means that this morning he saw a light . . . (FIRST JUAN *nods, then adds something else in* MARTINCILLO's *ear.*) He saw a great light. And that, just between Your Lordship and me, he can go and tell to his grandmother because today is misty. (FIRST JUAN *whispers something else in* MARTINCILLO's *ear.*) But he wants the Lord Bishop to tell him whether that light is a thing of the Spaniards and the Church, or if it's that the idols are announcing their return.

FRIAR JUAN (*smiles, looking upward*): Take him away, Brother. Speak to him for a long time, as you know so well how to do, and tell him that only God can make the light—the one God who brought us here to teach them the truth and show Paradise to them. And be eloquent. Now go. (*His smile increases.*)

It is evident that FIRST JUAN understands and he, too, smiles broadly. He kisses FRIAR JUAN's hand, then MOTOLINÍA's, and goes to the door with MARTINCILLO.)

FRIAR JUAN (*with abrupt good humor*): Ha, thus I please them both and free ourselves of them. (MOTOLINÍA *smiles, but* FRIAR JUAN's *smile vanishes when he turns to the door where* FIRST JUAN *is again whispering with urgency in* MARTINCILLO's *ear. Impatiently.*) Now what?

MARTINCILLO (*excusing himself with a somewhat exaggerated gesture of innocence*): This I don't understand, Lord Bishop. It's something about a voice, something about a flower——. (*In pantomime he questions* FIRST JUAN *who points to the door and they both exit.* FRIAR JUAN *and* MOTOLINÍA *laugh a moment, but they both grow serious when they see* MARTINCILLO *return with* FIRST JUAN *and* SECOND JUAN *who is a somewhat younger Indian than the other.*)

FRIAR JUAN: What does this mean——?

MARTINCILLO (*with the same gesture of exaggerated innocence*): This other one, Lord Bishop, brings still another story. He says that he, too, saw the light but also heard voices.

FRIAR JUAN: Let him wash out his ears and leave us in peace. Go now, I have other matters that——.

MOTOLINÍA: Pardon, Friar Juan, but perhaps there's some connection between that light and those voices. We might try to investigate——.

FRIAR JUAN: I'm afraid, Friar Toribio, that the conquest has left nothing more than the imagination to these unfortunate sons of ours. If you could see the many things of this sort that I do!

MOTOLINÍA: Allow me. Try to ask them in some way or other, Brother Martín, where they saw that light and what precisely they did see.

MARTINCILLO: I don't mean to be irreverent, Friar Toribio, but that's very difficult, Couldn't Your Paternity who makes up dictionaries——?

MOTOLINÍA: Just among ourselves, my pronunciation is . . . well, even poorer than I am. Now make an effort, Brother.

MARTINCILLO *prepares for a big questioning in pantomime, but* SECOND JUAN *who understands Spanish rather well points with his right hand over his shoulder to indicate the north.*

SECOND JUAN: Tepeyácatl.

FRIAR JUAN: What's that?

MOTOLINÍA: I don't really know, but I've heard the name. It's some hill—toward the north, if I'm not mistaken —some distance beyond Tlatelolco.

FRIAR JUAN: Tell them that everything is God's work, Brother Martín, and for them to calm down and pray a little. Then give them something.

FIRST JUAN and SECOND JUAN say something to each other, shaking their heads while talking. MOTOLINÍA lends an ear. The two Indians exit with MARTINCILLO.

MOTOLINÍA: I hope the news I'm going to give you won't put you in a worse temper, Friar Juan. You already know that I understand the Nahuatl and Otomí tongues well. What those innocents have just said is that they're going to stay there in your waiting room because they don't want to go and won't go.

FRIAR JUAN: Come now! With the Chinese-like patience of this race they'll stay there indefinitely. More than once I've thought that they also resemble a bit the Arab infidel who passes endless hours at the entrance of his mosque. (*He rings a bell.*) They're also a little like flies at the end of summer, God forgive me.

MOTOLINÍA: Couldn't it be that they've lost the ability to fly or even move themselves—perhaps because of our fault, as you said?

FRIAR JUAN: So you agree? I'm glad. (MARTIN-CILLO *enters.*) Have they gone?

MARTINCILLO: No, Lord Bishop. And they won't go. They keep on talking all the time between themselves and they've sat down on the floor as in a parlor.

FRIAR JUAN: Then may it be God's will. Offer them some refreshment. But now that you're here, tell me, Brother Martín—but in just a few words—was it you who permitted yourself to call Friar Toribio here today? And if so, for what reason, for what object, with what authority, and by what right? Tell me at once.

MARTINCILLO: Forgive me—but I don't understand this. If you'll just let me think a moment, Lord Bishop——.

FRIAR JUAN (*raising his eyes heavenward*): You're going to take time. You lack training, Brother.

MOTOLINÍA: Friar Juan, you're hard.

FRIAR JUAN: Not any more so on others than on myself, Friar Toribio. But don't worry.

MARTINCILLO: Ah, now it's all clear!

FRIAR JUAN: What is?

MARTINCILLO: I don't have a reason nor an object nor authority nor the right to permit myself to call Friar Toribio here. So it's clear that if I did, it was because you ordered me to—there.

FRIAR JUAN: When?

MARTINCILLO: I don't remember, but even though I'm a lay brother, I'm not entirely an ignoramus. That's why I always make a note of your orders in a little book I keep about me—so as not to pay later on for the peccadillos of bish . . . er, that is, of other sinners.

FRIAR JUAN: And where's that little book?

MARTINCILLO: Pardon. (*He turns his back and raises the skirt of his habit high in an eager search while making modest movements. When attempting to use both hands, the skirt falls and he has to raise it again.* FRIAR JUAN *and* MOTOLINÍA *look the other way so as not to be seen smiling.*) Ah, here we are! (*He turns around again and leafs through a small book which is bound with untanned leather. His superiors face him again.*) That's it . . . yes . . . I was about to bet . . . (FRIAR JUAN *clears his throat loudly*) but only with myself, that I was right. (*Reading.*) "Remind Friar Juan to remember to send for Friar Toribio about the matter of the performances." (*He sighs with relief.*)

FRIAR JUAN: And on what date did you make that note, Brother Martín?

MARTINCILLO (*choking a bit*): Well, the . . . the
. . . twenty-eighth of——.

FRIAR JUAN: Now tell the truth.

MARTINCILLO: The twenty-eighth of October, Lord
Bishop.

FRIAR JUAN: The twenty-eighth of October. Ah.
And what's the date of today, Brother Martín?

MARTINCILLO: Well . . . it's the Feast of St. Constance and of St.——.

FRIAR JUAN: What date?

MARTINCILLO: The twelfth of December, my lord.

FRIAR JUAN (*making a rapid calculation*): That's to
say it's forty-six of the Lord's days since you made a note
that you should remind me of something. Forty-six days
. . . (*finally exploding*) and you never reminded me of anything! If you serve God as you do me, you've but little
hope of going to Paradise. Why didn't you remind me of
it then?

MOTOLINÍA: Oh, come now, Friar Juan. What does
it matter?

MARTINCILLO: I forgot, Lord Bishop. That's my
misfortune, Friar Toribio. When I make a note of something, I always forget it.

FRIAR JUAN: But, after all, you did send for Friar
Toribio.

MARTINCILLO (*humbly*): Yes.

FRIAR JUAN (*exasperated*): When?

MARTINCILLO (*as quickly as he can*): Well, you'll
see, Friar Juan. Day before yesterday I had to make a note
of something else which I don't remember either, and
always when I make a note of something, I read what I
made a note of before. Then I took note of this matter and
as one of our Indians was going to Tlatelolco, I asked him
to give the message to Friar Toribio—and Friar Toribio
came, and all worked out well.

FRIAR JUAN: You'd better go now, Brother Martín
—or I'll not be responsible for myself. (MARTINCILLO *exits
quickly.*)

MOTOLINÍA: Don't be angry, Friar Juan. It'll all work out for the best.

FRIAR JUAN: I hope so.

MOTOLINÍA: But what was it about the performances?

FRIAR JUAN (*thinks a moment*): Well . . . the truth is I don't remember, so I'll say before you do what you must be thinking—divine punishment.

MOTOLINÍA: God preserve me.

Both laugh briefly but frankly.

FRIAR JUAN: Ah, of course! But what I was just going to say to you before about the miracle plays which you so much——.

The rising sound of voices speaking excitedly in Otomí and Nahautl is heard offstage.

FRIAR JUAN (*continuing*): And now, Friar Toribio, what's happening? This blessed bishop's palace seems more like a mill or a baker's shop——.

MARTINCILLO (*entering*): Pardon, Lord Bishop— but there's another one out there.

FRIAR JUAN: Another what? You always speak in riddles.

MARTINCILLO: Another Indian who insists upon seeing you. And I'm not to blame.

FRIAR JUAN: Has he told you what he wants and why precisely he must talk with me?

MARTINCILLO: Only that what he has to say is for the ears of the bishop and not for those of a lay brother. This one speaks a little Castilian.

FRIAR JUAN: Just try working under such conditions, Friar Toribio.

MOTOLINÍA: Well I understand you. But aren't these poor little ones our most important work?

MARTINCILLO (*under his breath*): Just what I say.

FRIAR JUAN: Quiet. You know I always hear you. Well, then, let this other one come in. He's called Juan, too, isn't he? Another godchild. (MOTOLINÍA *smiles.*) And, of course, you're right, Friar Toribio. They are our most important work.

MARTINCILLO: But this one's name is Juan Felipe. (*He opens the door and makes a gesture.*) Pst!

> JUAN FELIPE *enters. He is* THIRD JUAN *and is evidently in a state of excitement. Before* MARTINCILLO *can prevent it,* FIRST JUAN *and* SECOND JUAN *trail in to stand, silent and expectant, upstage while* THIRD JUAN *goes to centerstage.*

FRIAR JUAN: Here I am, Juan Felipe. What do you want, my son?

THIRD JUAN (*with an effort overcoming his timidity and excitement*): Tata Bishop, Tata Bishop! I find xóchitl that makes blood. (*He holds out his right hand in the blood-reddened palm of which lies a red rose.* MOTOLINÍA *draws near.* FRIAR JUAN *takes the rose and goes downstage right followed by* MOTOLINÍA. *The two examine the rose in silence.*)

FRIAR JUAN: Do you see the same thing I do, Friar Toribio?

MOTOLINÍA: I see a rose. It's not a flower of Tenochtítlan.

FRIAR JUAN (*reflects a moment. His face lights up suddenly and he turns to* THIRD JUAN): Tell me, Juan Felipe, where did you find this . . . xóchitl?

THIRD JUAN (*smiles*): Up there . . . Tepeyácatl.

FRIAR JUAN: Do you understand well what I'm asking you? Do you understand Spanish well?

THIRD JUAN: Tongue of God . . . tongue of Truth.

FRIAR JUAN (*turning somewhat helplessly to* MOTOLINÍA): I want clarity, Brother.

MOTOLINÍA: Allow me. (*He takes* THIRD JUAN *aside and questions him briefly in a low voice while all the others watch. He returns, adjusting his habit.*) He expressed himself quite well, Friar Juan. He found that rose near the

Tepeyácatl, although farther on beyond the hill—more to the north.

FRIAR JUAN: Just a moment. (*He goes to his desk and looks in the drawer for a paper which at last he finds. He then returns downstage to* MOTOLINÍA *so as to be out of hearing of the others—especially of* MARTINCILLO. *All watch him with mounting curiosity.*) It's useless—I know from experience—to argue with these Indians, imaginative beings that they are who're always in flight from reality, from the Spanish reality which—it must be said, Friar Toribio—we're imposing upon them. Of course, you recall our council with Las Casas, Gante, Sahagún, and the others, and also the preparations which we finally agreed upon so as to carry out the blasphemous command of the emperor.

MOTOLINÍA (*his eyes opening wide*): The gardener, Friar Juan——.

FRIAR JUAN: Who was to have planted the roses in another place—toward the south. The gardener . . . (*A brief pause.*) Brother Martín. (*Filled with a vague apprehension despite his show of calm,* MARTINCILLO *goes to* FRIAR JUAN.) Brother, bring Friar Antonio here at once. And bring with him the gardener Alonso de Murcia, but let him wait outside. And stop up your ears and cut out your tongue. That's important. Do you understand?

MARTINCILLO: My lord, now you want a corpse for your servant-companion.

MOTOLINÍA: Brother Martín, be——.

FRIAR JUAN: Brother Martín!

Startled, MARTINCILLO *exits. The three Indians fall back upstage but follow* FRIAR JUAN *and* MOTOLINÍA *with their eyes as the faithful fix theirs on the images in church.*

MOTOLINÍA: I see that you're very much agitated, Friar Juan. What's passing through your mind?

FRIAR JUAN (*slowly*): I have here the minutes of that ill-starred council, Friar Toribio. In it, I let myself be convinced, as you know, by the men I respect most in the world and by the only thing that can really convince me which is the service of God over and above the intrigues of courtiers and politicians.

MOTOLINÍA: And I know that you did well.

FRIAR JUAN: As you heard, I've just sent for Friar Antonio. No doubt you remember him? (MOTOLINÍA *nods*.) He doesn't know what's really at the bottom of this matter. I've let him think that it's only about a ceremony similar—as you said then—to a miracle play. He doesn't know anything more. But I have here in the minutes a note which informs me that the gardener Alonso de Murcia received orders . . . I swear to you that with the very real sorrows of the Indians and the problems of their life, I'd forgotten about this farce——.

MOTOLINÍA: Brother Juan! In the first place, I know you did well to let us convince you.

FRIAR JUAN: ——this mystery play, if you prefer—this imposture in place of my own conviction. The gardener received orders to plant rose bushes in a wasteland, toward the south, which is called the Pedregal, or Rocky Ground, of St. Angel, where perhaps centuries ago the natural forces of a volcano, moved by the Divine Plan, destroyed the lives of innumerable pagans.

MOTOLINÍA: I advise you to calm down.

FRIAR JUAN: And where the volcanic rock makes it absolutely impossible to plant anything. But, nevertheless, the gardener promised to do so. Well then. Here I have a note in the minutes that's precise and clear . . . (*showing it*) and in this another hand, Toribio de Benavente, I have a rose that was cut in the north, on the road near the Tepeyácatl. What am I to think?

MOTOLINÍA: I understand. But prayer is thought, Brother.

FRIAR JUAN: Ah, no! Don't tell me that. I pray every hour of my life. At this moment my very bowels are at prayer, and they tell me that when the hand of man interferes with holy things it should be cut off and burnt and the ashes scattered to the four winds. God is truth and reason. Human imposture should suffer all the punishments, all the——.

The door opens while FRIAR JUAN *is speaking and* FRIAR ANTONIO *enters followed by* MARTINCILLO.

MARTINCILLO: Friar Antonio, my lord.

FRIAR JUAN (*regaining his composure and dignity*): Draw near, Friar Antonio. (FRIAR ANTONIO *silently obeys and waits.*) When our Clarisse Sister and Master Alonso de Murcia arrived, I asked you to keep them constant company and to inform them about the things of New Spain which they didn't know of. Both of them have important tasks to perform which were entrusted to them by our Holy Church, but I have cause to think that the gardener hasn't done what he was instructed to. Do you know whether he goes out often and if so where?

FRIAR ANTONIO: You didn't tell me to go along with him whenever he went out, my lord, but I do know that he has had to go many times to a place on the road to the south which he calls the Pedregal, or Rocky Ground.

FRIAR JUAN: But he goes to other places, too?

FRIAR ANTONIO: I don't know. He's a layman and as such he doesn't have to follow our rules to the letter, but he always returns in time for vespers.

FRIAR JUAN: Thank you. Please wait. (*He turns to* MARTINCILLO *who has been standing with the Indians upstage.*) Let the gardener come in, Brother.

MARTINCILLO *opens the door and beckons. The gardener enters. The three Indians draw closer together, silent and still observant.*

FRIAR JUAN: Draw near, Master Alonso.

ALONSO (*approaches, drops to one knee, and kisses* FRIAR JUAN's *hand*): Lord Bishop——.

FRIAR JUAN: Rise. (ALONSO *obeys.*) Upon your

arrival here, Master Alonso, our authority entrusted to you a difficult task for sacred ends (ALONSO *smiles*), knowing that you could carry it out because you're an experienced gardener of Murcia which is the flower garden of Spain. What was that task, Master Alonso?

ALONSO: To plant roses, Lord Bishop, which are the most extraordinary and majestic . . . the queen flowers of flowers . . . and to plant them in a desert place. It was a challenge to my ability as a humble gardener, but above all as a servant of God and His Church.

FRIAR JUAN: And have you done that?

ALONSO: My lord, that the rosebushes have caught like fire in grassland will assure you of it. Send some one there who'll come back and tell you about this marvel. I'm not boasting, not I. I think this soil here in New Spain is good for anything that's planted. The most beautiful roses I've ever seen have been born here—and in wasteland.

FRIAR JUAN: What do you call that wasteland?

ALONSO: It's that southern area which you yourself indicated to me, Lord Bishop. That area which these good people of the plateau call the Pedregal.

FRIAR JUAN: Are you sure?

ALONSO: As sure as of the everlasting presence of God, Lord Bishop.

MOTOLINÍA: We're all fallible because we're human, Master Alonso. Think well on your answer.

ALONSO: I've nothing to think on it, by Your Paternity's leave. I was given my orders and I carried them out like a soldier . . . of gardening if not of the army, but like a soldier of Christ.

FRIAR JUAN (*sadly*): Liar!

ALONSO (*wounded*): Lord Bishop!

FRIAR JUAN: Liar, I repeat. Liar! What have I here that you see in this hand?

ALONSO (*turning pale*): A red rose, lord, that has faded. Forgive me, but the death of a flower wounds me as much as that of a Christian.

FRIAR JUAN (*trenchantly*): This rose as you call it, Master Alonso, does not come from the Pedregal of St. Angel, (ALONSO *is greatly disturbed.*) Can you tell me, without lying to Christ, where it could come from?

ALONSO (*on the defensive*): I swear to Your Lordship that I don't know.

MOTOLINÍA: Careful, Alonso. False swearing is beyond redemption.

FRIAR JUAN: Were there roses in Tenochtítlan before, for reasons that I don't want to mention now, you came to this land in a military ship? Were there roses?

ALONSO: No, my lord. I studied all the orchards and gardens. There were no roses.

FRIAR JUAN: Then explain to me how this one which is dying in my hand and which causes you such sorrow could come to me from the north road, from a point that these three innocent Indians call the Tepeyácatl.

> Upset and worried, ALONSO DE MURCIA *appears not to be able to hit upon the answer. There is a hurried movement and consultation amongst the three Indians, after which* THIRD JUAN *goes to* MOTOLINÍA *and whispers in his ear.*

FRIAR JUAN: I'm waiting for your answer, Master Alonso.

MOTOLINÍA: Allow me, Lord Bishop, and you, Master Alonso de Murcia. These Indians live in the direction of the Tepeyácatl, but, they tell me, much farther away from the *tepetl*, that is, the hill. They're in agreement about having seen Master Alonso around that spot where he visits an Indian hut. (ALONSO *makes a gesture of protest.*) And more, according to this poor little Juan Felipe, the rose you hold in your hand comes from there.

ALONSO: A lie!

FRIAR JUAN: My daily prayer of every hour is that God allow me to be kind and just, and keep the sinner alive for his redemption, and never to sacrifice a human life which I can't put back with my own hands. Master Alonso, don't force my Christian patience so far as to commit you to the Tribunal of the Holy Inquisition.

MOTOLINÍA: Master Alonso, consider that the truth is a flower more precious than those you plant and cultivate and love so much. Speak, I implore you.

ALONSO (*defeated*): Very well, then, Lord Bishop. I'm a man—a creature of God and also of the Devil. I serve the altar, but I have my appetites. My appetites led me to an Indian girl who lives beyond the Tepeyácatl, about two leagues on. She still believes that we Spaniards are like gods, and so before she'd submit to me she asked me for a miracle. Well, then, at the door of her hut I planted a rosebush that blossomed at the same time that her womb did.

FRIAR JUAN: And you confess thus that promiscuity, that clandestine mating, that——?

ALONSO: My lord, you didn't leave me any other way out. So like the soldiers and many others, I'll give another Spaniard to New Spain.

MOTOLINÍA: Who'll be an Indian, above all.

ALONSO: What does that matter so long as he's born and lives because of me?

FRIAR JUAN: You're a man of your own time—of this senseless time, Master Alonso. I'll see you in confession and on trial. I can do nothing against those damnable goings-on, but to have planted rosebushes there is a grave matter. Perhaps you left a wife in Spain?

ALONSO: Yes, my lord—but what I am as a man came here with me.

FRIAR JUAN: Miserable sinner. May God forgive you. And did you plant more rosebushes in other places? This time tell the truth, or you'll pay for the lie.

ALONSO: Only in the Pedregal and at the hut of my Indian, Lord Bishop.

MOTOLINÍA: Can you swear to that?

FRIAR JUAN: Are you certain that on the Tepeyá-catl itself you didn't——?

ALONSO: By the life of the son which I've begotten here, by the life of Spain which throbs in me like blood, by the flowers which are my reason for being—by the roses, if you will—I didn't plant any more. I swear it.

FRIAR JUAN *walks about for a while. He looks at the rose in his hand, then goes to the balcony. He closes his hand, crushing the rose which he lets fall, and steps on it.*

FRIAR JUAN (*returning to* MOTOLINÍA): You're a polyglot, Toribio. I want these people to go. Send them away. Tell them that nothing has happened—that neither God nor their ancient dead idols have anything to do with this new flower which is only a blessing of nature that they're to enjoy because it's beautiful. Tell them that if its thorns draw blood it's because God wishes it to be treated tenderly, and that it protects itself as they do from us. And leave me alone for a while. I must meditate. (MOTOLINÍA *goes to the Indians and tells them what the bishop has said. His gestures are calm but at the same time forceful. The Indians appear to yield.*) Brother Martín. (MARTIN-CILLO *goes to* FRIAR JUAN *who indicates with a gesture that he is to send everyone away.*) Master Alonso, you'll see me in confession tomorrow. Now go, all of you. Go. And I don't want ever again in my life to hear the name "Tepe-yácatal," or whatever it's called.

Toward the end of these lines, FOURTH JUAN (JUAN DARÍO) *enters unseen. In his left hand is gathered up the front of his tilma: the loose, outer garment worn by Indian men which has a hole that permits it to be slipped over the head and which falls to the front and back, the sides being open.* FOURTH JUAN *is serene and soft, rather as if dazzled, but not undecided. He joins the group which gradually takes on the character of the popular religious pictures which depict some miraculous recovery or event such as are seen as votive offerings in many churches. He remains silent.*

At FRIAR JUAN'S *words to* MARTINCILLO, *he, like a twentieth-century traffic officer, organizes the group for its exit.*

FRIAR JUAN: No, on thinking better of it, don't you go, Friar Toribio. Let us meditate together, if you will. Meditation is a matter—where have I read it?—that requires more than one head.

MOTOLINÍA *stops. In response to the signs* MARTIN-CILLO *makes to them with his hands,* FIRST JUAN, SEC-OND JUAN, THIRD JUAN, *and* ALONSO *move toward the door while spreading out like a fan. It is then that the silent figure of* FOURTH JUAN, *who is standing in the middle of the doorway like a runner who has reached his goal, is revealed to* FRIAR JUAN, MOTOLINÍA, FRIAR ANTONIO, *and the audience.*

MARTINCILLO: And you, who are you?

At the sound of MARTINCILLO'S *voice,* FRIAR JUAN, *who has gone to his desk to put the minutes of the council in the drawer, turns around slowly.* MOTOLINÍA *does likewise.* FRIAR JUAN *moves slowly toward* FOURTH JUAN *and repeats mechanically* MARTINCILLO'S *question.*

FRIAR JUAN: And you, who are you?
FOURTH JUAN (*he speaks Spanish rather well with only some grammatical lapses which he makes up for with a smile that radiates a calm certainty*): I'm Juan Darío, *Tata* Bishop.
FRIAR JUAN: And what are you looking for here?

MOTOLINÍA *goes to* FOURTH JUAN *while looking at him searchingly.*

FOURTH JUAN: I have message for you, *Tata* Bishop. Only for you. I come from far.

MOTOLINÍA: Where have you come from, son?

FRIAR JUAN: Are you beside yourself, Friar Toribio? I'm afraid that I'm falling into Martincillo's sin, but I'll wager you that this one also comes from the Tepcyácatl.

FOURTH JUAN (*kneeling*): You, like God, know everything.

FRIAR JUAN (*blushing*): Yes, of course, I'm His bishop and because of that I'm infallible—and a wizard. But what are you looking for here, Juan Darío? Tell me quickly what your message is.

FOURTH JUAN: I live in Tepeyácatl by hill. I know that man. (*He points to* ALONSO *who, as all the others, has stopped to listen on seeing* FRIAR JUAN *question* FOURTH JUAN.) He has Indian wife. (FRIAR JUAN *turns to* ALONSO *who bows his head in resignation.*) Message only for you.

FRIAR JUAN (*impatiently*): Friar Toribio, can you make those people leave so we can finish with this matter?

MOTOLINÍA: I was thinking, forgive me, Friar Juan, that now there're four Indians who're talking to us about Tepeyácatl. It's as though the four cardinal points had come together.

FRIAR JUAN (*his patience exhausted*): So, but at any rate will you try to make them leave?

MOTOLINÍA *goes to the Indians and speaks to them in a low voice.* FRIAR JUAN *and* FOURTH JUAN *wait like statues in a mysterious duet. The three Indians move their heads in negation and say something. It is evident that they want to know what is going on.*

MOTOLINÍA: They won't go, Friar Juan. I know that. They've been impressed by something and are determined. The conquistadores themselves could threaten them with death and even kill them, but they won't move. Poor little ones.

FRIAR JUAN: Yes, Motolinías. (*He reflects a moment.*) Juan Darío, tell them to go.

FOURTH JUAN (*smiling*): They brothers. (*He goes*

to them and speaks to them. Strong shaking of their heads by the three Indians. ALONSO, FRIAR ANTONIO, *and* MARTIN-CILLO *wait expectantly.* FOURTH JUAN *returns to* FRIAR JUAN.) They don't want.

FRIAR JUAN: Then you can't give me your message. Or better, you come out with me.

FOURTH JUAN: Must be here—before *Tata.* (*He points to the crucifix hanging on the wall.*)

FRIAR JUAN: Then make them go.

FOURTH JUAN: I haven't . . . (*searching for the word*) the power. (*Looking out front.*) There. (*He moves downstage. Intrigued,* FRIAR JUAN *follows him and* FOURTH JUAN *kneels.* MOTOLINÍA *remains in midstage but watches attentively.*)

FRIAR JUAN (*moved in spite of himself*): Speak, then, Juan Darío.

FOURTH JUAN (*speaking in a tone of voice that would seem to be inaudible to the three Indians,* FRIAR ANTONIO, ALONSO, *and* MARTINCILLO): *Tata,* at hillside very beautiful lady say to Juan Darío, poor little one, say, "Juan Darío, here I want beautiful house, very beautiful. I'm your Mother, poor Indian Juan Darío. Tell *Tata* Bishop I want here beautiful house for Mother of God and Indians." I tell *Tata* Bishop now.

FRIAR JUAN (*takes this in slowly, then goes to his desk for the minutes which he glances through.* FOURTH JUAN *remains kneeling.* FRIAR JUAN *shows signs of anger*): Come, get up from there, man. Friar Toribio——.

MOTOLINÍA: Brother . . . (*The two come together downstage left.*)

FRIAR JUAN: This is a curse, Benavente. And may Our Lord God forgive me. I've just remembered that when we held that council an Indian was listening behind the door. Do you remember that? Was he one of these four who're here now?

MOTOLINÍA (*doubtfully*): I couldn't say. Perhaps Friar Antonio——.

FRIAR JUAN: Friar Antonio——.

FRIAR ANTONIO *steps out of the group and goes to him.*

FRIAR ANTONIO: My lord?

FRIAR JUAN: Think about this well. Could one of these four Indians be the one you found that afternoon listening at my door when I was with Prior Las Casas and the——.

FRIAR ANTONIO: The one I called an idiot, Lord Bishop? No. I could swear not. Is there something——?

FRIAR JUAN: Nothing. Thanks. Withdraw. (FRIAR ANTONIO *returns to the group.*) Brother, that one (*pointing to* FOURTH JUAN) assures me that he talked with *the lady.*

MOTOLINÍA: Ave María!

FRIAR JUAN: We've already spoken of their imagination, Brother. An end must be put to this. (*He returns energetically to* FOURTH JUAN.) How is it that you speak Spanish, Juan Darío?

FOURTH JUAN: I study it in Tlatelolco. Motolinía teaches. He not know me because Aztecs all same.

FRIAR JUAN: Do you know him?

MOTOLINÍA (*smiling*): He has already explained the matter to you.

FRIAR JUAN: But now you come from Te——. (*He pauses.*)

FOURTH JUAN: ——peyácatl. (*Lowering his voice, he faces front.*) Beautiful lady say——.

FRIAR JUAN: Stop. Where did you see that lady? Tell me.

FOURTH JUAN: At foot of hill. She looked like Indian lady, but beautiful.

FRIAR JUAN: Are you certain that it wasn't by the house where the Spaniard's—er, wife lives? (*He indicates* ALONSO *with a glance.*)

FOURTH JUAN: No there. Far—one league—two league.

FRIAR JUAN: And in what language, in what tongue did she speak to you?

FOURTH JUAN: I not know, but I understand.

MOTOLINÍA: Is this a true miracle, Friar Juan?

FRIAR JUAN: I'm a believer, Brother. But this time I doubt. I have reason to doubt. (*He glances through the minutes.*) The . . . er, miracle play which was planned entirely against my will was to take place at the Pedregal on St. Silvester's Day, the thirty-first of December. What is the date of today?

MOTOLINÍA: The twelfth. Recall that Martincillo——.

FRIAR JUAN: Yes, I remember, and I thank God for Martincillo's earlier forgetfulness. Because of it, he brought you to my side today. Master Alonso——.

ALONSO (*approaching*): My Lord Bishop——.

FRIAR JUAN: By the Most Holy Sacrament and under pain of excommunication, tell me again how many rosebushes you've planted.

ALONSO (*trembling*): I've already told you, my lord. Three big ones in the Pedregal for some reason I wasn't told about and a small one back of and far from the hill of Tepeyácatl for the Indian girl who's going to give me a little mestizo of my own flesh and blood.

FRIAR JUAN *paces back and forth a moment. Finally he snaps the middle finger and thumb of his right hand.*

FRIAR JUAN: That's it. I should have taken it into account before. I knew well that nothing good could come from the king's idea. To mix women into such a matter . . . God! Tell me, Juan Darío, what was that lady like?

FOURTH JUAN (*thinking, then smiling*): Beautiful——.

FRIAR JUAN: Yes. What else?

FOURTH JUAN: Sweet. Voice like music in canes of lake.

FRIAR JUAN: What else?

FOURTH JUAN: She like Indian—but with *citlali*

. . . no, no, with light. I see her now. (*His expression shows this.*)

FRIAR JUAN: An end must be put to this at once. Now I'll tell you, Friar Toribio, what I think. Friar Antonio?

FRIAR ANTONIO (*approaching again*): Lord Bishop.

FRIAR JUAN: As far as you know, has our Clarisse Sister left this house at any time?

FRIAR ANTONIO: I couldn't say, my lord. I don't know.

FRIAR JUAN: Go to the rear cloister with Brother Martín. Ask permission for him to enter with you, and request the Sister to come here accompanied by you both. (*From where he is standing,* MARTINCILLO *indicates that he wants to say something.*) Go now without a word and come back at once.

FRIAR ANTONIO *and* MARTINCILLO *exit.*

MOTOLINÍA (*perplexed*): Do you think that——?

FRIAR JUAN: I think—God forgive me—that this intrusion of the temporal power into the power of the Church is giving premature bad fruit. I think that the men of the sword who're more loyal to Charles and his interests than they are to God might have arranged all this. In some way they came to know of the emperor's intentions. What do you think?

MOTOLINÍA: Should I think, Friar Juan, perhaps I'd not believe. Yet I do believe, although with no grounds at all for it, and with nothing of reason or knowledge to hold on to, that something is happening here which is outside and beyond ourselves.

FRIAR JUAN: My whole effort, Brother, has been to tie two ends together because, for me, what our time requires is religion and reason. If the human being must be, because he is, an animal of reason, it's necessary to implant the religious sentiment in him. Without that, he'd be nothing than an animal without a real purpose. There must be instilled in him the exercise of reason without which religion would revert in him to animality, to sheer instinct. I fear everything that comes from the valiant captains who are destroyers, Brother, and everything that comes from the Cortéses who, to assert their authority, used to cut off the hands of the emissaries of the Indian princes, and who practice promiscuity with Indian women as if the pelvis of a virgin could be distinguished and separated from those of other women because of the different color of the skin. And, furthermore, who are men that allowed themselves to pass as gods to the Indians.

MOTOLINÍA: It horrifies me to think of this—much less even to say it—but I see that you're on the verge of apostasy, Friar Juan.

FRIAR JUAN: You're naïve, poor little Brother. God is essence, of course. But if God isn't reason, it would mean that reason is a thing of the devil. Live in your own time and stop living on alms of the past.

MOTOLINÍA: Friar Juan!

FRIAR JUAN: Go ahead and protest. Aren't you aware of how we are being used? We convert the Indian to the Faith of our Lord. We fill his ears with hymns and his breast with prayers. We promise him Paradise. And all for what? So that he'll go down into the mines to dig out gold and silver, or else into the quarries to cut stones for the building of a few churches and many palaces—and burst out singing the holy name of God while laboring thus. And how many of our weaker brethren in other lands—who're totally unlike you and Las Casas, or Gante, or Olmos, or Alonso de la Veracruz, or Martín de Valencia, or Sahagún, or even myself—may even now be abandoning themselves to the good life, to chocolate and gold! I repeat, I'm not speaking of us who see everything here close at hand and whose consciences are crucified every hour of the day and night—but of the many and many of those who are probably laughing at you and me in Spain and—God forgive me—perhaps even in Rome itself!

MOTOLINÍA: Friar Juan, it does me harm just to listen to you and to see you so far away from our Faith. Call me stupid and naïve and Poor Little One, if you please, but I believe that you're sick.

FRIAR JUAN: Of course I'm sick. I'm sick, Brother, of a new illness, an illness of our century. I'm sick of a corruption which all Europe is apt to succumb to. Its name is America or Mexico.

The sound of spurs causes all to turn to the door which is opened, without a knock having been given, by a LIEUTENANT *of brusk manners and harsh voice.*

FRIAR JUAN: What does this intrusion mean? How dare you enter here without being announced?

LIEUTENANT (*insolent and looking about*): You receive Indians and friars with welcome. I'm an officer and hidalgo. (*He salutes in a rough manner.*) I've come as the emissary of Captain General Don Hernando Cortés who's left his residence in Coyoacán to honor you with his visit.

FRIAR JUAN (*trembling with anger, but just managing to control himself*): The captain general of New Spain will be welcome to this bishop's palace as a respectful son of the Church—and just like any Indian. (*The* LIEUTENANT *makes to speak.*) Wait a moment. What is the reason for his visit?

LIEUTENANT: The captain general knows about everything that goes on in his dominions. Very early this morning news of what's happening in Tenochtítlan reached his ears. Swarms of Indians—which is like saying swarms of infectious flies—have surrounded his palace to tell him I don't know what nonsense or fable about some woman who's appearing to the Indians to squeeze more tithes out of them for the Church.

MOTOLINÍA: Lieutenant, do not——!

FRIAR JUAN: Leave off, Friar Toribio. This poor man of the sword doesn't know that the tongue of a bishop has more armed virtues than a whole army. Lieutenant,

Master son of . . . son of something . . . hidalgo, that is . . .
leave at once. You dishonor my house which is the House
of God where the sword has neither voice nor power.
When your captain general who also bears the title—
although I don't know why—of Favorite Son of the
Christian Church comes here, he will be admitted to my
presence. But he alone!

LIEUTENANT: Forgive me for laughing, but——.

FRIAR JUAN: If you know what a Basque is, pic-
ture to yourself a Basque bishop (*raising his fist*) possessed
of all the fury of God . . . I told you—go!

LIEUTENANT: I'm the lieutenant of the captain
gene——.

FRIAR JUAN: Beneath this as yet unfinished roof
there's room for no army except Christ's. When you wear
a cassock without dishonoring it, you also will be welcome.
I told you—go!

> FRIAR JUAN *moves with all his energy toward the*
> LIEUTENANT *who falls back and leaves in anger. The*
> *Indians smile broadly.*

MOTOLINIA: You're beside yourself, Brother. Is this
the behavior of a bishop?

FRIAR JUAN: Does a man—and more, a man of the
Basque country—stop being a man because he's a bishop?
The episcopacy isn't a matter of vestments, Brother, but of
human attributes. It's not an ornament, but a matter of
war—above all here. Don't you see all this clearly now?
Don't you see that Cortés is well prepared for what without
a doubt he himself has got up? Now he's coming to collect
the tithes of the "miracle" while accusing the Church itself
of fraud. Here we've only just heard Juan Darío, but there
in Coyoacán they're already fully informed of everything.
Don't you see it?

MOTOLINÍA: Forgive me, Friar Juan, but I've seen
fires in the grassland. Just let a stalk or a blade of grass take
fire from the heat of the sun or from a flint spark, and all

the others will blaze up as we'd like for the Indians themselves to take fire from the flame of the Christian faith.
Who, then, can check the fire that spreads? Who can stop
the blood that flows? Who can hold back the water that
floods over the river banks?

FRIAR JUAN: Are you trying to tell me something?
If so, Friar Toribio, just what is it?

MOTOLINÍA: I don't really know, Friar Juan—I
don't know. But I do know that anger, although it's your
natural element, is a blind factory of errors.

FRIAR JUAN: True. Juan de Zumárraga, Juan of
Reason, Juan of Anger. I'll never be punished enough by
the Divine Mercy. And mark it well, Brother Toribio, that
God's mercy is the sinner's greatest punishment. It's worse
than God's lightning because you have to live with His
mercy—and under it—forever!

MOTOLINÍA (*crossing himself*): May He forgive you,
Friar Juan.

FRIAR ANTONIO *returns. He is alone and has the appearance of being possessed of a strange and uncon-
trollable agitation.*

FRIAR JUAN (*turning around while at the same time
being moved to anger for yet another reason*): Have you
come without the Sister?

FRIAR ANTONIO: Forgive me, Lord Bishop. I can
stand it no longer. I'm going to leave the order—with or
without your permission.

FRIAR JUAN: What's the matter with you now?
Have you lost all sense of——?

FRIAR ANTONIO (*interrupting him*): I believe so,
my lord. Charles and his minister and even our own cardinal jolted my faith strangely there in Spain, Then, afterward, I caught on to certain matters here, and now this
crazy nun——.

FRIAR JUAN: Will you get on with explaining
yourself?

FRIAR ANTONIO: She's crazy beyond a doubt and says she's always in an ecstasy and that she's the Mother of God . . . I can't shut my eyes any longer to what's going on. I don't want to be an accomplice in a fraud, nor a witness to . . . I beg of you—let me go at once.

FRIAR JUAN: Ah, now this. Very well. It's the best thing you can do, foolish man. You'll go to the soldiers, of course. But I've no time for your matter now. Where is the Sister?

MARTINCILLO, *bewildered, enters quickly and hears the question.*

MARTINCILLO: The Sister is following me and talking to herself, but I'm more upset than if I'd desecrated the Most Blesséd Sacrament, Lord Bishop.

FRIAR JUAN: What new foolishness has got hold of you now?

MARTINCILLO: Just go to the balcony, my lord. Look at that mass of Indians down there—a sight never seen before. If the Italians or the French or the Andalusians should see it, they'd think it's a procession or a riot, and they'd enjoy watching it.

FRIAR JUAN: Be quiet, Brother.

FRIAR JUAN *goes upstage. The Indians,* FRIAR ANTONIO, *and* ALONSO *make way for* THE NUN *who enters. She is a young, brown-complexioned Sevillian with large black eyes so dilated as to suggest that she suffers from goiter. Her habit gives the impression of being light and translucent. She holds her hands together on her bosom as in prayer, in a manner suggestive of what is later to be the image of the Virgin of Guadalupe without the Infant. She is, to all appearances, in a trance that was provoked perhaps by her awareness of having been summoned to face a group of men. The three Indians prostrate themselves, their faces touching the floor.* ALONSO *who is, after all, superstitious himself ends up by imitating their example. There is something of saintliness, of a kind of merchandisable divin-*

ity which emanates from the seemingly haloed figure
of the Clarisse Sister. Only FRIAR JUAN, MOTOLINÍA,
FRIAR ANTONIO, *who is erect and exalted,* MARTINCILLO,
who is apart from the group, and FOURTH JUAN *remain
standing in their places while observing the newcomer.
Without a word,* THE NUN *moves halfway downstage
center. Her smile is one of absolute beatitude. Her
gaze is lost in the distance. Her hands flutter briefly,
then come together again in their original position.
Her trance seems continuous and totally out of this
world.*

FRIAR JUAN (*taking in the entire situation at once
and resolved to clarify it immediately*): Good morning,
Clarisse Sister. (THE NUN *pays no attention. She appears
not even to have heard.*) Good morning, Clarisse Sister.
(THE NUN *remains silent.* FRIAR JUAN *repeats with more
emphasis and in a louder voice.*) Good morning, Clarisse
Sister.

THE NUN (*apparently coming out of her trance while
speaking in a soft, musical voice like one who is hypnotized,
or a medium*): Good morning, Brother Bishop.

FOURTH JUAN, *in the grip of a powerful fascination,
observes* THE NUN *fixedly. With his left hand he continues to clasp his folded tilma to his breast.*

FRIAR JUAN (*with deliberation and marvelous coolness in the manner of a surgeon who is preparing to oper-
ate*): Juan Darío, Juan Darío, Juan Darío. (FOURTH JUAN
at last looks at him.) Juan Darío, is this the lady you saw
at the foot of the hill of Tepeyácatl? Is this the beautiful
lady?

Still in her trance the, Sevillian NUN *slowly fixes the
velvety look of her dilated, marvelously black eyes on*
FOURTH JUAN *who twists about but does not, however,
prostrate himself nor turn away his eyes with which
he is devouring the spectacle. Their gazes meet for a
long moment.*

FRIAR JUAN: Look at those other Indians, Friar Toribio. (*With bitter irony.*) May God damn me if they don't look like the Adams of some unknown Eve—all except Juan Darío. Is this, Juan Darío, the lady you saw? The lady who gave you a message for me?

FOURTH JUAN (*swallows in distress. With a visible effort he tears his eyes away from the apparent vision. Slowly*): Looks like . . . yes, looks like. But she is not, *Tata* Bishop.

> THE NUN *feigns to be still in an ecstasy, although she notices that* FOURTH JUAN *has stopped looking her in the eyes.*

FRIAR JUAN (*to* MOTOLINÍA): I was certain, you know, that the Sister—poor demented soul that she is— had made a mistake and appeared before the date agreed upon and in another place. What do we know about what goes on in a sick spirit? (*To* FOURTH JUAN.) Think well on it. Are you sure, Juan Darío?

FOURTH JUAN (*with the same slowness as if chanting a prayer or savoring a sweet*): Looks like . . . no, she is not, *Tata* Bishop. She is not.

FRIAR JUAN: You heard her voice when she spoke to me. Isn't that her voice . . . (*an expressive pantomime before* FOURTH JUAN's *questioning look*) the voice in which she spoke to you? The voice?

FOURTH JUAN (*moves his head in negation while smiling softly*): No.

FRIAR JUAN: How can you be certain?

FOURTH JUAN: Other voice . . . more . . . more sweet . . . more . . . light. And she hasn't *xóchitl*.

MOTOLINÍA: A flower? What flower, what *xóchitl*?

FOURTH JUAN: *Xóchitl* what makes blood . . . This——.

> FOURTH JUAN *turns to face* FRIAR JUAN, MOTOLINÍA, THE NUN, *the Indians,* ALONSO, FRIAR ANTONIO, *and* MARTINCILLO *while at the same time turning his back*

to the audience. He unfolds his tilma, *then with both hands holds out red roses, many of them, to* FRIAR JUAN *and* MOTOLINÍA. *At the same time,* THE NUN *collapses before the unfolded image of the Guada-lupana which is imprinted on the tilma and is still invisible to the audience.*

FOURTH JUAN: Lady say, "Give *xóchitl* to *Tata* Bishop so he make my house here. Is sign I send."

FRIAR ANTONIO *falls to his knees. His lips silently form the word "Miracle" and he makes the sign of the cross.*

The growing noise of the crowd is heard offstage. The light increases gradually. FRIAR JUAN *meditates with as much intensity as a surgeon operates or a miner tests a vein of metal. He seems to grow taller with his medi-tation. The small group of Indians have seen the image and again prostrate themselves with the exception of* FOURTH JUAN *who remains kneeling on one knee.* ALONSO, *on both knees, examines the roses in bewilder-ment.*

FRIAR JUAN (*speaking at last*): What is this, Friar Toribio?

MOTOLINÍA: You've frightened me so with your violence that I hardly dare to tell you, Friar Juan.

FRIAR JUAN: At any rate, tell me.

MOTOLINÍA: It's a . . . miracle (*a gesture by* FRIAR JUAN) or it appears to be a miracle.

FRIAR JUAN: A miracle? Deceit and fraud! Blas-phemy against faith and reason!

MOTOLINÍA: Please, hear me. At my request, as you know, we decided upon a miracle play for the thirty-first of December, the Feast of St. Silvester, and in the Pedregal of St. Angel, toward the south. (*Another gesture by* FRIAR JUAN.) Allow me. All this is in your minutes. But the apparition takes place on the twelfth of December of 1531 at the foot of the hill of Tepeyácatl, toward the north, and not on a solemn feast day. What greater clarity could be asked?

FRIAR JUAN: Now I'm certain. Those people have used another woman, not even, if you please, a nun because there aren't any more here . . . an Indian girl perhaps. In-human, sacrilegious intrigue. A play of Charles V and Cortés which must be denounced. (*He looks toward the balcony and, seeming to gather all his forces in his clenched fists, goes to it.*)

MOTOLINÍA: What are you going to do, Friar Juan? In God's name, what are you going to do?

FRIAR JUAN opens the balcony window. The tumult below increases without it being possible to distinguish what the voices are shouting in Nahuatl. Little by little, however, the word "Tlamahuizolli!" repeated with an increasing volume of sound, becomes clear.

FRIAR JUAN: What're they shouting, Toribio?

MOTOLINÍA (*listens a moment, then smiles*): I get it now. They're shouting, Friar Juan, *Tlamahuizolli!* which means a surprising event, or a marvelous happening—in other words, a miracle! (*Drawing back, FRIAR JUAN retires from the balcony while raising his hands to his forehead. The light increases.*) What's the matter with you, Friar Juan?

FRIAR JUAN (*after wringing his hands for a moment*): Charles or no Charles, Cortés or no Cortés, now I see it all as though my head had been split apart to let the light in, Benavente.

MOTOLINÍA: I don't understand you . . . even less now.

FRIAR JUAN: The thirty-first of December, the twelfth of December—what does it matter? Human agencies, how could they exist, how function without God? Like a great blow of the cross upon my chest I feel something, Brother, in that outroar that's coming in to us from the plaza.

MOTOLINÍA: I beg you to explain yourself.

FRIAR JUAN: We'll say nothing, Benavente. We'll let the proud crown of Spain think that everything took place as it had arranged. We'll let Spain believe that she invented the miracle.

MOTOLINÍA: You're not yourself.

FRIAR JUAN: You wouldn't be either if you could see what I do with these eyes of mine. The truth must be kept hidden from Charles—from all of them—Brother, because from this very moment Mexico has ceased to belong to Spain—forever! And that is God's miracle.

MOTOLINÍA: And now you do believe in miracles?

FRIAR JUAN: There's only one miracle, and I feel it now. My reason is shouting it to me.

A VOICE (*offstage*): Captain General Don Hernando Cortés is approaching. Make way! Make way!

While THE NUN *remains on the floor, but conscious now and at prayer, the Indians,* FRIAR ANTONIO, ALONSO, *and* MARTINCILLO *follow* FRIAR JUAN *and* MOTOLINÍA *to the balcony.* MARTINCILLO *crosses himself frantically. The tumult of voices grows. The light of the midday sun gives the impression of bursting through the very walls and of spreading everywhere.* FOURTH JUAN *slowly moves to face the audience to show his* tilma. *Something stops him, however, and, as though bathed by a childlike flood of well-being, he goes to the balcony where* FRIAR JUAN *is making ready to bless the people in the plaza.*

FRIAR JUAN (*to* MOTOLINÍA): All at once I see these people crowned with light, with faith. I see faith already running through all Mexico like a river without banks. That is the miracle, Brother!

CURTAIN

One of These Days . . .

A Nonpolitical Fantasy in three acts

Cast of characters

The Captain
Secretary of State
Mr. Nobody (José Gómez Urbina)
Secretary of War
Secretary of Public Education
Secretary of Finance
Secretary of Economics
Secretary of Agriculture
Secretary of Communications
A Lieutenant
Chief Justice of the Supreme Court
President of the official party (General Meléndez)
Speaker of Congress
Home Secretary
Ambassador of the Federated States of Demoland
Florentino Balandro
Voice of the Ambassador to the Southern Cross
Voice of the Announcer
Counselor Aguirre ⎫
General Eloy   ⎪
Dr. Suárez Meza   ⎬ *Ex-presidents*
General Avalos   ⎪ *of*
General Puebla   ⎪ *Indoland*
Counselor Germán ⎭
Colonel Judas
Two Soldiers
Voices of the People

PLACE: *Indoland, a Latin American republic of growing impor-
tance. The action takes place in the conference room of the
presidential palace.*
TIME: *One of these days . . .*
ACT ONE: *The night of the crime, at a quarter after one.*
ACT TWO: *Three months later: morning, afternoon, and evening.*
ACT THREE: *Two days later: daytime.*

Act I

*When the curtain rises, another appears on which is painted the flag of Indoland which consists of two horizontal stripes: one green, the other red. Across the colors is the emblem of the country: a rearing white stallion, its mane blowing in the wind, that raises its right hoof against an enormous toad that is sitting on its hind legs like the smart animals of the animated cartoons. A big star shines above the stallion's mane. Below the flag, on a waving strip, is the motto: "Indo-*land Undivided and Free."

The second curtain rises on a completely dark conference room in the presidential palace as the wall clock is striking the first quarter after one. A moment later, voices are heard offstage.

VOICE OF THE CAPTAIN: This way, sir, if you'll be so kind.

VOICE OF THE SECRETARY OF STATE (*above the noise made by his tripping over a heavy chair*): The devil!

A door is heard being opened. THE CAPTAIN *enters downstage right and switches on the lights. In the background, French windows open onto three balconies. A grandfather clock stands between two of the balconies. Three massive doors, two on the left, the other on the right, are embellished with brightly polished metal plates and knockers. Heavy green curtains with gold trimmings hang at doors and balcony*

windows, between which stand high-backed Spanish
Colonial armchairs. The walls are decorated with gilt
moldings of the period of the 1900s. On the ceiling,
from the center of which hangs an immense French
chandelier, there is a painting of angels and mytho-
logical figures colored mainly in rose and blue. A glass
case standing between two of the balconies holds the
green and red flag of Indoland. In the center of the
room are a conference table and twelve chairs. In addi-
tion to crystal ashtrays and various sets of thermos
jugs and glasses, there is a microphone in the center
of the table.

THE CAPTAIN: I hope you haven't hurt yourself,
Mr. Secretary of State.

SECRETARY OF STATE (*entering*): I hope so more
than you, Captain. (*Carefully he rubs his left knee.*)

THE CAPTAIN: Don't you want to sit down, sir?

SECRETARY OF STATE: What I want is for you
to explain this to me, if you can. I was dragged out of bed
after midnight because of what is an urgent matter, or so
I was told by the person who telephoned.

THE CAPTAIN: I am that person, sir.

SECRETARY OF STATE: Ah? So it was *you* who
gave me to understand that there's some matter under way
of the greatest urgency and that the whole Cabinet has
been called for a meeting!

THE CAPTAIN: Right, sir.

SECRETARY OF STATE: Really, it's not right. I
come here and find not a soul present but you, and not
even a light burning. I almost break my kneecap and, to
make matters worse, I'm the first Cabinet member to
arrive.

THE CAPTAIN: You were the last to be notified,
Mr. Secretary.

SECRETARY OF STATE: Well, that would explain
things. But can you tell me where my colleagues are?

THE CAPTAIN: No doubt on their way here, sir. Some have to come in from out of town.

SECRETARY OF STATE: So? I thought that in the new régime the secretaries wouldn't have country houses any more.

THE CAPTAIN: If you'll permit me to venture an opinion——.

SECRETARY OF STATE: Venture whatever you care to. I'm not forcing you to. But just remember that he who takes no risks never crosses the seas.

THE CAPTAIN: Very well, sir. I only wanted to say that it isn't easy to go back to being poor after the years of revolution we've had.

SECRETARY OF STATE: There's something in that which . . . Yes, decidedly there's something to what you say. (*With surprise.*) You're quite a philosopher, Captain.

THE CAPTAIN: In countries at peace, as ours is, the army enjoys quite a bit of well-paid idleness, Mr. Secretary. I take advantage of my leisure to read——.

SECRETARY OF STATE: History?

THE CAPTAIN: No, sir. All history books are the same. Any one of them shows us quite clearly that history repeats itself. I prefer to read the philosophers because no two of them write alike or say the same thing.

SECRETARY OF STATE: True, true, especially if one thinks of contemporary ones. But tell me, have you any idea what the reason for this most . . . most unexpected meeting is? After all, it's Saturday.

THE CAPTAIN: Sunday, sir.

SECRETARY OF STATE (*glancing at his watch*): Sunday already. Yes, it's almost half-past one. But, after all, there're working days and hours, and also days for resting. What the devil! Please explain——.

THE CAPTAIN: I would if I could, sir. I'd be able to if, for example, I'd read the explanation in a book because books claim to explain everything. But I only followed orders from a chief and chiefs have the mania of never giving explanations.

SECRETARY OF STATE: Well, you can at least tell me who gave you the order.

THE CAPTAIN: With the order, sir, I received another.

SECRETARY OF STATE: Yes? What?

THE CAPTAIN: Not to tell anyone who had given the first order.

SECRETARY OF STATE: Well, that's fine indeed!

The SECRETARY *takes out a cigarette case and offers a cigarette to the* CAPTAIN *who refuses it but lights the* SECRETARY'S *who then walks back and forth for a while in silence. The* CAPTAIN, *standing as on guard, watches him. A third person enters almost noiselessly downstage right. Of the* CAPTAIN *it could be said that he is a handsome example of the new military generation which combines athletics with the martial tradition, and both with a note of social refinement. It could also be said of the* SECRETARY OF STATE *that he has had a European education and has the appearance of an intellectual along with that of a good-looking man who is well fed and well bronzed by the sun, and that his smiles blend with acidity in an air of unquestionable authority along with good-humored condescension. Nothing much, however, could be said of the third person who has just entered. He is a man of medium age, medium height, and is mediumly well dressed and fed. Moderately dark-skinned, his description on a passport might read: features, regular; eyes, brown; mouth, regular; distinguishing marks, none. We will, then, identify him for the present by the name of* MR. NOBODY.

MR. NOBODY: Good evening, gentlemen. (*The* CAPTAIN *turns to look at him but does not move from his post.*

The SECRETARY OF STATE *stops and turns around.*) Mr.
Secretary . . . (*A half bow.*) Captain——.

SECRETARY OF STATE: Good morning, rather.

MR. NOBODY: You're right, sir. Good morning. (*He
half smiles.*)

THE CAPTAIN: Good evening. Can I help you?

MR. NOBODY: I don't know whether you can or not.

THE CAPTAIN: Are you looking for someone?

MR. NOBODY: I don't know about that either.

THE CAPTAIN: Well, then?

MR. NOBODY: I was summoned here. That's all I
know.

THE CAPTAIN (*taking a list from the breast pocket of
his jacket and glancing over it*): Pardon me, but I was ordered to telephone everyone and . . . I don't remember you.

MR. NOBODY (*in a moderately ironical tone that is
also somewhat humble*): I don't have a telephone at my
house. I received this. (*He, in turn takes a paper from his
pocket and gives it to the* CAPTAIN.)

THE CAPTAIN (*after a glance at the paper*): Right.
Pardon me, but I hadn't had the pleasure of . . . (*He returns the paper.*) Won't you sit down?

MR. NOBODY: Thank you very much. (*He sits down
in a chair between the two doors on the left.*)

SECRETARY OF STATE: Captain——.

THE CAPTAIN: Mr. Secretary? (*He goes to the
SECRETARY who asks him, by raising his eyebrows in the
usual gesture of such a query, who* MR. NOBODY *is. The
CAPTAIN replies with a shrug of the shoulders that is universally recognized as a way of expressing that one does
not know. The clock strikes the half hour.*)

SECRETARY OF STATE (*looking at his watch*): I
think it's high time something should be happening. After
all, this isn't a waiting room.

THE CAPTAIN: I'm certain that the others won't be
long now, sir.

SECRETARY OF STATE: I've an interesting obser-
vation to make in reply to that. In my profession, Captain,
which is, as you know, diplomacy, one learns to be silent;
but in yours one learns something more important—to wait.

THE CAPTAIN: One learns that in the ranks, Mr.
Secretary.

SECRETARY OF STATE: As you haven't been able
to answer two of my questions, perhaps you can the third.

THE CAPTAIN: Perhaps.

SECRETARY OF STATE: Who else has been summoned here?

THE CAPTAIN: The whole Cabinet, sir, except . . .
(*Voices are heard offstage.*) Ah, you see? They're coming.

Both turn toward the door downstage right. MR. NO-
BODY *rises like a soldier, but a civilian, after all, he be-
gins turning his hat about in his hands in a somewhat
nervous manner. Enter, downstage right, the* SECRE-
TARY OF WAR, *in civilian country dress, and the* SECRE-
TARY OF PUBLIC EDUCATION.

THE CAPTAIN (*saluting*): General . . . Mr. Secretary——.

SECRETARY OF WAR: I couldn't possibly leave the
ladies halfway through their game of canasta and with the
steepest damned pool I've ever seen.

SECRETARY OF PUBLIC EDUCATION: I had an
urgent matter to finish, too. But you (*to the* SECRETARY OF
STATE) are always on the dot.

SECRETARY OF STATE: An occupational disease.
A diplomat often wonders why he should be exactly on
time when the real fun invariably begins a couple of hours
later.

A discreet cough causes all to turn toward MR. NOBODY.

MR. NOBODY: Mr. Secretary . . . General——.

*These reply with surprised expressions and nods, then,
by means of a look, inquire of the* SECRETARY OF STATE

who the person is that has just spoken to them. The
SECRETARY OF STATE, *in turn, shrugs his shoulders.*
MR. NOBODY *sits down again.*

SECRETARY OF WAR: Well, what's this all about?

SECRETARY OF PUBLIC EDUCATION: Something
urgent, it seems. But what? Tell us.

SECRETARY OF STATE: I know as much, or,
rather, as little as you. As proof that neither I nor my
ministry is at the bottom of this affair—whatever it is—
I'll have you know that they roused me out of bed at
midnight.

SECRETARY OF PUBLIC EDUCATION: Not an international problem, then. As for me, Public Education is
a boiling pot of conflicts but they're all entirely budgetary.
Such matters are taken care of during regular office hours
or during a strike. General?

SECRETARY OF WAR: The army, gentlemen, is
immersed in the most disquieting state of peace. But with
a new government, especially when it's one of civilians, I
suppose the battle must go on day and night.

SECRETARY OF PUBLIC EDUCATION: And above
all, against the ghosts of its predecessors.

SECRETARY OF STATE: Especially if they're still
very much around. I've tried to question the captain about
this meeting, but to no avail. He's incorruptible.

THE CAPTAIN: As ignorance is, sir.

SECRETARY OF PUBLIC EDUCATION: That's a
good feint, Captain.

SECRETARY OF WAR: To me the matter is quite
clear. The president works too much. To work is a good
thing, but it mustn't be overdone.

SECRETARY OF STATE: Someone once said that
man's greatest ambition is to avoid work.

SECRETARY OF PUBLIC EDUCATION: That's an
ambition he'll carry out up to a point of exhaustion, my
dear friends.

All laugh. MR. NOBODY *provides a slight echo. Other laughs are heard offstage. The* CAPTAIN *salutes as the* SECRETARIES OF FINANCE, ECONOMICS, *and* AGRICULTURE *enter downstage right. The first two are in evening dress, the last in informal country dress.* MR. NOBODY *comes to his feet as if moved by an inner spring. Exchange of greetings ad lib.*

SECRETARY OF WAR: I'm sure that these two (*indicating the* SECRETARIES OF FINANCE *and* ECONOMICS) are the responsible parties. Money is at the bottom of all our evils, isn't that right, my dear Secretary of Finance?

SECRETARY OF PUBLIC EDUCATION: And Economics is the pharmacy where all remedies are sold.

SECRETARY OF STATE: Indeed it is, but at what prices, gentlemen, at what prices! And you see? These two weren't sleeping, as I was.

SECRETARY OF FINANCE (*laughing*): As a matter of fact, the private bankers were giving us a banquet——.

SECRETARY OF ECONOMICS: With interest, gentlemen. With interest. (*Laughs all around.*)

SECRETARY OF WAR: Now this is what I call democracy. The engineer has come straight from his ranch.

SECRETARY OF AGRICULTURE (*laughing*): The truth is I haven't. The president sent me to make a week-end inventory of my predecessor's fish hatcheries.

MR. NOBODY *coughs again. All look at him.*

MR. NOBODY: Mr. Secretary . . . Mr. Secretary . . . Mr. Secretary——.

THE THREE: Good evening. (*They turn with questioning glances to the* SECRETARIES OF PUBLIC EDUCATION *and* WAR *who shrug their shoulders.* MR. NOBODY *sits down again.*)

SECRETARY OF AGRICULTURE: Who is he?

SECRETARY OF FINANCE: Can we speak freely with him here?

SECRETARY OF PUBLIC EDUCATION: I suppose so, as he's here.

SECRETARY OF STATE: I know that he was summoned, too, but I don't know who he is.

SECRETARY OF WAR: Well, we were wondering what's the purpose of this gathering. I'm certain now that it has to do with Finance.

SECRETARY OF FINANCE: Not as far as I know.

SECRETARY OF WAR: Then with prices.

SECRETARY OF ECONOMICS: No, because, thanks to the measures that have already been taken, food prices are going down.

SECRETARY OF FINANCE: There's really no problem now in that direction except to find the food.

SECRETARY OF WAR: I don't think, gentlemen, that we ought to make light of this matter.

SECRETARY OF PUBLIC EDUCATION: Well, don't forget, General, that at the beginning every new government makes a show of the infectious good humor that comes from the people. They never lose hope.

SECRETARY OF STATE: It's a fact that hope is always reborn in them, even though they lose it again as each government ends. That naturally puts the people in a bad humor which seems to infect those who're leaving office.

SECRETARY OF COMMUNICATIONS (*from downstage right*): Good evening, gentlemen. (*He approaches the group. Greetings ad lib.* MR. NOBODY *rises.*)

MR. NOBODY: Mr. Secretary——. (*The* SECRETARY OF COMMUNICATIONS *bows slightly, then with a glance asks the others who the man is. The others all shrug their shoulders.* MR. NOBODY *sits down again.*)

SECRETARY OF COMMUNICATIONS: Do you know why we have been called here at such an ungodly hour?

THE OTHERS (*all speaking at the same time*): Ah!

So you do.—What's it all about?—Come on, man. At last
someone who knows.—Tell us. Do you know?—Come on,
let's have it.

SECRETARY OF COMMUNICATIONS: No. No. I
don't know. I was only asking. (*General disappointment.*)
But one thing about this strikes me especially. (*A show of
general attention.*) This morning, or that is, yesterday
morning, the president telephoned to tell me that he'd
spend the weekend at his estate at La Estrella, and that
he'd expect me there tomorrow—that is today—for lunch
when he'd go over certain urgent plans with me.

SECRETARY OF STATE: That's odd.

SECRETARY OF FINANCE: He doesn't
change plans easily.

SECRETARY OF ECONOMICS: What
could have happened ?

SECRETARY OF WAR: Without some
serious reason——.

SECRETARY OF AGRICULTURE: I don't
understand a word of it.

> *All
> speak
> at
> once*

SECRETARY OF COMMUNICATION: And furthermore, he called me again yesterday afternoon from La
Estrella to tell me that Captain Peláez would accompany
me there.

THE CAPTAIN (*going up to him*): I, sir?

SECRETARY OF COMMUNICATIONS: If you're
Captain Peláez, yes, you.

THE CAPTAIN: I find this strange. I escorted the
president to his motorcar when he left at noon for La
Estrella, but he said nothing about this to me.

SECRETARY OF COMMUNICATIONS: Are you
Captain Peláez, the expert in military communications?

THE CAPTAIN: Yes, Mr. Secretary.

SECRETARY OF COMMUNICATIONS: Then no
doubt you're the one he meant.

A feeling of growing uneasiness is registered by the

SECRETARIES. MR. NOBODY *also gives moderate signs of uneasiness from his chair. The clock strikes three-quarters of the hour.*

THE CAPTAIN: I'm certain that all this will be cleared up in no time now.

SECRETARY OF WAR: If you know something, tell it.

The door upstage right opens and a LIEUTENANT *enters who, somewhat bewildered on seeing so many important officials present, goes up to the* CAPTAIN, *salutes and then holds out a folded sheet of paper to him.*

THE CAPTAIN: What's this?

THE LIEUTENANT: A teletype message for you, Captain.

THE CAPTAIN (*after unfolding and reading the message*): This message was sent from La Estrella at nine-thirty in the evening. Why is it being delivered to me only now?

THE LIEUTENANT: We didn't know where to find you, Captain, until Colonel Hernández of Communications just told us that you'd be on guard duty at the palace.

THE CAPTAIN: And how did the colonel know that?

THE LIEUTENANT: I haven't the least idea, Captain.

THE CAPTAIN: Thank you. That's all, Lieutenant.

THE LIEUTENANT: Yes, sir. (*Salutes and exits.*)

SECRETARY OF STATE: I suppose you still can't tell us anything, Captain?

SECRETARY OF WAR: As secretary of war and your superior officer——.

THE CAPTAIN: That isn't necessary, General. (*He reads the message.*) "By orders of the president, you will proceed to the residence of the secretary of communications at nine o'clock tomorrow morning, Sunday, and escort him to the president's estate at La Estrella."

SECRETARY OF FINANCE: Well, now we're just where we were before.

SECRETARY OF EDUCATION: Like with the rate of exchanges, which is comforting.

SECRETARY OF ECONOMICS: But why, then, have we been summoned here?

SECRETARY OF STATE (*to the* CAPTAIN): You told me that it was for a Cabinet meeting.

SECRETARY OF AGRICULTURE: And me the same.

THE CAPTAIN: Just so, gentlemen.

SECRETARY OF AGRICULTURE: I think that no one except the president himself is authorized to call a meeting of us secretaries.

SECRETARY OF WAR: Correct. How do you explain this, Captain?

THE CAPTAIN: In this whole matter, General, I've been only a simple intermediary. As I've already explained to the secretary of state, when I was ordered to call you together I was also strictly ordered not to say anything else.

SECRETARY OF WAR: Well, I order you now to tell us everything you know.

THE CAPTAIN: I've already told you all I can, General, but on my own, I'll add one thing.

SECRETARY OF COMMUNICATIONS: Go ahead. What are you waiting for?

SECRETARY OF STATE: I was right, a soldier knows how to wait.

SECRETARY OF PUBLIC EDUCATION: Let's have it, Captain.

SECRETARY OF FINANCE: Speak up, man.

SECRETARY OF ECONOMICS: Let's economize on time, at least, gentlemen.

THE CAPTAIN: I must make it clear that what I have to say is neither a key to what you're wondering about nor a revelation. Any revelation would be entirely out of place.

SECRETARY OF WAR (*irritably*): You don't act like an officer, Captain, but like a . . . a philosopher. Get on with you.

SECRETARY OF STATE: Admirable penetration, General. A soldier is also a man of instinct. If you please, Captain, explain.

THE CAPTAIN: It's really very simple. The order I received, together with the list of your names, was this: Summon them all to a Cabinet meeting to be held at one o'clock sharp in the morning so that all will be assembled by two. And——.

SEVERAL VOICES: And——?

THE CAPTAIN: That's all. But allow me to remind you that several secretaries were out of town and also the mayor. Because of this, I don't think that everyone will be here by two o'clock.

SECRETARY OF WAR: That doesn't matter. What is important——.

THE CAPTAIN: Pardon me, General. (*He turns toward the clock; all the others do the same.*) It's two o'clock.

> *The clock strikes two and immediately a bell is heard ringing in a way that expresses authority on the part of the ringer. The* CAPTAIN *walks with a smart military stride to the door upstage left and exits.* MR. NOBODY *rises. General movement on stage, coughs and clearing of throats. Exchange of cigarettes and the striking of lighters. No one speaks. The* SECRETARIES *all line up, their eyes fixed on the door which is opened in a moment by the* CAPTAIN *who stands aside at attention. The scene immediately takes on an air of solemnity. The* SECRETARIES *draw themselves up and forget their cigarettes. In a moment there enter the* CHIEF JUSTICE OF THE SUPREME COURT *who wears a goatee and is dressed in an old-fashioned black suit; the* SPEAKER OF CONGRESS *who is still a young man and is dressed*

smartly in navy blue; and the PRESIDENT OF THE OFFI-
CIAL PARTY *who wears the uniform of a general. After
taking a few steps forward, these three form a compact
line of their own.* MR. NOBODY *coughs in vain: no one
turns to him.*

CHIEF JUSTICE: Good evening, gentlemen. (*Ad
lib responses of* "Good evening." *The* CHIEF JUSTICE *turns
to his two companions and whispers something. Both nod
gravely.*) Although I regret the absence of several Cabinet
members, these gentlemen (*indicating the* SPEAKER OF CON-
GRESS *and the* PRESIDENT OF THE OFFICIAL PARTY) and I
consider that the most important members are present,
so we will open this meeting with you. Please be seated.

The SECRETARIES *take seats around the table, leaving
four seats empty at its head. The* SPEAKER OF CONGRESS
and the PRESIDENT OF THE OFFICIAL PARTY *sit in two
of the empty chairs. The* CHIEF JUSTICE *remains
standing.*

SECRETARY OF STATE: Mr. Chief Justice——.
CHIEF JUSTICE: Yes, Mr. Secretary of State?

The SECRETARY OF STATE *goes up to the old man and
whispers something to which he nods his head affirmatively, then turns to look at* MR. NOBODY *who is standing before his chair and twirling his hat about in his
hands. The* SECRETARY *returns to his chair. The* CHIEF
JUSTICE *whispers something to the* PRESIDENT OF THE
OFFICIAL PARTY *who then looks at* MR. NOBODY *who is
growing more uneasy. The* PRESIDENT OF THE OFFICIAL
PARTY *shrugs his shoulders and whispers to the* SPEAKER
OF CONGRESS. *The latter also looks at* MR. NOBODY,
then rises and goes to him with outstretched hand.

SPEAKER OF CONGRESS: My dear friend——.
MR. NOBODY (*somewhat nervous on finding himself
being paid so much attention*): Yes, Mr. Speaker?

SPEAKER OF CONGRESS (*with a slight smile*): I'd like to ask a favor of you.

MR. NOBODY: If I can be of any service——.

SPEAKER OF CONGRESS: You can. Although it was at my instance that you were summoned to this meeting, its importance requires that we dispense with your presence until later on. I must beg of you, therefore, to go to the antechamber and wait patiently there until you're called. Captain Peláez——.

> *The* CAPTAIN *goes up to* MR. NOBODY, *takes him courteously by the arm and accompanies him to the door downstage right which he opens. Exit* MR. NOBODY. *The* CAPTAIN *closes the door, then stands before it on guard. The* SPEAKER OF CONGRESS *returns to his seat. The* CHIEF JUSTICE *also sits down.*

SECRETARY OF WAR: May I ask who that man is?

CHIEF JUSTICE: You'll know in due course General. (*He takes out an immaculate white handkerchief from his coat pocket, carefully wipes his eyeglasses and puts them on again, then replaces the handkerchief in his pocket. The silence that surrounds him is of the kind that the classics called "marvelous."*) Gentlemen, I'll be brief because the solemnity of this occasion imposes brevity. Furthermore, words aren't what we need now. (*He rises.*) Before declaring this session open, in agreement with the Speaker of Congress and the president of the official party of the Republic, who represents the executive power, I must request of you that you stand and take the solemn oath that nothing we discuss here will be made public unless authorized by us three authorities. I request you, therefore, to repeat after me: "I solemnly swear, as an Indolander and patriot, to maintain the most absolute silence regarding the reason for and the import of this Cabinet meeting, and if I shouldn't do so, may the country call me to account." (*The* SECRETARIES *repeat the rhetorical phrases with some display of bewilderment and surprise. All of*

them are red-faced as they sit down again. The CHIEF
JUSTICE *also sits down.*) Thank you, gentlemen. I now declare this Cabinet session open. (*In a changed tone.*) Somewhat more than two months ago—two months and a week,
to be exact—all those present had the honor of being called
to serve, each in his own capacity, the new president of our
country, a servant of the fatherland whose reputation for
rectitude and whose program for reform and moral aggran-
disement made us unconditionally his. We all undertook
to collaborate with him with an enthusiasm and an opti-
mism that rarely have been seen in our country. But in
countries such as ours, we are all, as you know only too
well, the playthings of volcanoes and we're also creatures
of the tropics. The unexpected happens here every day, as
it has done before in our history and as it has just done
again. It is now my painful and overwhelming duty, Messrs.
Secretaries, to inform you that President Matías, our guide
and the hope of the Republic, met his death a short while
ago.

> *The news sinks in gradually, then provokes an out-*
> *burst. All the* SECRETARIES *jump up, gesticulating and*
> *speaking together ad lib.*

THE SECRETARIES: Impossible!—What has he said!
—This is incredible!—Absurd!—It can't be!—No, no, no,
no!—It's impossible!—How?—Why?

SECRETARY OF WAR: This is terrible, but I always
said that he was overworking himself.

SECRETARY OF STATE: But how——?
SECRETARY OF FINANCE: The heart?
SECRETARY OF ECONOMICS: What?
What——?
SECRETARY OF PUBLIC EDUCATION:
He was well today! I know it.
SECRETARY OF COMMUNICATIONS:
In perfect health! I saw him.
SECRETARY OF AGRICULTURE:
How did it happen? How?

All at the same time

ALL AD LIB: How? How? How?

CHIEF JUSTICE: Order, gentlemen. Order, please. *(Some of the* SECRETARIES *sit down again. Others remain standing, exchanging glances and making gestures.)* I'm only halfway through my task. I beg of you to listen further. I spoke before of the unexpected as the factor which governs life in our country. Prepare yourselves, gentlemen, to learn more that is even worse. The president of the Republic was assassinated at eleven o'clock last night at his estate at La Estrella.

Now neither astonishment nor outburst has limits.

THE SECRETARIES *(ad lib):* Assassinated?—Horrible!—How?—By whom?—The Archangelists!—No, no, no, without a doubt that traitor of a General Jaimes!—Impossible!—No, no, the Communists!—No, the reactionaries, that's plain.—Assassinated!

CHIEF JUSTICE: Gentlemen, silence, please. But my emotion prevents me from going on. I beg the Speaker of Congress, who was almost an eyewitness to the event, to take my place as spokesman.

The excitement diminishes gradually. All take their seats, still giving evidence, however, of great consternation, as each speaks.

SECRETARY OF WAR: I swear to avenge the death of our president!

SECRETARY OF PUBLIC EDUCATION: Our martyred president!

SECRETARY OF STATE: What a position this puts us in in the eyes of the world!

SECRETARY OF AGRICULTURE: I'm crushed, stupefied.

SECRETARY OF ECONOMICS: It's obvious: this is a crisis without limits.

SECRETARY OF FINANCE: Bankruptcy, We've gone backward twenty years—no, fifty!

SECRETARY OF COMMUNICATIONS: Nationwide grief and disgrace.

SPEAKER OF CONGRESS: Please, gentlemen. I invoke my position as Speaker of Congress to inform you in detail but in the most absolute secrecy, for the time being at least——.

SECRETARY OF PUBLIC EDUCATION: But who will keep the newspapers quiet?

SPEAKER OF CONGRESS: The necessary pressure has already been brought to bear in that quarter. The press won't break the news for a few more hours. Only the publishers of the most important dailies have been informed of the assassination. They've also been warned that if any of them should publish a single word on his own about what has happened, his paper will be closed down and confiscated. No one's going to play with this national emergency.

PRESIDENT OF THE OFFICIAL PARTY: It would be advisable to let these gentlemen know——.

General silence and anxious expectation.

SPEAKER OF CONGRESS: Yes, of course. Because of the heat in the La Estrella region, the president was, as you all know, accustomed to working until late at night on the terrace of his home where he had a desk and proper lighting installed. At eleven o'clock last night when he was still working for the fatherland, he was struck down by the bullets of submachine guns fired from two motorcars that drove by slowly, then sped off after the assassination. (*General murmurs. The* SPEAKER OF CONGRESS *gestures for silence.*) The first motorcar, gentlemen, I say this fully ashamed of it as I am, was manned by two officers of the National Army.

SECRETARY OF WAR: Impossible! This is slander! the army is loyal to the national institutions. Those men were bandits disguised as officers.

PRESIDENT OF THE OFFICIAL PARTY: Please, my dear friend——.

SPEAKER OF CONGRESS: The army officers were seen and their trail is being closely followed. In the second motorcar, where there was also a submachine gun, two school teachers——.

SECRETARY OF PUBLIC EDUCATION: What!

SPEAKER OF CONGRESS: Pardon . . . they were identified as two known Communist agitators who receive salaries from the Ministry of Public Education.

SECRETARY OF PUBLIC EDUCATION: I deny most energetically that——.

CHIEF JUSTICE: Save your energy, Mr. Secretary. You gentlemen still haven't heard all.

SPEAKER OF CONGRESS: Shall I continue? (*General assent.*) This indescribable assassination of an idealist who was a good and honorable man has imposed two grave problems on the country. The first is that justice be done——.

CHIEF JUSTICE: It shall be, fall who may!

SPEAKER OF CONGRESS: As the chief justice has just said, nothing and no one can stop us. Because the assassination took place outside the capital, the guilty person or persons are subject to the death penalty. And to make sure that justice really is done, it's indispensable, gentlemen, that we all stay on as members of the government. Now for the other grave problem: the immediate succession to the presidency.

SECRETARY OF STATE: That's provided for in the Constitution. The home secretary——.

SECRETARY OF PUBLIC EDUCATION: Absolutely loyal to our assassinated chief——.

SECRETARY OF AGRICULTURE: And a great friend of every one here.

SECRETARY OF FINANCE: I don't see that there's any problem.

SPEAKER OF CONGRESS: The chief justice warned you, gentlemen, that there's still more that's going to be terrible for you to hear. Our friend the home secretary was with the president on the terrace——.

SECRETARY OF AGRICULTURE: No!

SPEAKER OF CONGRESS: ——and also fell to the assassins' bullets!

ALL THE SECRETARIES TOGETHER (*ad lib*): Terrible!—He who'd have been the next president!—And so full of enthusiasm!—Such a man!—This is terrifying!—It's crushing!

SPEAKER OF CONGRESS: Let's save our comments for later, gentlemen. I repeat that we're faced with a national emergency and we must meet it as men. The next immediate successor would have been the home secretary's undersecretary after having been duly installed as Secretary. But . . . pardon me, this affects me personally because it concerns my brother-in-law . . . Counselor Pozos stepped out on the terrace at the moment the crime was committed. No, wait—(*He raises his hand to silence the general protest which begins.*) The rain of bullets missed him so he was able to get to his motorcar and set out in pursuit of the assassins. (*Expectant silence.*) He did in fact overtake them and tried to block their escape at a curve of the road. The first motorcar managed to get by, but the second crashed into my brother-in-law's and both cars plunged over the cliffside. The bodies of the two Communist school teachers were identified in the wreck.

SECRETARY OF WAR: And Pozos was——?

SECRETARY OF PUBLIC EDUCATION: Injured... killed?

SPEAKER OF CONGRESS: Killed while doing his duty. (*Voices rise all around.*) No! No, please! Not a word more or I'll lose control of myself and that mustn't happen. For Indoland's sake I mustn't. My brother-in-law and the home secretary will be avenged, as will the president. So, gentlemen, you have the other problem which is: who is to be president now?

SECRETARY OF FINANCE: I'll not make any comment. I'm too overwhelmed . . . But, in short, as authorized by the Constitution, the chief justice may be automatically appointed provisional president of the Republic and then call for a new election. (*Murmurs of approval.*)

CHIEF JUSTICE: Mr. Secretary of Finance, the Constitution and I are old friends. I'm almost the only survivor of those who drafted it after we won the revolution. I know it by heart. I've fought for it and never have I forgotten my duty to it. But I'm seventy-seven years old and I've very high blood pressure which even whiskey can't lower. I need rest. I must live at a lower altitude if I'm to survive. In other words, gentlemen, although I'm still sound in mind and spirit, just about all of my body that I could give to my country would, in a very short while, be a corpse. Under the pressure of affairs of state, my blood pressure wouldn't permit me to last a month. Dr. Siegfried has just assured me of this.

SECRETARY OF ECONOMICS: Well, what then?

SECRETARY OF AGRICULTURE: There's a solution. If you gentlemen will allow me——.

CHIEF JUSTICE: Mr. Engineer, don't let it upset you if I tell you that I'm way ahead of you. You're young, but time will cure that, don't worry. What you're going to propose is what we (*indicating himself and the* SPEAKER OF CONGRESS *and the* PRESIDENT OF THE OFFICAL PARTY) have already discussed for more than two hours because I myself suggested that General Meléndez, president of the official party, assume the provisional presidency.

SECRETARY OF AGRICULTURE: Exactly.

SECRETARY OF STATE: It makes sense. It's logical.

SECRETARY OF PUBLIC EDUCATION: I agree.

SECRETARY OF COMMUNICATIONS: Perfect.

SECRETARY OF ECONOMICS: Then there's no problem.

SECRETARY OF WAR: Of course not.

SECRETARY OF FINANCE: There's no problem at all. I repeat it.

All together

PRESIDENT OF THE OFFICIAL PARTY (*standing up*): Will you permit me, gentlemen? (*General silence.*) I thank you very much for what you've just said, but I've had much political experience—as you well know—and the fruit of it all is my ambition to serve my country in the presidency as its most humble incumbent. But there're two immediate obstacles to this. The first is my military status. It was a cultured civilian that the people of Indoland overwhelmingly elected.

SEVERAL SECRETARIES: That's no obstacle.—This is an emergency.—You must assume this responsibility.— Of course.—It's all clear.

PRESIDENT OF THE OFFICIAL PARTY: Gentlemen, again, many thanks. But the second obstacle is that a reform of the national Constitution would be required which would be possible if Congress hadn't been in recess since . . .

SECRETARY OF PUBLIC EDUCATION: An emergency session would resolve the whole matter in three days.

PRESIDENT OF THE OFFICIAL PARTY: In three days without government, Mr. Secretary, a revolution of absolutely unpredictable consequences could break out. Don't forget, gentlemen, that our immediate predecessors are far from being in agreement with us and have criticized us openly. And furthermore, who would assure us that General Jaimes, who boasted so of having really won the recent election, wouldn't try to seize power by a *coup d'état* in forty-eight hours, or less? And don't forget the reactionaries and the Communists who're capable of any alliance that would make it possible for them to take advantage of the raging torrent of a revolution, should one break out. No, we must settle the whole matter this morning. We three (*indicating himself, the* CHIEF JUSTICE *and the* SPEAKER OF CONGRESS) have already thought about all these problems very much indeed, believe me, gentlemen. The hundreds of speeches I've made about the stability of our national institutions have never deluded me. It was just *now* that these institutions were due to come to life.

SECRETARY OF ECONOMICS: I think that in this case subtleties of a political nature mustn't be entered into, nor——.

PRESIDENT OF THE OFFICIAL PARTY: Allow me, Mr. Secretary. There's also a third obstacle which is the simple fact that I won't be a mere shooting star. In all frankness, I inform you colleagues now that I plan to launch my own candidacy for the presidency and that I can count on a national organization that's able to put me there. So that's that. (*He sits down.*)

General disconcertion.

SECRETARY OF PUBLIC EDUCATION: Then what?

SECRETARY OF AGRICULTURE: What solution is there?

SECRETARY OF FINANCE: A junta to govern?

SECRETARY OF ECONOMICS: I don't see any solution.

SECRETARY OF STATE: Nor do I.

SECRETARY OF WAR: Perhaps, yes——.

SECRETARY OF STATE: No, not that.

SECRETARY OF WAR: I haven't finished yet.

SECRETARY OF STATE: No, but that just won't do.

All at the same time

SPEAKER OF CONGRESS: I must call you to order, gentlemen.

SECRETARY OF STATE: Pardon me, but in an earlier period the secretary of state was the one indicated to——.

SECRETARY OF PUBLIC EDUCATION: That was under a different Constitution, my dear friend, the one of the dictatorship.

SECRETARY OF WAR: Pardon, but the secretary of war——.

SECRETARY OF AGRICULTURE: That Constitution is even older, General.

SECRETARY OF FINANCE: I think it's high time to break with tradition and show that a secretary of finance can reach the presidency of the Republic even though it be provisional.

SECRETARY OF ECONOMICS: At the stage of development that our country and the world have now reached, it's rather the secretary of economics who could best take over the steering wheel——.

SECRETARY OF PUBLIC EDUCATION: And why not the secretary of public education, my friends? After all, it's we who've made the people literate and they'd show their gratitude——.

CHIEF JUSTICE: Gentlemen! Gentlemen! I was about to say—you'll pardon me this in consideration of my age—children! Children! To begin with, although I don't for one moment question the merits or the capacity of any one of you to govern—nor even less your good intentions— in the case of deciding on any one of you, we'd only find ourselves facing the same bull whose horns haven't been blunted. This is just another way of saying that by convening an emergency session of Congress we'd only meet with the same hazards and risk the same dangers now confronting us. As the president of the official party has already said, the matter of who is to be the new president must be settled definitely *today*. Now, let's be sensible and remember that the legitimately elected president was assassinated when he'd hardly begun his duties. The French have a saying that "He who has drunk once will go on drinking." This is equivalent to our own saying that "He who makes one hamper makes a hundred." Who could prove to us that the emergency in which we now find ourselves may not be repeated in a short while from now? From the history of Indoland it is clear that the cult of violent death is a tradition with us. Now who of you truly believes that he can serve his country by dying such a death?

Coughs, humms, the twisting of mouths, biting of lips, etc. amongst the SECRETARIES.

THE SECRETARIES: Humm, that's so.—Yes, yes, to be sure.—It's the truth. Surely, but . . . —There's not just one "but," but many "buts."—And what would be accomplished, after all, by dying in such a way?—What's important is to work for our country.—And to do that, you have to be alive.

SECRETARY OF STATE: Absolutely right. I think we've all understood the situation. And now, Mr. Chief Justice, I, as secretary of state—that's to say, as the target of the international press that this very morning will take not only my office by storm but my home, too—consider it pertinent to ask you if you authorities have reached some agreement? Have found a solution? In short, I'm asking if you've found the way out.

CHIEF JUSTICE: We have reached an agreement.

SPEAKER OF CONGRESS: We have the solution.

PRESIDENT OF THE OFFICIAL PARTY: Yes, we've found the way out.

SECRETARY OF PUBLIC EDUCATION: May one know——?

SECRETARY OF FINANCE: We must know.

SECRETARY OF AGRICULTURE: This is as important as the country's agriculture itself.

SECRETARY OF ECONOMICS: As vital as its economy.

SECRETARY OF COMMUNICATIONS (*ironically, after his manner*): May I, as secretary of communications, request that this agreement, this solution, this way out be communicated to us?

SECRETARY OF WAR: I think it's time that you speak to us clearly. The peace of the nation is at stake.

An expectant pause.

CHIEF JUSTICE (*to the* PRESIDENT OF THE OFFICIAL PARTY *and the* SPEAKER OF CONGRESS): Gentlemen, who's to bell this cat?

PRESIDENT OF THE OFFICIAL PARTY: I think that the Speaker of Congress, as the younger, should speak first. That's how it's done in councils of war.

SPEAKER OF CONGRESS: But I'm of the opinion, General, that you, as president of the official party which put our late president in office, should——.

PRESIDENT OF THE OFFICIAL PARTY: In that case, without the slightest hesitation, I delegate all my authority to the oldest and most respected among us.

SPEAKER OF CONGRESS: I do the same.

CHIEF JUSTICE: Then I'm damned. I saw this coming, though. Very well, gentlemen. I beg you to listen to me without explosions or exclamations which would only make my blood pressure rise to the bursting point. It's customary and bureaucratic routine, as well as absolutely in keeping with the Constitution, that when the head of a ministry fails to perform his duties because of absence, sickness, or death, the next in authority be automatically named as minister: that is, the undersecretary. In this most unfortunate case, however, material circumstances prevent us from following the usual procedure. But the same custom would prevail in the sense that if the undersecretary should also be absent, or otherwise engaged, sick, or deceased, his immediate subordinate would take charge of the ministry. That person is, of course, the executive officer. That's all. The Speaker of Congress and the president of the Official party share my point of view. Now it's for you gentlemen to speak.

SECRETARY OF FINANCE: An executive officer as president of the Republic?

SECRETARY OF COMMUNICATIONS: A subordinate of ours? It'd be the first time in our country's history.

SECRETARY OF ECONOMICS: Absurd. Absolutely senseless.

SECRETARY OF AGRICULTURE: What special ability or distinctions does he have?

SECRETARY OF PUBLIC EDUCATION: It'd look like making sport of the country.

SECRETARY OF STATE: The press would come down on us with a bang.

SECRETARY OF WAR: No. No. No. What reason could there be for——?

CHIEF JUSTICE: There're three reasons. The first is that the press, as the secretary of state has just said, would come down on *us*. That is to say, it's *we* who'll still be carrying on in this government.

SPEAKER OF CONGRESS: The second reason is that it would permit us to solve the problem easily in five minutes. Then, after three months, while the provisional president will have had our advice and help to count on, a new election will be held.

CHIEF JUSTICE: The third reason, gentlemen, and, in my opinion the most important one, is that all the members of this Cabinet would still be *alive* and could, therefore, be candidates.

SECRETARY OF STATE: Why not hold a new election at once? Why wait for three months?

CHIEF JUSTICE: Because justice must be done in the assassination of President Matías. Don't you gentlemen think that it'd be better to leave this task to a man who has no political commitments and who'll be leaving office in a short while?

SECRETARY OF FINANCE: Suppose that, as we said earlier, this same emergency should be repeated and he, too—— (*He makes an expressive gesture suggesting assassination.*)

CHIEF JUSTICE: Would *you* lose anything?

SPEAKER OF CONGRESS: An unknown president

is likely to be less of an immediate target. He arouses the people's curiosity——.

SECRETARY OF AGRICULTURE: Let's not forget, gentlemen, that in our country the mere investiture of any man as president has magic powers very superior to those attributed to certain kinds of armor in the books of chivalry. Who can tell us that, once in as president, this executive officer wouldn't be capable of putting one over on us and send us all——?

PRESIDENT OF THE OFFICIAL PARTY: An indispensable condition is that he must agree that there are to be no changes in the Cabinet. Another indispensable contion is that we all remain united.

SECRETARY OF PUBLIC EDUCATION: The vacant posts in the Ministry of the Interior will have to be filled, and——.

SPEAKER OF CONGRESS: Wouldn't it be up to us to recommend the most suitable persons? I think that in view of my position in Congress and because of my family connection with the unfortunate Pozos, the undersecretaryship should go to me.

SECRETARY OF FINANCE: Earlier, there are many who thought that our ambassador in London would be given that post.

SECRETARY OF ECONOMICS: Or rather——.

CHIEF JUSTICE: This is a mere detail, gentlemen. What is essential is your support of the decision taken by us authorities.

SECRETARY OF STATE: But I think that a simple question is in order before we decide about this matter. Just who is this executive officer of the Ministry of the Interior?

CHIEF JUSTICE: The first sensible question so far. (*He turns to the* SPEAKER OF CONGRESS *and to the* PRESIDENT OF THE OFFICIAL PARTY.) Who is he, gentlemen?

PRESIDENT OF THE OFFICIAL PARTY: Well . . . Hmmm. He was appointed personally by the defunct president. I don't believe that I recall his name. By the way, what is it, Mr. Speaker?

SPEAKER OF CONGRESS: Come now! Hmmm . . . (*He draws a notebook from his coat pocket and glances through it.*) Ah, ah, yes! Here it is, José Gómez Urbina.

SECRETARY OF AGRICULTURE: Just plain that? No title?

SECRETARY OF PUBLIC EDUCATION: Isn't he an attorney?

SECRETARY OF WAR: He's not a general?

SECRETARY OF FINANCE: Not a doctor either?

SECRETARY OF ECONOMICS: No degree of any kind . . . no Ph.D. or Sc.D. even for *ignoramus causa?*

SECRETARY OF STATE: No, it can't be. This wont' go over well abroad. It won't impress anybody.

SECRETARY OF ECONOMICS: A . . . a chemically pure, unknown fellow!

SPEAKER OF CONGRESS: "Antiseptic" is the word.

SECRETARY OF PUBLIC EDUCATION: But, but . . . a nobody . . . a Mr. Nobody——.

PRESIDENT OF THE OFFICIAL PARTY: Gentlemen, gentlemen. This historic conference is being tape recorded. Let's not say anything we may regret later on.

SECRETARY OF AGRICULTURE: But the office of chief executive of the nation entrusted to a mere bureaucrat . . . No, it just can't be!

SECRETARY OF WAR: To a Gómez . . . what? to a plain gómezurbina. (*He pronounces the two names as without capitals while running them together.*)

SECRETARY OF FINANCE: To a man without any professional title? This is strong stuff!

CHIEF JUSTICE: But, gentlemen, just consider the tremendous unusualness of it all: the presidency, the supreme mandate, the magical investiture, all turned over to a plain *citizen.* I can foresee the people's enthusiasm, the hopes which will blossom in every heart. After this historic moment, it will no longer be necessary to be a general or an attorney to be president of the Republic. As in other countries, it'll be possible to go to the presidency straight from chopping wood or from a haberdasher's shop that's in bankruptcy. This is nothing less than the beginning of democracy: of Plato's Republic, if you please, here in our very midst.

SPEAKER OF CONGRESS: It's the perfect solution!

PRESIDENT OF THE OFFICIAL PARTY: Reached this very moment!

SPEAKER OF CONGRESS: The emergency warded off.

PRESIDENT OF THE OFFICIAL PARTY: And without violating the Constitution.

CHIEF JUSTICE: The lives, the work, and influence of every one of you made safe. The best interest of the country itself commands, gentlemen.

SECRETARY OF STATE: But let's not be hasty. All this deserves serious reflection. Yes, it must be given the most serious reflection.

SECRETARY OF PUBLIC EDUCATION: I'm afraid that if we do think it over really seriously, we won't ever accept it.

SECRETARY OF AGRICULTURE: It's like marriage: the full plunge in or nothing.

SECRETARY OF FINANCE: We mustn't joke about our country's destiny, gentlemen. But . . . just what shall we do?

SECRETARY OF COMMUNICATIONS: This situation reminds me of a forest fire: he who stops to think about them when caught in one, gets burnt to ashes.

SECRETARY OF ECONOMICS: But just what do we know about this man?

CHIEF JUSTICE: That we can teach him, if not all we know, at least that we are indispensable to his government. And we'll see to it that he'll have justice done to the assassins of Matías and that he'll follow our advice. He'll cap the storm . . . with our assistance.

PRESIDENT OF THE OFFICIAL PARTY: Now would you gentlemen doubt the wisdom of one of the few survivors of our Revolution, of one who helped draft our Constitution itself, and one of the most brilliant minds Indoland has produced in a hundred years? Let's be reasonable, gentlemen.

SPEAKER OF CONGRESS: And practical. Nothing's been accomplished by doubt in spite of all the philosophers who've ever lived, so let's be affirmative, positive.

CHIEF JUSTICE: Above all, Messrs. Secretaries, let's be clear. The techniques of our national politics have evolved tremendously. We don't any longer kill those whom we can't convince. We don't any longer justify violent action as my schoolmate who was also my comrade-in-arms and companion in the Constitutional Convention did by saying that "The Revolution is the Revolution." We now let the doubters, the sceptics, the critics live in their Diogenes' tubs. We're modern. We've simply cut that kind of person out of the budget, out of preferences, and out of public works contracts. We've even improved on the ancient civil death by transforming it into economic death. We hate the use of force which isn't reconcilable with the elements of our ancient culture or with our present-day political civilization. We've learned how to choose. If we can't have the future president with the present Cabinet, we'll limit ourselves to having him without it. You can change a Cabinet like a shirt, but not so a president. (All *appear preoccupied and give the impression of biting their nails.*) What do you say; shall we qualify the executive officer of the Ministry of the Interior as the secretary, then work together with him as our new president, or shall we go back to our homes—if we manage to keep them—and just wait there for something to happen?

SECRETARY OF STATE: You're a devil.

CHIEF JUSTICE: I'm more than that, my dear friend, and, incidentally, I'm what makes the Devil himself angry. I'm a very experienced old man.

SECRETARY OF WAR (*as though coming out of deep thought*): What I'd like is to see this Gomitos . . . this Señor Gómez . . . so I can size him up.

SPEAKER OF CONGRESS: You've already seen him.

SECRETARY OF WAR: I have?

PRESIDENT OF THE OFFICIAL PARTY: In this very room.

CHIEF JUSTICE: Only a half hour ago.

All look at one another, understanding.

SECRETARY OF WAR (*breaking the silence*): That guy none of us knows! It can't be!

CHIEF JUSTICE: What can't be, General, is, rightly enough, just what a miracle is. Things to be seen . . . But if you gentlemen haven't any more objections——.

PRESIDENT OF THE OFFICIAL PARTY: I request officially that we vote on the chief justice's proposal. Those who agree will please raise their right hands.

SPEAKER OF CONGRESS: And those who don't agree have already been informed of the opinion of us authorities.

PRESIDENT OF THE OFFICIAL PARTY: Will you vote now, gentlemen?

Some slowly, grumbling to themselves; others as swimmers who plunge headlong into the water, the six SECRETARIES *raise their right hands*

CHIEF JUSTICE: Well, this dish of rice is now cooked. (*He breathes contentedly.*)

PRESIDENT OF THE OFFICIAL PARTY: Captain Peláez?

The CAPTAIN *steps forward and stands at attention.*

THE CAPTAIN: General?

PRESIDENT OF THE OFFICIAL PARTY: Show Señor Gómez Urbina in.

The PRESIDENT OF THE OFFICAL PARTY *stands and all the others do likewise while the* CAPTAIN *opens the door downstage right, exits, and says:*

THE CAPTAIN: This way, Señor Gómez Urbina, if you'll be so kind.

Darkness in which after a moment is heard:

THE VOICE OF THE SPEAKER OF CONGRESS: Citizen José Gómez Urbina, do you solemnly swear to up-hold the Constitution of the United States of Indoland and to have it upheld? And do you solemnly swear to de-fend the integrity of the national territory and to encourage by every means possible the peace and well-being and the high standard of living of the people?

THE VOICE OF GÓMEZ URBINA (*after a brief pause, trembling*): I . . . I so swear.

THE VOICE OF THE SPEAKER OF CONGRESS: If you do as you have sworn to, may the nation reward you. And if you do not, may it call you to account.

Lights. The uproar of voices, cheers, and the sound of a march blend as the curtain falls.

CURTAIN

Act 2

The same conference room as in Act 1. Three months later. The action takes place in the morning, the afternoon, and the evening.

Perhaps the sun—the sun at spring's end—that pours into the room from the enormous balconies is responsible for the sense of of lightness and the impression of quiet happiness that seem to float in the air. The only dust perceptible in the ancient viceregal palace is, in fact, the dust in the sunbeams. In other words, it can be said that the characters are living in a new era.

As the curtain rises, the CAPTAIN *is standing guard before the door upstage right. A new character, the* HOME SECRETARY, *is walking back and forth from one balcony to another. After a moment he looks at his watch, then raises his eyes to heaven.*

HOME SECRETARY: Captain, did you explain to the president that my matter is of vital importance?

THE CAPTAIN: The president understands everything after the first few words, Mr. Secretary. He's trying now to rearrange his schedule so he can give you a few moments. He has another very busy day ahead of him, but that puts him in an excellent humor.

HOME SECRETARY: Always an observer, Captain. The president enjoys working, but I'm afraid that I don't. And what's more, I've my own waiting room full of nervous governors who're getting restless, and I've a meeting scheduled with them that ought to be taking place now.

THE CAPTAIN: I'm certain that in a moment——.

The door upstage left opens and PRESIDENT GÓMEZ
URBINA *appears. The* CAPTAIN *draws back so as to let
him pass. It could not be said of the* MR. NOBODY *of
Act 1 that he has grown taller—this could not happen
at his age, of course—but the way he carries his head
gives the impression of increased height. He is dressed
modestly as in Act 1, but somehow his very clothes
seem to be surrounded by an aura of light. He proceeds without nervousness now in a slow, pleasant,
and quiet manner, as well as with a simplicity so perfect as to give the impression of being a work of well-
disciplined art. His personality is no longer blurred nor
average: from it emanate strength, assurance, and confidence.
The* CAPTAIN *resumes guard at the door downstage
right.*

GÓMEZ URBINA: Good morning, Mr. Secretary,
and a beautiful morning it is. So you're no longer happy
with our regular weekly conference, but must have more?
I didn't expect such zeal of you. (*Without speaking, the*
HOME SECRETARY *hands him a sheet of paper.*) What's this?

HOME SECRETARY: My resignation, Mr. President.

GÓMEZ URBINA: So? (*After a pause.*) That will be
all, Captain.

THE CAPTAIN: Yes, sir. And, pardon me, but the
chief justice, the president of the official party and the
Speaker of Congress are beginning to look impatient.

GÓMEZ URBINA: Is that so? Well, tell them, if
need be, that I have at their disposal all the tons of patience they may need. (*He smiles.*)

The CAPTAIN *draws himself up to attention and exits.*

GÓMEZ URBINA (*striking the fingers of his left hand
with the sheet of paper he holds in his right hand*): I'm
the only one who can afford to make jokes here, Mr. Secretary.

HOME SECRETARY: You know me well enough to know that I'm incapable of——.

GÓMEZ URBINA: When a serious man starts joking, there's no end to it. (*With a change in manner.*) Mr. Secretary Del Roble, you are, as you already know, the only man I was able to introduce into this prefabricated Cabinet of mine. I've been hoping that as my secretary of the interior, you'd stay with me to the end. What's the meaning of this? (*He indicates the sheet of paper.*)

HOME SECRETARY: Simply that I find I'm not going to be able to see all the way through the special mission you entrusted me with . . . the mission for which you really called me to your Cabinet. My conscience won't let me go on deluding you nor myself.

GÓMEZ URBINA: The mission which I especially entrusted to you consists of discovering the intellectual authors of the assassination of my predecessor, President Matías. I can't believe that an experienced and mature justice like you who wouldn't let me alone until he'd proved my complete innocence in the alleged crime of which I was accused several years ago, would forgo making known the guilty parties in the assassination. It's easier to hunt down the guilty than to clear the innocent. I think you're not being altogether frank with me, and I'm sorry about this.

HOME SECRETARY: Be that as it may, by decision is irrevocable and I beg you to accept——.

GÓMEZ URBINA: When you were the judge and I was the accused, you made me talk in spite of myself and saved me by main force. Have I ceased to be a man to you now because I've become president? And remember, above all, that I've pledged myself to all Indoland that justice will be done and I can't go back on that pledge. Now if, after having reminded you of what I have, you still want to quit, then quit. I'll find some other way of doing what I must.

HOME SECRETARY: Still the same stubborn fellow
. . . er . . . Mr. President. On that other occasion you've
just referred to I was keen on proving your innocence because I concluded that you were being stupidly loyal to
guilty friends. But this is an entirely different matter, and
I can't and won't lend myself to——.

GÓMEZ URBINA: This is better. Do you want me
to tell you now what has happened? (*The* HOME SECRETARY
waits in silence.) You've already solved the case. (*A
pause.*) Am I wrong?

HOME SECRETARY: Are you a president or a witch
doctor?

GÓMEZ URBINA: A president, of course, though
only provisionally, which means that I see more clearly and
am not so bad as some of my predecessors because I'll last
in office less time than they did. Come on now, my friend,
speak up.

HOME SECRETARY: It makes me boil with indignation that you don't realize that everything concerning you
in this whole matter is either a felony . . . or a mockery.
It's all very easy to make a president of some unknown
party—pardon me, I must speak frankly—that is, of an unknown without political commitments, then use him as a
cat's paw to pull the chestnuts out of the fire. You're right
about the case of the assassination. It is solved. I know the
names of the men implicated and have proof of their guilt.
But even you won't be able to see that justice is done in
this case.

GÓMEZ URBINA: Why not? Or have you gone over
to the side of those who hold that justice isn't for man to
do? (*Without speaking, the* SECRETARY *hands him another
paper which he reads slowly.*) Is this evidence final and
absolute? (*The* SECRETARY *nods in agreement.*) It will
stand up in court without the least possibility of a doubt?
(*Again the* SECRETARY *nods in agreement.*) Then there's
nothing to prevent me from keeping my word and punish-
ing the guilty.

HOME SECRETARY: But do those names of men in high positions, some of them with immense personal fortunes rooted like cancerous growths in the life of our country, mean nothing to you?

GÓMEZ URBINA (*quietly*): I'm simply aware of the fact that I'm the president of the Republic and that I'm pledged to see justice done.

HOME SECRETARY: Ah, you're not only stubborn, but so naïve that you seem to be rather the inhabitant of another planet. Haven't you learned yet what men are like? Are you still ignorant of what our politics really are? And, finally, don't you realize that those men would grind you to pieces in an hour? I'm sorry to be the one to have to tell you this, but what I'm going to say now is the absolute truth. You were made president simply to call a new election and to be the scapegoat in the matter of justice being done to Matías's assassins. But that isn't all I have to tell you. I'll put it into these few words: you simply haven't the authority nor the strength to go through with what you're so determined to in having justice really done in this case. And now again I'll ask you to pardon my bluntness.

GÓMEZ URBINA (*calmly*): I don't think anyone else in this whole country would dare say such things to me. Thank you very much, my friend.

HOME SECRETARY: All that's really expected of you is mere routine: that you punish the actual assassins, then make an abstract and resounding speech against the reactionary forces. You can put all that over easily enough.

GÓMEZ URBINA: That would be to go along with injustice . . . the exact opposite of what I intend doing. Would you stay with me if such were the case?

HOME SECRETARY: Or else, to break your head against——.

GÓMEZ URBINA: Before my head is broken, I'll do some thinking about that, because if I don't, I won't be able to use it afterward. (*Slowly he tears up the resignation and puts the other sheet of paper in his pocket.*) Stay with

me at least until we've done what we've set out to do. I
ask this of you as a friend and as man to man.

Without a word, the SECRETARY *shakes* GÓMEZ UR-
BINA's *hand. The* CAPTAIN *enters.*

GÓMEZ URBINA: The man I shielded with my
silence in that other case was an honorable man, so this
isn't only a question of justice, but of paying off a debt to
him whom later we were to call President Matías.

THE CAPTAIN: Excuse me, sir, but those gentlemen——.

GÓMEZ URBINA (*light-heartedly*): Would rather
wait for the price of patience to go down, isn't that so?
Come to my private office. Mr. Secretary. Your information has come at precisely the right moment for action.
(*They go to the door upstage left.* GÓMEZ URBINA *turns
around.*) Show those gentlemen in here and ask them to
wait, Captain.

GÓMEZ URBINA *and the* SECRETARY *exit. The* CAPTAIN
then opens the door downstage right for the CHIEF JUS-
TICE, *the* PRESIDENT OF THE OFFICIAL PARTY, *and the*
SPEAKER OF CONGRESS *who enter in that order.*

PRESIDENT OF THE OFFICIAL PARTY (*turning to
the* CAPTAIN): Are you positive, Captain, that you made it
quite clear to the president we've been waiting here for . . .
(*looking at his watch*) half an hour? And does he know
that this is the first time I've ever been kept in a waiting
room?

THE CAPTAIN: If you'll permit me to say this, General, in President Gómez Urbina's administration there're
no waiting rooms. He himself says so.

PRESIDENT OF THE OFFICIAL PARTY: Well, I
I didn't know he's a humorist, too!

THE CAPTAIN: Oh, he's extraordinary. During his
work day, which is often longer than sixteen hours, he
always has time for a joke. There're those who think that

he's even wittier than Churchill. Two of our president's
sayings already have become famous. One is, "Where I am,
there is the presidency" and the other is, "I feather my nest
in any old tree." The second saying he admits having taken
from the archbishop on purely constitutional grounds: "It's
good enough to be state property."

CHIEF JUSTICE (*laughing*): I suspected as much.
But I must admit that I'm uneasy—oh, not because of
politics—but because I'm a purist.

PRESIDENT OF THE OFFICIAL PARTY: A purist?
What does that mean?

CHIEF JUSTICE: Take it easy, General. It's nothing to do with eating. It's just that I've heard my great-
grandchildren, who attend preparatory school instead of
learning to play billiards—as my generation did—apply to
the president a word of indubitable colloquial origin. This
is a very serious matter because there's a relation between
words and facts which defines——.

SPEAKER OF CONGRESS: Well, what word are you
talking about?

CHIEF JUSTICE: When speaking of Señor Gómez
Urbina, the people say "He's a great *vaciado*": that is,
"He's a great one to spill his guts."

PRESIDENT OF THE OFFICIAL PARTY: But just
what does that mean?

SPEAKER OF CONGRESS (*to the* CHIEF JUSTICE): I
was afraid it might be something else. (*To the* PRESIDENT
OF THE OFFICIAL PARTY.) For our brand of beatniks it
means that a person is all right, in other words, OK.

CHIEF JUSTICE: But there's shades of meaning to
it, General. A big *vaciado* is a kind of exceptional type, a
paragon.

PRESIDENT OF THE OFFICIAL PARTY: I don't
see why this is so important.

CHIEF JUSTICE: As a good political orator, you
believe only in the meaning of words when you use them
in a speech. To me, what I was just saying means that the

people are with the president, which in turn means that we're faced with a fact without precedent. It's clear now that Don José is an Indolander through and through——.

SPEAKER OF CONGRESS: Well, we must admit that his speech at the removal of President Matías's predecessor's statute at the university was unusual for its courage and clarity. For example, that phrase of his about the judgment of posterity; that only a world without descendants and given over entirely to the present, would forget . . . Really scourging! As an orator I——.

A *bell rings. The talking stops. The* CAPTAIN *exits downstage left and returns a moment later.*

THE CAPTAIN: Gentlemen, the president will finish an urgent matter in just a few moments and will come on to you at once. (*He exits downstage right.*)

CHIEF JUSTICE: Good. As they say in the customs, "Have you anything to declare?"

PRESIDENT OF THE OFFICIAL PARTY: I'm dumbfounded. Anyone would say that that little captain is already a major general.

SPEAKER OF CONGRESS (*looking at his watch*): As for me, I have the feeling that I'm dreaming. What about you gentlemen?

CHIEF JUSTICE: At my age one no longer dreams, one remembers. I'm an old man——.

PRESIDENT OF THE OFFICIAL PARTY: So much so that you told us you were dying and got us into this mess, yet there you are——.

CHIEF JUSTICE: For likings, colors, and death there're no hard and fast rules, General, therefore, you'll pardon me if I go on living. But let's be frank now. During the past three months I've seen the president ten or twelve times . . . but only on social occasions. How long is it since any of you've seen him Straight to the point now and no rhetoric.

PRESIDENT OF THE OFFICIAL PARTY: I've seen

him only once. That was a month and a half ago and he
said just one thing to me.

SPEAKER OF CONGRESS: The same with me, only
it was a month and a week ago.

PRESIDENT OF THE OFFICIAL PARTY: No, a
month and three weeks ago.

CHIEF JUSTICE: And what, in short, did he say to
you two?

PRESIDENT OF THE OFFICIAL PARTY *and*
SPEAKER OF CONGRESS (*both speaking at the same
time*): "The country will settle down, so we'll wait a while
longer before exposing it to the dangerous excitement of
electioneering by a crowd of candidates. There're more
urgent problems in the national life than . . ." (*Both stop
and look at each other in surprise.*) Ah, but he promised
that soon——. (*Again they interrupt themselves and look at
each other.*)

CHIEF JUSTICE: It's beyond doubt that in Indoland we collect presidential words like so many precious
stones. But the promises of presidents tend to fall into
wells, gentlemen, like so many stones. The situation is
critical.

PRESIDENT OF THE OFFICIAL PARTY: Critical?
It can't stand any more——.

SPEAKER OF CONGRESS: We agree: it can't stand
. . . The call for an election can't be postponed any longer.

PRESIDENT OF THE OFFICIAL PARTY: I'm disturbed about the interview that's to take place today and
that's been so pointedly announced by the press.

CHIEF JUSTICE: What I'm concerned about, gentlemen, is that justice be done to the assassins of President
Matías. It's quite clear to me that this case must be settled
finally before another election is called. As to the interview,
don't be upset, General. We both know the reason for it.

PRESIDENT OF THE OFFICIAL PARTY: Are you
insinuating——?

CHIEF JUSTICE: At my age one can't waste time in insinuations.

PRESIDENT OF THE OFFICIAL PARTY: Mr. Chief Justice, as a soldier I'm frank and play with my cards on the table. The fact that Demoland has just elected a general as its president points the way for us to follow, and I——.

CHIEF JUSTICE: And you are a general. Agreed.

PRESIDENT OF THE OFFICIAL PARTY: Furthermore, I made it quite clear on that historic night when we put our foot in . . . when we gave in so foolishly to your proposal that we invest Gómez Urbina as provisional president——.

SPEAKER OF CONGRESS: Please, gentlemen, no personalities. We'll ask the president for an explanation of this private interview that he has granted to the ambassador of the Federated States of Demoland——.

PRESIDENT OF THE OFFICIAL PARTY: Without consulting us!

CHIEF JUSTICE: Are we perhaps oracles?

SPEAKER OF CONGRESS: Let's not lose any more time in talking about the interview. Now for the other point we're to take up with him: the calling of an election. As we all know, the country is expecting a demonstration of democracy by us.

CHIEF JUSTICE: Pardon me a moment. Your ideas are good, but your psychological penetration is feeble. What the country wants is to have no more elections.

PRESIDENT OF THE OFFICIAL PARTY: This is no time for jokes. It's unbelievable that an individual who came into office by sheer accident could so upset the natural life of the country.

CHIEF JUSTICE: Do you call politics natural? And as for joking, I'll have you to understand that I've been quite serious all along. I maintain that it's of prime importance to urge on the trial of the assassins. This is the key to all the rest.

SPEAKER OF CONGRESS: Well, on second thought, it's evident that you're right.

PRESIDENT OF THE OFFICIAL PARTY: Granted. The next government shouldn't be faced with this problem.

SPEAKER OF CONGRESS: Once public opinion has been satisfied about it, the people can devote all their attention to the election.

CHIEF JUSTICE: I'm happy to see that at last we're in agreement.

SPEAKER OF CONGRESS: Ah, but we must be firm with him.

PRESIDENT OF THE OFFICIAL PARTY: Inflexible, my friend.

A bell rings twice. The CAPTAIN *enters downstage right, crosses the stage and opens the door upstage left where* GÓMEZ URBINA *appears.*

GÓMEZ URBINA: Good morning, gentlemen and colleagues.

Greetings and handshakes all around.

CHIEF JUSTICE: On grounds of purely academic curiosity, Don José, would you explain your use of the word "colleagues"?

GÓMEZ URBINA: With pleasure. You're chief justice, that is president of the Supreme Court; the general here is president of the official party; the Speaker is president of Congress; and I'm president of the country . . . for the time being. We're all presidents in Indoland.

PRESIDENT OF THE OFFICIAL PARTY (*with a forced laugh*): I've always held that you have a great sense of humor.

SPEAKER OF CONGRESS: Far superior to that of Churchill.

GÓMEZ URBINA: But let's not exaggerate, my friends . . . he has never been a provisional president of Indoland and so he missed some curious experiences. I liked better what you said about me, Mr. Chief Justice. With the sanction of a scholar, it's more pleasing to me to be "a great one to spill his guts."

CHIEF JUSTICE (*without losing composure*): Permit me to congratulate you on having such a sharp ear, Mr. President.

GÓMEZ URBINA (*unperturbed*): Thank you very much. And now, gentlemen, as I have but little time, let's get on to the business that brings you here.

PRESIDENT OF THE OFFICIAL
PARTY: It's simply that, Mr. President, the press publishes——.

SPEAKER OF CONGRESS: There is, as we well know, much unrest in the country about the coming election and——.

Both speaking at the same time

GÓMEZ URBINA: One at a time, if you'll be so kind. I agree with the chief justice that, first of all, my predecessor's assassins must be punished. As usual, our colleague here goes straight to the bottom of matters.

CHIEF JUSTICE: Are you possibly thinking, Mr. President, that I interfere too much——?

GÓMEZ URBINA: Worse for the country and worse for you if you don't do so. In my home town we have a picturesque name for men such as you. It's *entresiliche*, the "meddlesome" person who butts into everything. He's a kind of commonsense patriarch.

CHIEF JUSTICE: I'll make a note of that for the dictionary of the people's sayings that I'm compiling.

GÓMEZ URBINA: Now to get on with our business, gentlemen. The problem as planted for us in the case of the assassination is the nature of justice itself with its two eternal aspects—shall we call them? There's practical, swift justice with all its immediate consequences. There's also immanent justice with its aspect of transcendency. But to leave off philosophizing, I'm now in a position to inform you gentlemen that the actual assassins of President Matías are in the hands of the law.

PRESIDENT OF THE OFFICIAL PARTY: Then they must be shot at once!

SPEAKER OF CONGRESS: Practical, swift justice, as you say.

GÓMEZ URBINA: What is the opinion of the Court?

CHIEF JUSTICE: The Court is waiting to hear what else you have to say, sir.

GÓMEZ URBINA: If only the others knew how to wait, too . . . Very well, then, two high-ranking officers of the Indolandish army have confessed their direct responsibility for the assassination.

PRESIDENT OF THE OFFICIAL PARTY: So! But this, of course, changes matters!

GÓMEZ URBINA: Really, General Meléndez? But, whether mistaken or not, these unfortunate men are loyal to their convictions and absolutely refuse to shed any light on the identity of what we'll call the intellectual authors, who were responsible for their crime. We have enough leads, however, to assume who the guilty one or ones are. But now it's for the chief justice to inform you gentlemen if mere assumptions are sufficient to go on in such a case. And what would you say if it should turn out that several members of the present Congress were implicated?

SPEAKER OF CONGRESS: I must protest in the name of——.

GÓMEZ URBINA (*pleasantly*): We're only assuming, nothing more, Mr. Speaker. We'll not talk now about the Communist teachers who were killed when their car plunged into the ravine after the assassination. The assumptions, or, more correctly, the convictions held by the secret tribunal which I authorized to investigate the assassination have opened up to us an almost unlimited perspective. If it should turn out that a political rival of Matías's with a grudge——.

PRESIDENT OF THE OFFICIAL PARTY: That forage appropriations thief must be hanged! I know who he is.

GÓMEZ URBINA: You're thinking of one possibility, General. But this case reminds me of what happens when a person begins going through an old family trunk. He's likely to end up by finding something he wouldn't have wanted to. Right, isn't it? Well, then, what would you do if we were to continue bringing out more dirty linen and all at once some friends of the president who preceded Matías were to come to light?

SPEAKER OF CONGRESS: We shouldn't let that stop us.

GÓMEZ URBINA: Wait a moment, my dear colleague. I haven't finished yet. Or what if suddenly there should come out of this sort of Indoland Pandora's box a former president of the country?

CHIEF JUSTICE: Hell! (*without emphasis. The word just slipped out.*) Hmmm, pardon me, Mr. President.

GÓMEZ URBINA: But you said it, Mr. Chief Justice! And if it should turn out that such men were implicated in plotting against the president, that would be worse, or wouldn't it? As for the army officers in question, I'm afraid that if we give any publicity to their arrest, it won't be possible to keep the army under control.

PRESIDENT OF THE OFFICIAL PARTY: Of course not. The loyalty of the armed forces is unimpeachable.

GÓMEZ URBINA: Furthermore, if, as I indicated earlier, some members of Congress should be implicated, as now seems probable, the door would be opened to tremendous political agitation.

SPEAKER OF CONGRESS: Naturally. The official family of the Revolution would violently resent any imputation of disloyalty.

GÓMEZ URBINA: And if more, we should also stumble upon a governor, the following would surely happen. The army, Congress, and the local governments would all demand the punishment of the really guilty ones so as to clear themselves of any possible stain. But as it isn't possible to try anyone on mere suppositions, there isn't a direct way of getting at those men . . . at least not for the present.

PRESIDENT OF THE OFFICIAL PARTY: What do you propose then?

GÓMEZ URBINA: The chief justice has the answer on the tip of his tongue. I beg him to give it.

CHIEF JUSTICE: In a case like this there's nothing to do but wait, think, and investigate. Above all, to wait as long as necessary. After all, the time of governments isn't measured with the same clock that men's time is.

GÓMEZ URBINA (*pleasantly*): Just ask the unfortunates who have to sit around in waiting rooms about that. (*Discreet laughs.*) So, gentlemen, regarding your first point I find myself compelled to wait. And this, Mr. Speaker, is precisely the reason why I'm failing in my immediate duty of calling a new election. It's evident that it would be absurd to take this step without first having seen justice done. But it's no less evident that if I accede to your wishes and do call on election, an armed uprising will follow quicker than a jet plane can fly. If you insist, however, I'll just resign and you gentlemen can face the music.

SPEAKER OF CONGRESS: No. No. Not even to be thought of.

PRESIDENT OF THE OFFICIAL PARTY: National suicide, that's what it would be.

CHIEF JUSTICE: It is indisputable, gentlemen, that the president is right.

GÓMEZ URBINA: Many thanks, Mr. Chief Justice. Now as to your other point, General Meléndez, it amazes me that you'd be surprised at my granting a private interview to the ambassador of the Federated States of Demoland.

PRESIDENT OF THE OFFICIAL PARTY: How so, Mr. President?

GÓMEZ URBINA: I've been informed of the three secret talks you've had with him to convince him that Indoland, in imitation of his own country, should be governed by an officer of your bureautic prestige.

PRESIDENT OF THE OFFICIAL PARTY: I've already said very clearly that——.

GÓMEZ URBINA: General, in love and war, each to his own way. I don't reproach you for wanting to sit in the president's chair. I simply urge you to buy an ounce of patience. I know it's said, because members of my government have spread it around, that I came to power by mere chance. But what's wrong with that? Chance is a citizen of Indoland with full rights. And so is the national inertia which, according to some others, brought me to power.

SPEAKER OF CONGRESS: Nothing is farther from our thoughts than such ideas, sir.

GÓMEZ URBINA (*smiles*): Thank you, Mr. Speaker. But the presidency itself is somewhat of a lottery. Either one wins or one doesn't. There's nothing of "almosts," nor of refunds, nor of two persons sharing the same ticket . . . all of which add up to the masturbation of the Indolanders. In fact, this country shouldn't be called Indoland at all, but Indolenceland.

PRESIDENT OF THE OFFICIAL PARTY: I must say that in this particular lottery, you've drawn a winning number, Mr. President.

GÓMEZ URBINA: Not yet, because it simply remains to be seen whether or not my presence in this government is a mere matter of chance or of destiny. I myself don't know as of now. But this I do know that I am here . . . and here I am going to stay for the necessary time.

PRESIDENT OF THE OFFICIAL PARTY: But your interview with the ambassador——?

GÓMEZ URBINA: He requested it at your own suggestion, General. I don't know what his purpose is.

SPEAKER OF CONGRESS: If I'm not being indiscreet, or——.

CHIEF JUSTICE: Or *entresiliche*—meddlesome?

GÓMEZ URBINA *smiles.*

SPEAKER OF CONGRESS: ——may I inquire what you propose to resolve in this interview? After the press has sounded such a national alarm about it, we here must know what——.

GÓMEZ URBINA: Wouldn't it be better to ask the ambassador what his idea is? May the chief justice contradict me if I'm not right when I say that wise old men talk about what they've done, while young damned fools talk about what they intend doing. Isn't that so, Mr. Chief Justice?

CHIEF JUSTICE: I don't know whether or not I should say this to you, Mr. President, but . . . you're really older than I am!

GÓMEZ URBINA: You flatter me, my dear colleague. (*He looks at the wall clock.*) And now, gentlemen, I beg you to go to my private office and wait. You'll find a friend there. The time has come for my interview with the ambassador of Demoland.

The three bow and go to the door upstage left which the CAPTAIN *holds open for them.*

GÓMEZ URBINA (*when they reach the threshold*): Gentlemen, pardon me. (*The three turn around.*) I forgot something. For his own amusement, I allowed Captain Peláez to install secret microphones throughout the palace.

Disconcerted, the SPEAKER OF CONGRESS *and the* PRESIDENT OF THE OFFICIAL PARTY *exchange startled glances while the* CHIEF JUSTICE *strokes his goatee and smiles. As they exit, the* CAPTAIN *closes the door behind them and goes to* GÓMEZ URBINA *who smiles reflectively as he rubs his hands energetically.*

THE CAPTAIN: Mr. President?

GÓMEZ URBINA: It's time, Captain, but first I'll see the secretary of state.

During the CAPTAIN'S *absence,* GÓMEZ URBINA *takes out a cigarette, looks at it a moment and lights it. Then, with an energetic gesture, he crushes it in an ashtray on the table without even having taken a draw from it. He smiles again. The door downstage right opens and the* SECRETARY OF STATE *enters. He walks quickly to* GÓMEZ URBINA *and shakes his hand.*

SECRETARY OF STATE: Mr. President.

GÓMEZ URBINA: Good morning, my dear friend. You seem nervous.

SECRETARY OF STATE: I am, because to get here I had to run the gantlet of a score of local reporters and an equal number of foreign correspondents. They're in a frenzy.

GÓMEZ URBINA: And the ambassador?

SECRETARY OF STATE: While I was offering myself as a target to the international press, he entered by the secret door leading into the Patio of the Statue of the Liberator and went on without interference to your private presidential salon.

GÓMEZ URBINA: Splendid. How do you find him?

SECRETARY OF STATE: Chewing gum . . . and very self-assured.

GÓMEZ URBINA (*reflectively*): Did he let anything slip about the object of his visit? (*The* SECRETARY *moves his head in the negative.*) Well, show him in, please.

The SECRETARY *goes to the door upstage right, opens it, and bows. A moment later the* AMBASSADOR OF THE FEDERATED STATES OF DEMOLAND *enters dressed informally in a light grey flannel suit. He is about forty-eight years old, simple and of limited ability. His lips are set in a habitual smile that is somewhat artificial but agreeable. He speaks Indolandish with a slight accent which lends a vaguely musical quality to his words.*

THE AMBASSADOR: Hello, President.

GÓMEZ URBINA: How are you, Mr. Ambassador? (*They shake hands.*) Please be seated. (*Turning to the* SECRETARY OF STATE.) Will you wait in my private office, my dear friend?

> The SECRETARY *bows without speaking and exits upstage left. The* CAPTAIN *stands guard at the door downstage right.*

THE AMBASSADOR (*nodding casually toward the* CAPTAIN): Can we speak freely in front of him?

GÓMEZ URBINA (*smiling*): You wouldn't want me, Mr. Ambassador, to dispense with my shadow . . . or with my reflection in the mirror, which is what Captain Pelaéz is to me, would you?

THE AMBASSADOR (*laughing*): Oh, very good, very good! An armed shadow, eh?

GÓMEZ URBINA: Captain, show the ambassador that you aren't armed. (*The* CAPTAIN *obeys to the amusement of the* AMBASSADOR.) And now be so kind as to wait outside. (*The* CAPTAIN *exits downstage right.*) Will you have a drink, Mr. Ambassador?

THE AMBASSADOR: Oh, not this early in the morning, but thanks just the same.

GÓMEZ URBINA: I must tell you that I like the idea of this informal talk with you, Mr. Ambassador. If I'm not mistaken, you're new in the foreign service, aren't you?

THE AMBASSADOR: I'm an old war horse in politics, but was just recently called in from the pasture. My party was out of office for twenty years.

GÓMEZ URBINA (*half-seriously, half in jest*): You don't look as though you were very close to the picador's lance.

THE AMBASSADOR: What? Oh, yes. You mean like those broken-down old nags they use in the bullring. No, I'm still kicking. (*Both laugh a moment.*)

GÓMEZ URBINA: And now will you be so kind as to tell me how I can be of service to you?

THE AMBASSADOR: Yes, of course. Thanks. As you've said, I'm new to this particular service and because I am, I use new ways of going without things . . . more direct, more open. I've come to make a suggestion to you, Mr. President.

GÓMEZ URBINA: I'm listening with interest.

THE AMBASSADOR (*good-naturedly*): I think that you, too, are new in your own particular service—shall we say?—and so, as horse to horse, but horses that are still in there kicking, I want to give you some advice.

GÓMEZ URBINA: Well, go on.

THE AMBASSADOR: The Federated States of Demoland has big investments in this country, as you well know. This isn't a matter to be played with at present, as you also must know. The restlessness that's evident in Indoland because you haven't called an election yet can encourage Communist outbreaks. And this is something that the Federated States of Demoland can't and won't permit. If you want to save your skin—oh, pardon, just a manner of speaking—and go down in history as a great man, you should call an election immediately. The sooner, the better. Yesterday, if possible, as you people say. (*He laughs at his own joke.*)

GÓMEZ URBINA (*with no show of emotion*): Yes?

THE AMBASSADOR: There's another matter, too, and remember, I'm speaking as your friend—I like you, what the devil!—and I'm also speaking as an admirer of your great little country. (*He pauses and smiles.*)

GÓMEZ URBINA (*also smiling*): I'm still listening.

THE AMBASSADOR: The truth is—in my opinion, and my opinion is that of the Federated States of Demoland, so it's the opinion of the country that has shown the way to democracy to the whole world—the truth is that you people should follow our latest example. The job of president isn't for civilians any longer. The world situation now demands that government of the free countries be confided to military experts. My personal advice is that you'll do well to favor the candidacy of General Meléndez, a magnificent man, a revolutionary officer who's known personally to our president, the general. Did you know that one day our president asked your Meléndez why he wasn't the president of Indoland, and that Meléndez replied, "Right. Right you are. Why am I not?" (*He laughs at his joke.*)

GÓMEZ URBINA: Ah ha. (*He reflects a moment while looking at his hands as though they were a goldsmith's scales on which precious stones are weighed.*) And ——? (*He pauses.*)

THE AMBASSADOR: And my government would welcome you with pleasure as ambassador in Demópolis because evidently you'd still be alive. Understand? What do you say to this? (*He makes a sound with his tongue against his teeth.*) Do you like the idea?

GÓMEZ URBINA: Is that all, Mr. Ambassador?

THE AMBASSADOR: Well, man, I think that's enough, isn't it? (*He laughs contentedly.*)

GÓMEZ URBINA (*rises and goes to the door upstage left which he opens. Calling*): Mr. Secretary of State!

SECRETARY OF STATE (*appearing and closing the the door behind him*): Mr. President?

> GÓMEZ URBINA *pauses a moment. He looks at his hands while lifting them as if they were precision scales. The* AMBASSADOR *observes the scene with increasing amusement.*

GÓMEZ URBINA: I must say that the ambassador of Demoland speaks an almost perfect Indolandish, but I doubt that he understands it as well as he speaks it. In the understanding of languages there enters an ineffable national sentiment, Mr. Ambassador. I'm going to ask you, therefore, Mr. Secretary, to translate into Demolandish what I have to say now.

The AMBASSADOR *shows his amusement.*

GÓMEZ URBINA: Be so kind as to stand, Mr. Ambassador, while you listen to me.

Disconcerted, incredulous, the AMBASSADOR *looks at him and blinks.* GÓMEZ URBINA *remains motionless as a statue. As the* AMBASSADOR *at length understands that this is serious, he rises slowly and assumes an attentive attitude of simple diplomatic dignity.*

GÓMEZ URBINA: Mr. Ambassador, first of all we're not in one of those films that the North Americans shoot in Hollywood where it's always the foreign hero who comes in and saves some country that isn't his from destruction. (*He pauses and nods to the* SECRETARY OF STATE.)

SECRETARY OF STATE (*proceeds with his translation with absolute seriousness so as to give the impression of speaking a real language*): Rm. Rodassabma, tsrif fo lla ew era ton ni eno fo esoht smlif taht eht North Americans toohs ni Hollywood erehw ti si syawla eht ngierof oreh ohw semoc ni dna sevas emos yrtnuoc taht si ton sih morf noitcurtsed.

GÓMEZ URBINA: We aren't, as you said, "a great little country," but a little great country. Our national wealth is enormous and our poverty isn't of the spirit nor of the mind.

SECRETARY OF STATE (*as before*): Ew era ton, sa uoy dias, 'a taerg elttil yrtnuoc', tub a elttil taerg yrtnuoc. Ruo lanoitan htlaew si suomrone dna rou ytrevop si ton fo eht tirips ron fo eht dnim.

The AMBASSADOR *moves as though to speak, but* GÓMEZ URBINA'S *next words silence him.*

GÓMEZ URBINA: In Indoland we believe that every country is or should be the master of its own destiny, and that it and it alone can and should solve its internal problems without outside interference. In the face of your in-

experience in diplomacy—and even though I, too, like you—
I must inform you that your passport is at your disposal,
anytime.

SECRETARY OF STATE (*gasps, then proceeds with
his translation as before*): Ni Indoland ew eveileb taht
yreve yrtnuoc si ro dluosh eb eht retsam fo sti nwo
ynitsed, dna taht ti dna ti enola nac dna dluosh evlos sti
lanretni smelborp tuohtiw edistuo ecnerefretni. Ni eht
ecaf fo rouy ecneirepxeni ni ycamolpid—dna neve hgouht
I, oot, ekil uoy—I tsum mrofni uoy taht rouy tropssap si ta
rouy lasopsid, emityna.

THE AMBASSADOR: You don't seem to know what
you're doing, President. You forget the strong ties of friend-
ship and, even more, the mutual interests that bind our
countries together. Your act has no precedent in the history of our diplomatic relations. Not even when your
country expropriated the strategic minerals of its soil was
such extreme action as yours taken. As your friend and
neighbor, and in the name of Demoland, I must advise you
to think over what I've just counseled you and also that
you give some thought to Indoland's foreign debt to us.

GÓMEZ URBINA: I wish you a happy trip back to
your homeland, Mr. Ex-Ambassador to Indoland.

SECRETARY OF STATE (*as before*): I hsiw uoy a
yppah pirt kcab ot ruoy dnalemoh, Rm. Xe-Rodassabma ot
Indoland.

> The AMBASSADOR *stops himself on the point of saying
> something more, draws himself up, bows stiffly, and,
> then purpling, draws himself up again. He exits down-
> stage right. The SECRETARY OF STATE seems to have
> been hypnotized. At last he speaks.*

SECRETARY OF STATE: But, Mr. President, are
you aware of what you've just done?

GÓMEZ URBINA (*smiling*): I request you to busy
yourself at once with the ex-ambassador's passport, Mr.

Secretary. You know that Demolanders don't like to be kept waiting.

SECRETARY OF STATE: But, Mr. President, this is disaster . . . unlimited disaster. It's——.

GÓMEZ URBINA: It's nothing more than a necessary bad moment we'll just have to put up with for a while. You may go now, but come back at six o'clock this evening.

SECRETARY OF STATE: This situation you've created is so grave that it calls for immediate diplomatic intervention, Mr. President. There may still be time to——.

GÓMEZ URBINA (*interrupting him*): Time is the fatherland's, Mr. Secretary.

The SECRETARY *exits downstage right like a man who has just been stunned by a sledge hammer and is on the point of falling. A moment later enter the* PRESIDENT OF THE OFFICIAL PARTY *and the* SPEAKER OF CONGRESS, *both intensely excited; also the* CHIEF JUSTICE *who smiles philosophically while stroking his goatee; and the* HOME SECRETARY *who is serious and preoccupied.*

PRESIDENT OF THE OFFICIAL PARTY: What have you done, Mr. President? To have gone through with such a mad thing . . . and without the approval of the official party!

SPEAKER OF CONGRESS: Nor of Congress!

GÓMEZ URBINA: What's important now, gentlemen, is that what I've just done is done. So it's simply up to you to decide whether or not you're going to support me.

SPEAKER OF CONGRESS: The whole country will have to back you up . . . but it's . . . it'll be suicide!

GÓMEZ URBINA: To "back you up" is a vulgar expression, Mr. Speaker. It indicates that all of you think I've made a mistake.

PRESIDENT OF THE OFFICIAL PARTY: For Indoland's sake we'll have to cover up somehow for you, but the people won't stand for what you've just done. It's insanity!

SPEAKER OF CONGRESS: As Speaker of Congress I say that it's a gesture . . . no, an act of recklessness that's the very opposite of governing.

GÓMEZ URBINA: But I insist that you tell me whether you think I've made a mistake. And don't forget that it was you who made me president. But why? Because of my incompetence? If so, just what did you expect of me? That I'd give in when faced with a serious showdown? Did you want a president of Indoland, who was placed in office by you along with your colleagues, to obey the orders of another country's ambassador? Small chance of that! But you haven't said anything yet, Mr. Chief Justice.

CHIEF JUSTICE: I was thinking, sir, that we've spent more than half a century saying that what you've just done wasn't possible.

GÓMEZ URBINA: Well, if I've made a mistake or have been incompetent, as some of you evidently think, I don't see it so clearly as you do. Perhaps that's because the mistake or incompetence is mine and, therefore, I lack perspective. According to my own conscience, though, I've done only what I knew I must do. But now it's time, I insist, for you gentlemen to have your say.

SPEAKER OF CONGRESS: As far as I'm concerned, I'm not answering for anything. It's likely, though, that Congress, when convened to meet this emergency you've created, will demand your immediate resignation.

PRESIDENT OF THE OFFICIAL PARTY: Our party is meeting now. As its president, I'll have to bow to the delegates' decision. If they demand that you resign, it'll have to be that way.

GÓMEZ URBINA: As the Mexican Juárez said, "One does not resign from an office such as this: it is taken from one . . . if there're those who can." So first let's see what the people have to say.

PRESIDENT OF THE OFFICIAL PARTY: The people . . . if they really counted, we wouldn't be here.

GÓMEZ URBINA (*to the* HOME SECRETARY): You're very quiet, Mr. Secretary. Do you still find me lacking in authority and strength, as you told me a little while ago?

HOME SECRETARY: As you already know, I'm expected at my meeting of governors. What shall I tell them?

GÓMEZ URBINA: You have some real news for them now. How do you think they'll react?

HOME SECRETARY: As I see it, this is what they'll do. Those who are wobbly in office will support you so as not to fall, and those who feel sure of themselves will be for you so as to keep from wobbling themselves. Just leave this little job up to me. I am, as they say, "hep" to my governors.

SPEAKER OF CONGRESS: Demoland will now naturally demand that we pay our foreign debt.

GÓMEZ URBINA: Captain Peláez?

THE CAPTAIN: Mr. President?

GÓMEZ URBINA: Please call the secretary of finance on my private phone and ask him to come here at once.

PRESIDENT OF THE OFFICIAL PARTY: Armed intervention in at least two strategic ports seems inevitable.

GÓMEZ URBINA (*to the* CAPTAIN): Also tell the secretary of war and the secretary of communications that I want them here immediately.

CHIEF JUSTICE: The question of prices, sir, is now more important than ever.

GÓMEZ URBINA: Captain, tell the secretary of economics that I want him here, too.

THE CAPTAIN (*on the point of bursting with enthusiasm*): Very well, Mr. President. (*He reaches the door upstage left but turns and, urged on by an irrepressible impulse, returns quickly to* GÓMEZ URBINA *whose hand he shakes energetically.*)

GÓMEZ URBINA: What's this, Captain?

THE CAPTAIN: Pardon, Mr. President. I just wanted to make certain that I'd understood correctly. And, sir——.

GÓMEZ URBINA: What else?

THE CAPTAIN: The newspaper reporters. There're more than fifty of them out there in the waiting room. What are you . . . what are we going to do with them?

GÓMEZ URBINA: Why don't you suggest to them that they go to the Demoland embassy to see the ex-ambassador? Demolanders are the masters of the art of publicity. (*The* CAPTAIN *smiles and exits upstage left.*) And now, gentlemen and colleagues, if you'll allow me . . . I have work to do.

The PRESIDENT OF THE OFFICIAL PARTY *and the* SPEAKER OF CONGRESS *look at each other, then exit downstage right: the former raising his hands to heaven, the latter letting his fall in discouragement. The* HOME SECRETARY *shakes* GÓMEZ URBINA's *hand energetically. Smiling, the* CHIEF JUSTICE *returns from the door for which he also had started.*

CHIEF JUSTICE: And do you know, Mr. President, who was one of those asses that most often said this simply never could be?

GÓMEZ URBINA (*returning the* CHIEF JUSTICE's *smile*): You yourself, Mr. Chief Justice.

The lights dim into darkness which is followed by an immediate return of dimmed light. GÓMEZ URBINA *goes to a side table and turns on a radio set. He sits down before it and remains motionless, his chin in his hand, like the meditative one in Rubén Darío's poem on "Time." The light should be dim so as to give the impression of shadows to those onstage. The* CAPTAIN *enters, looks at the wall clock, opens the case and moves the hands, letting each hour, quarter, and half hour strike until six o'clock. He then closes the case and goes to open the door downstage right. Enter, also as shadows, the* SECRETARIES OF FINANCE, ECONOMICS, *and* WAR *who take their places at the conference table. Meanwhile,* GÓMEZ URBINA *has remained in his same position while listening to the radio from which issues the excited* VOICE OF THE ANNOUNCER.

VOICE OF THE ANNOUNCER: In the face of the choice arrogantly given to our government by the Federated States of Demoland, the choice being that Indoland should pay its foreign debt or run the risk of armed intervention, our entire population has hurried to the Central Bank and its branches throughout the nation. Teachers, workers, commercial employees, civil servants, and government officials have all given a day's pay. Industrialists and businessmen have made generous contributions. Housewives have turned in their jewelry and even their wedding rings. Children have gladly opened their savings banks to the nation. The middle and lower classes have been outstanding in their enthusiastic generosity. And here's a touching detail: some members of the aristocracy have given up their most precious possessions which are nothing more or less than their pawnshop tickets. Popular enthusiasm knows no limits. The cry of "Indoland first!" is on the lips of everyone: of all ages, classes, and religious beliefs. Stay tuned in and we'll give you more news as soon as we get it. Indoland first!

GÓMEZ URBINA *switches off the radio. The* CAPTAIN *then turns up the lights.*

GÓMEZ URBINA (*rising, calm and smiling*): A great invention the radio, gentlemen. By merely turning a switch one puts an end to it all and comes back to the world of silence which is so necessary, at least to some of us human beings. But now, even with the radio switched off, somehow I have the impression that I hear the voices of the people still going on. Has my order been carried out, Mr. Secretary of Finance?

SECRETARY OF FINANCE: Mr. President, we're working on the account of the contributions now being made. Telegrams are pouring in without end from all over

the country. (*Looking at his watch.*) I calculate that before
another half hour we'll have reached seventy-five million
indos.

GÓMEZ URBINA (*smiling*): Chicken feed, Mr. Secretary. Indoland's debt is three hundred million demos.
Three times eight——.

SECRETARY OF FINANCE: I know, Mr. President.
We're doing everything humanly possible and even impos-
sible. But the people really don't have to be spurred on.
The truth is simply that they haven't got the money.

GÓMEZ URBINA: What people well-saddled with
government ever have any money left over? Now let's hear
what the secretary of economics has to tell us.

SECRETARY OF ECONOMICS (*rising*): Mr. President, I've just come from a meeting with the production
groups of the country that lasted for more than five hours—
since your order was brought to me—until a few moments
ago. The grain depots are being opened up to the market,
the monopolies are being dissolved, and the cornerers of the
market who are being forced out of business are beating
their breasts. Tomorrow ten thousand emergency shops
where basic necessities will be sold at a tenth of their official cost will be opened up all over the country. The
peasants and small allotment farmers have agreed to barter
their products, regardless of loss. In accordance with the
new emergency law, anyone who tries to hoard food is put
in stocks in the public squares and denounced as a false
Indolander. It was even suggested that a sign with the
Mexican word *Malinchista*, you know: "Traitor," be hung
about the necks of all those who don't cooperate with the
nation, or who criticize our actions in any way whatsoever.
There are those who even proposed that tar and feathers
be used, but the proposal was unanimously defeated because that's an old Demoland custom.

GÓMEZ URBINA: The ridiculous takes distinctive
forms in every country . . . it's a national characteristic of

any people. Very well, thank you. And now, Mr. Secretary of War?

SECRETARY OF WAR: During the past few hours all your orders have been carried out, sir. The army, aside from the military security forces in the capital, has been strategically stationed on the frontier and in the seaports. The air fields are also fully covered. National Guard units were formed immediately in each state: in every city and town and even in the smallest villages. As of now, the women's corps are in the lead, having obeyed orders as one man . . . pardon, as one woman. (GÓMEZ URBINA *walks about moving his head in the affirmative.*) I think it my duty, however, to inform you that some of our military chiefs, although ready to give their lives for their country, would prefer an army officer for president, especially at a time like this.

GÓMEZ URBINA: Yes? Hmmm . . . Then those officers must be kept here in the capital. I don't hold with becoming a general all at one stroke . . . as I came to be president. The army wouldn't like that any more than I. (*The* SECRETARY OF COMMUNICATIONS *enters.*) Ah! What news, Mr. Secretary of Communications?

SECRETARY OF COMMUNICATIONS (*almost breathless*): Mr. President, all means of communication, land, sea, and air—telephonic, telegraphic, radiotelephonic, and cablegraphic—are now in charge of civilian committees of experts who were organized on an emergency basis. Our radar has been alerted. Civilian transportation services have been suspended until further orders. And here's a batch of congratulatory messages from Europe which prove that we're on the right track.

GÓMEZ URBINA: I'm glad to hear about all this. I've tried several times to communicate with you by our private line, but there was no answer.

SECRETARY OF COMMUNICATIONS: Pardon, Mr. President, but that line is out of order.

GÓMEZ URBINA: And what about the home secretary? By now he should——.

The CAPTAIN *exits downstage right, pressing himself close to the wall so as to let the* HOME SECRETARY *pass him.*

HOME SECRETARY (*enters without haste but energetically*): I have the great pleasure to inform you, Mr. President, that the governors who were here in the capital have returned to their respective states disposed to give their all for their country . . . and especially to keep their mandates. Those who were absent have sent in their declaration of loyalty by telephone, telegraph, and radio. There is, as I anticipated, nationwide rivalry to support you.

GÓMEZ URBINA: Very well. But it's of basic importance to keep the closest contact possible with our frontier.

The CAPTAIN *returns, goes up to* GÓMEZ URBINA *and whispers in his ear. The latter smiles, then moves his head affirmatively.*

GÓMEZ URBINA: Go back to your posts, gentlemen, with my personal gratitude and that of the whole country. And you, Mr. Secretary of Finance, remember: three times eight——.

SECRETARY OF FINANCE: Understood, Mr. President, thirty-five.

GÓMEZ URBINA: At least. I'm pleased to see that you're so well acquainted with the flexibility of numbers. (*Laughter. The* SECRETARIES *leave in a group.*) Don't you go, Mr. Home Secretary.

GÓMEZ URBINA *slowly glances through the messages which the* SECRETARY OF COMMUNICATIONS *gave to him. He puts them on the table as the labor leader* FLORENTINO BALANDRO *enters downstage right preceded by the* CAPTAIN. *At a sign from* GÓMEZ URBINA, *the* HOME SECRETARY *moves upstage.*

FLORENTINO BALANDRO (*Advancing enthusiastically with outstretched hands*): Mr. President and colleague! I've just come from presiding over—pardon—from attending an assembly of the Federal Congress of Workers in which your name was linked with those of the greatest liberators and martyrs in Indoland's political life. Never in my long time as a Socialist leader have I witnessed an apotheosis to equal yours . . . not even when it comes to myself or other famous martyrs of organized labor.

GÓMEZ URBINA: I'm glad that, in spite of everything, equality does have some limit, Señor Florentino Balandro. And what, if it may be known, apart from meeting in assembly, are the many members of the FCW doing? The country is busy just now with preparations against possible occupation.

FLORENTINO BALANDRO: Mr. President, I'll come straight to the point. It's the general opinion of the assembly that at last the solemn moment, so long awaited by all, has come in which Indoland should sign a pact with the Asiatic Socialist Federation, and incorporate the principles of Karl Marx and his ideological descendants into a new Constitution. At the moment when two great powers —one of them inspired by worship of the golden calf and brute force, the other inspired by the will for peace and the desire to save mankind—are preparing to confront each other, Indoland's rôle isn't difficult to see. Not only is it not difficult to see, but it's crystal clear. And not only is it crystal clear, but it's dazzling. All of us hope that you've already seen this.

GÓMEZ URBINA: The rôle of Indoland, Señor Balandro, is indeed most clear at this time. It's simply for us to keep intact the territory geography has destined to us, and to maintain our national independence while doing so.

FLORENTINO BALANDRO: I wonder if I've heard you right?

GÓMEZ URBINA: You've never been accused of

deafness, my friend, and with that brilliant intellect of yours, you certainly haven't been charged with not being able to comprehend.

FLORENTINO BALANDRO: But I must confess that I haven't understood you. This is a unique opportunity to take a stand, Mr. President—to put an end to the imperialist, money pride of Demoland. What better shield could we have for that than the glorious emblem of the ASF—the Asiatic Socialist Federation? What better defense could we have for our frontiers?

GÓMEZ URBINA: Regardless of geography, my respected former leader and teacher, the frontiers of a country are where the men of that country itself fix them. What we're fighting for now is Indoland's own affair. It has nothing to do with the rest of the world.

FLORENTINO BALANDRO: Pardon me, Mr. President, but it isn't possible to speak like this when the speed of communications and armaments has reached the incredible developments that everybody knows about. It just can't be said any more that any nation has its own private life. But you're right about geography and frontiers. Our spiritual frontier has so expanded that it has brought us to stand shoulder to shoulder with the Asiatic Socialist Federation. And I want you to know, without any more loss of time, that the ambassador of that great federation is waiting for just one word from you, just one gesture of agreement on your part, for him to advise the great Asiatic Socialist Federation to begin immediate preparations for strong action in our defense.

GÓMEZ URBINA: As my grandmother, who was so wise that she seemed to be an old maid, used to say: "It would be better to wait sitting down because that way you won't get too tired."

FLORENTINO BALANDRO: Do you mean to say that you refuse——?

GÓMEZ URBINA: Have you never found yourself in the midst of a crowd and so close pressed that you felt that if you breathed you'd breathe right into the faces of the others?

FLORENTINO BALANDRO: I still don't under-stand——.

GÓMEZ URBINA: I mean to say that if you let your-self be led by the crowd, you'll be lost. When the crisis, whatever it may be, has passed, the crowd stops being that and breaks up into individuals again. But even while the crowd is still a crowd, you can, even though in the midst of it, always follow your own inner voices, your personal ideas, and your individual loves. The crowd can only swerve you out of your road, but not away from your destiny or ideas. It can tear you away from everything except your-self, unless, of course, you're bound to disappear.

The radio set on the table upstage sounds a call signal. The CAPTAIN *answers, presses several buttons, then goes up to* GÓMEZ URBINA.

THE CAPTAIN: They're calling you by radio from the Southern Cross, Mr. President.

FLORENTINO BALANDRO: Am I to understand then that you reject our proposal, and that you insist on maintaining the bourgeois state of things as they are?

GÓMEZ URBINA (*to the* CAPTAIN): One moment. (*To* BALANDRO) You must understand that up until now there has been a basic error here in our general concept of government. You must also understand that the people don't really exist for a president unless all the classes that go to make up the people are equally dear to him as sons. You must further understand that I gave this same answer to the Cardinal Primate who offered me the purple canopy —or in just plain language; the protection—of an alliance with Rome. It was, of course, to have been based on cer-tain conditions: religious, naturally. Mr. Home Secretary.

HOME SECRETARY (*advancing*): Mr. President?

GÓMEZ URBINA: Take care that there be no agi-tation whatsoever amongst our workers who're more important to the country in this crisis than ever before. And you, Comrade Balandro, must now understand that if I don't want to see Indoland invaded because of economic interests, still less would I want to see it invaded because of a political error. If you'll permit me . . . (*He goes to the radio and turns his back on* BALANDRO *who hesitates a moment, then shrugs and exits quickly. The sound of static is heard from the radio.*) This doesn't seem to be working well, Captain. Why do you think that mechanical things rebel so against us?

THE CAPTAIN: I think that it's we who defy the machine, Mr. President.

GÓMEZ URBINA: Still cultivating the philosophers?

The CAPTAIN *continues to work with the radio.*

HOME SECRETARY: I should like to ask you a question, if I may.

GÓMEZ URBINA: Of course you may.

HOME SECRETARY: Do you really know exactly where you want to go?

GÓMEZ URBINA: Who really knows that, my friend? For the present what matters to me is to settle this crisis without a revolution or a war. Either of those means would be the easy way out.

HOME SECRETARY: If there should be a revolution——.

GÓMEZ URBINA: In event one should prove to be indispensable, I'll head it myself. Don't worry about that.

THE AMBASSADOR'S VOICE FROM THE RADIO: Hello, hello, hello! The ambassador of Indoland to the Republic of the Southern Cross here. Are you there, Mr. President?

GÓMEZ URBINA: At my post. Carry on.

THE AMBASSADOR'S VOICE FROM THE RADIO: The breach in relations between the Republic of Indoland and the Federated States of Demoland, together with the imperialist attitude of Demoland, has moved the chief of

the Southern Cross to offer you an alliance for the creation
of the Continental United States which will oppose any
further expansion of Demolandish power. The conditions
of the alliance will be discussed later. What matters now is
the basis of the alliance; continental union.

GÓMEZ URBINA: Is the chief of whom you speak
the same one who ordered a newspaper plant to be burnt
yesterday?

THE AMBASSADOR'S VOICE FROM THE RADIO
(*increases gradually in nervousness and embarrassment*):
Mr. President, the chief is waiting for your answer before
immediately underwriting a loan to us of six hundred million argentos, more than a thousand million of our own
indos.

GÓMEZ URBINA: Thank the chief and tell him that
Indoland is engaged in a strictly family matter. Tell him,
also, that in such matters the opinions of outsiders always
run the risk of being mistaken. Inform him further that
when it comes to a matter of continental alliance, Indoland
will take the initiative because she prefers, as one of my
small-town aunts used to say, to be a mouse's head rather
than a lion's tail.

THE AMBASSADOR'S VOICE FROM THE RADIO:
Bu . . . bu . . . but . . . Mr. Pre . . . President, my personal
situation at this moment is most embarrassing. He is right
here with me.

GÓMEZ URBINA: Who is?

THE AMBASSADOR'S VOICE FROM THE RADIO:
The ch . . . ch . . . chief.

GÓMEZ URBINA (*to the* HOME SECRETARY *and the*
CAPTAIN): Did you both hear that? (*They both nod.* GÓMEZ
URBINA *speaks into the radio again.*) You are, to say the
least, an innovator in diplomacy. Present my compliments
to the chief and take the first plane home. You're relieved
of your duties as of now.

With a very firm movement, GÓMEZ URBINA *switches
off the radio. He sighs, then on thinking over what*

has happened, breaks into frank, youthful laughter in which the HOME SECRETARY *and the* CAPTAIN *join. The telephone rings and the* CAPTAIN *answers it.*

THE CAPTAIN: Hello, Yes, yes, sir. (*To* GÓMEZ URBINA) the secretary of finance, sir.

GÓMEZ URBINA (*taking the receiver*): Yes? (*Pause.*) How much? (*Pause.*) A hundred and fifty-eight million indos in a few more hours? But these people are masochists. We're still short a great deal, my friend. Remember: three times eight . . . (*He hangs up, breathes deeply, then sits down at the desk and reaches for pencil and paper.*) Let's see how well up on contemporary national history you are, Mr. Secretary, and you, too, Captain. Who were my immediate predecessors in the presidency? Only the living, though. Not those who've gone like poor Matías who died much too soon. Take pencil and paper, Mr. Secretary.

HOME SECRETARY: I think I see ahead to what you're going to do——.

GÓMEZ URBINA: You can't foresee anything, my friend. You're neither a witch doctor nor a president. Are you both ready?

The HOME SECRETARY *writes rapidly on a sheet of paper and passes it to* GÓMEZ URBINA *who reads silently what is written while moving his head in the affirmative.*

GÓMEZ URBINA: Captain, you will summon all these gentlemen at once for a meeting here at midnight.

A change of lights. The CAPTAIN *goes to the wall clock and moves the hour hand so that hours sound successively. Meanwhile,* GÓMEZ URBINA *slowly reads aloud the names on the list. As he pronounces each of the names, the men enter one by one like shadows in the half light and sit down at the conference table.*

GÓMEZ URBINA: Mr. Counselor Aguirre . . . Dr.

Suárez Meza . . . General Eloy . . . General Avalos . . .
General Puebla . . . Mr. Counselor Germán——.

> *The last named enters as midnight is striking. Meanwhile, at a nod from* GÓMEZ URBINA, *the* HOME SECRETARY *exits upstage left. On the last stroke of midnight, the light increases so as to illuminate the scene brightly. All seven characters are now seated at the table. The* CAPTAIN *stands guard at the door downstage right.*

GÓMEZ URBINA: Good evening to you all, gentlemen. I don't presume to call you colleagues because my time in office is short in comparison with your long terms. I shall, therefore, address you as ex-president compatriots. (*Murmurs of agreement from all.*) All of you are aware of what is now going on in our country and perhaps you blame me because of it. But is there any Indolander who wouldn't be pleased at the idea of being responsible for making such a big stir? I've taken the liberty—I don't say the authority—af calling you tonight to your former and I hope not forgotten domain to say to you: You know what I've done. And to ask you: Have I done well or badly, and, above all, can I count on your help?

> *The* EX-PRESIDENTS *look at one another. Some of them appear about to speak, but the first to do so is* COUNSELOR AGUIRRE.

COUNSELOR AGUIRRE: As an Indolander I'd like to think, my colleague, that you've done what you took to be your duty . . . that is, if there was no other recourse open to you. As a practical man who governed the country at the time of our religious wars, I find myself obliged, however, to dissent. Why must a nation with so many domestic problems have been launched into the storm of the kind of international problem you've created?

GÓMEZ URBINA: Have you never tried, Mr. Counselor, to get yourself out of one difficult situation by getting into another? I remember that when my teeth were aching in my adolescence I used to prick my arm with a pin until it hurt more than my teeth did. I suppose, though, that that was just an indigenous Indolander's odd way of doing things.

COUNSELOR AGUIRRE: That might be, my colleague, but there's a tremendous difference between the pain caused by one's own teeth—which is a private pain, as it were—and an earthquake that strikes on a national scale.

GÓMEZ URBINA: Quite right. As the expropriator of the sources of our strategic minerals, what have you to say to me, General Avalos?

GENERAL AVALOS: That the only thing we can expropriate, my friend, is what's in our own territory.

GÓMEZ URBINA: Isn't the independence of Indoland itself to be found here, General?

GENERAL AVALOS: After my stormy term as president, I've had time to read and I've discovered a curious thing. It's that up till now Indoland's independence was to be found in the street called the Golden Wall that's in the capital of the Federated States of Demoland. That's why I agree with what you've done. We're now going to free our independence from up there and bring her back, no matter by what means, to this desert home of hers where she'll really be mistress, even if it's only of a desert. Yes, you can count on me all the way.

GÓMEZ URBINA: Thank you very much. General Eloy?

GENERAL ELOY: I don't like idle talk, as you all know. Indolanders, like fish, usually die by the mouth. But now that you've asked me, I'll say this. I believe that frontiers are of vital importance when they're open to trade and especially to tourists. If your action leads to the closing of our frontiers, what kind of answer do you expect me to give you? The most I can say is that we'll just have to see this through together because we simply won't have any other choice, but I warn you that the whole affair'll end up in the red.

GÓMEZ URBINA: Another pessimist? But perhaps General Puebla who, as we know, refused a military pact with Demoland is with me?

GENERAL PUEBLA: My dear Don José, my government was a transitional one and, therefore, the opposite of the kind you're undertaking. You're giving battle. I didn't. I simply said "No." My predecessor, General Avalos, also like you put the country in an extremely dangerous position which could easily have led to chaos. Far be it from me, though, to reproach him for that. He merely acted in accord with the demands of the times. And it so happened that the people, who didn't think as he did about the matter, but as I did, supported him to the limit. In a similar case, they wouldn't have supported me precisely because they thought as I did. What I mean by this is that each government has its own moment of truth and its own form. It's the lot of a president to recognize these for what they are and to act accordingly.

GÓMEZ URBINA: I understand what you mean, but I must confess that I can't distinguish one form of our governments from another because they all seem to me to have had the same form with only minor differences in their curves. Counselor Germán?

COUNSELOR GERMÁN: I must tell you, colleague, that you've obliged me make a long plane trip here and that I'm afraid it has been to no avail. Our points of view are exactly opposite. Where I raised prices, you lower them. Where I was responsible for the value of our money falling, you raise it. Where I tried to create highly specialized industries, you revive the old crafts along with the barter system. Don't you, as one yourself, know that Indolanders suffer from the chronic fever to spend more than they have and, therefore, that they must be kept in reduced circumstances because when they do have any extra money they only waste it foolishly? As for Demoland, my policy was always clear and simple. "Lend me as much as you want to," I said in effect. "Because," I added to myself, "it's not I who'll have to pay it back, but my successors." Now you, instead of being content to spread the nation's debt over twenty successive governments, take upon your own shoulders the absurdly impossible task of liquidating the total sum. You're an Indolander but, pardon me, one in the worst sense of the word. You confuse boldness, which really is calculation, as I showed in my government, with supremacy which is an abstraction. But, be all that as it may, since you've called me here, how can I be of service to you?

GÓMEZ URBINA: In a way that you don't know about yet. I find the lesson you've just read me most interesting, but before replying, I must observe that we haven't yet heard the authoritative voice of Dr. Suárez Meza.

DR. SUÁREZ MEZA: My experience in office was really infinitesimal when compared with that of you gentlemen. My life as president was brief as that of the roses— shall we say?—but it taught me to make up for my mistake in not following the political advice of my elders while in office by following their financial advice to the letter after I left office. That's how I was able to invest my modest funds most profitably. Now in this crisis, my only advice to you is that the country must be saved.

GÓMEZ URBINA (*humbly*): Many thanks to all of you, gentlemen, but I must clear up at once the mistaken idea that seems to have arisen about this meeting. The problem which I've been so bold as to call you together to discuss isn't, unfortunately, one of a political nature. If it were, and therefore, simply a matter of trying to prevent something or other from happening, your advice would be invaluable to me. But the problem, or rather I should say the emergency, is of an economic nature. So I've called you together to ask your——.

Suddenly the door downstage right is opened so violently that it almost causes the CAPTAIN *to fall. Enter* COLONEL JUDAS *who is fat, and in full-dress uniform with all his medals. All turn at once to look at him. It is clear that* COLONEL JUDAS *is proud to attract so much attention from the distinguished company. He raises his right hand in which he exhibits a regulation army revolver as though it were an ornament of great value.*

COLONEL JUDAS: Pardon the interruption, gentlemen, but I'm looking for Señor José Gómez Urbina.

GÓMEZ URBINA (*Rising*): If you're looking for the president of the Republic, I am he, Colonel.

COLONEL JUDAS (*approaching him as if playing an amusing joke*): Ah, good! I didn't know you. In this case, Mr. President, you're my prisoner and all these ex-presidents are my hostages. (*General movement.*) It's useless for you to excite yourselves, gentlemen. For the salvation of the country, the capital garrison is now in loyal hands. I must ask all of you who have arms to put them on the table. (*Calmly,* COUNSELOR GERMÁN *takes a checkbook from his pocket and places it on the table.*) What's that?

COUNSELOR GERMÁN: My checkbook, Colonel. My only weapon. It's not loaded yet, so fill in for yourself the caliber of shot you want me to fire.

COLONEL JUDAS (*in a very military and angry manner*): This is no time for jokes, gentlemen. I'm sorry that some of you are my superior officers, but my instructions are precise. They're for me to take prisoner the so-called President Gómez Urbina and to take as hostages all those who are with him. If there should be any show of resistance (*he indicates his revolver*) . . . martial law.

THE EX-PRESIDENTS (*ad lib*): This is inconceivable!—who can have thought of such a disrespectful act?—Ridiculous?—And our former terms of office?—And our rank!—And our national importance?—And our money?—

Isn't anything in this country respected any more? GÓMEZ URBINA, *still standing, appears to be thinking profoundly.*

COLONEL JUDAS *places a hand on his shoulder.* GÓMEZ URBINA *shudders, recovers his breath and at last speaks.*

GÓMEZ URBINA: When a thing like this can happen, I must admit my defeat, gentlemen. I must also confess that all my former convictions have just crashed. All that remains is the conclusion I've reached as to who planned this bloody mockery. (*General movement amongst the* EX-PRESIDENTS. COLONEL JUDAS *raises his revolver again.*) I'll not name any names, though. I'm resigned and also prepared to act in keeping with what must be. But even so, what I can't do is make a spectacle of myself before the people. Nor will I serve as the butt of Indoland jokes which are our only truly national institution that I know of. Captain Peláez?

THE CAPTAIN (*advances a step and stands at attention*): Mr. President?

GÓMEZ URBINA: There's only one thing left for me to do now. If the colonel will permit it, lend me your revolver for just a moment. *The* CAPTAIN *moves agitatedly, reddens, and does not know what to do.*

THE CAPTAIN: By your express orders I am not armed, sir. If I were, this wouldn't have happened, or I'd be dead by now.

COLONEL JUDAS: Who'd have believed this? You're all man, Mr. President. I wouldn't miss out on such a historic occasion for anything in the world. (*With a magnificent gesture.*) Use my revolver, I beg of you.

GÓMEZ URBINA: Why not? Isn't it the victor's arms that the vanquished should make use of? (*He accepts the revolver from the* COLONEL *who hands it over to him ceremoniously as prescribed by the duel ritual.* GÓMEZ URBINA *looks at the revolver and smiles slightly as if he were about to become again the* MR. NOBODY *of the first act.*) I suppose you want to witness the act, Colonel, so go ahead, please. (*He nods toward the door upstage left.*)

COLONEL JUDAS: After you, Mr. President.

GÓMEZ URBINA *raises his shoulders slightly and walks with bowed head toward the door.* COLONEL JUDAS *follows him. The* CAPTAIN, *beside himself with agitation, follows them, while the six* EX-PRESIDENTS *look at one another as though they had been turned into pillars of salt. Not a word is spoken. When* GÓMEZ URBINA *reaches the door, he turns slowly but with a precise movement. Without apparent haste, or rather with the exactness and sureness of an Olympic champion, he raises the revolver and fires it point-blank at* COLONEL JUDAS *who falls with an expression on his face which indicates that he is the most surprised of all.*

GÓMEZ URBINA (*calm and inscrutable*): General Avalos, you will do me the favor of taking immediate command of the capital garrison. Shoot anyone who opposes you. You've full authority to proceed according to martial law in the state of emergency which I now declare.

GENERAL AVALOS: Then, sir, you don't need me for the other problem you called us here for?

GÓMEZ URBINA: You'd be of no use to me here because you haven't enough money. Go now and take command of the garrison. I'll expect a report from you shortly after you've left.

The EX-PRESIDENTS *meanwhile have been gradually recovering from shock which some show by taking out cigarettes and lighting them, others by moving their arms up and down, and still others by walking back and forth. They do not yet seem to have taken in altogether just what has happened so quickly.*

GÓMEZ URBINA: Captain, take charge of this revolver and have *that* (*with a motion of his chin he indicates the body of the* COLONEL) removed from here.

In the amazed silence that follows, GENERAL AVALOS *salutes smartly and exits. The* CAPTAIN *follows him to return immediately with two soldiers who pull offstage the body of the* COLONEL *as though it were that of a bull that has been valiantly killed in the ring. Another pause follows. The* CAPTAIN *resumes his position as guard at the door downstage right.*

GÓMEZ URBINA: Is all in order outside, Captain?

THE CAPTAIN: I didn't see any suspicious movements, sir. Apparently Colonel Judas came here alone, and I don't think the shot was heard because of the thickness of the walls and the double doors.

GÓMEZ URBINA: Thank you. A while ago, gentlemen, when I confessed that all my former convictions had crashed, I meant that I had to go against my own deepest feeling, because I realized that I had to kill a man. But, then, a president of Indoland is not to be trifled with nor betrayed. While in office he may, of course, be criticized, but that's all. And he's not to be molested after he has left office. (*He rubs his hands and continues in a sudden, unexpectedly pleasant tone.*) And now, gentlemen, if you don't mind, we'll talk about finances.

THE EX-PRESIDENTS (*murmur ad lib*): Uf!—Who'd have thought it!—What a man!—This is what's called having things in their right place!—I like the man! (*All sit down uncomfortably.*)

GENERAL ELOY: Allow me to congratulate you, colleague, on your courage.

GÓMEZ URBINA: Thank you. But just before we were interrupted, Dr. Suárez Meza was referring to the investment of his modest funds and ——.

COUNSELOR GERMÁN: Pardon me for also interrupting you, Mr. President and colleague, but when I think that that colonel could have killed you at any moment, I shudder. Now, as a practical man, I want to ask you if this attempted coup doesn't make you fear that there's some organized movement behind it—and possibly a strong one, at that—against you?

COUNSELOR AGUIRRE: There might be, of course. Those at the bottom of this inconceivable audacity must be identified in a thorough investigation.

GENERAL PUEBLA: I think it may be only an isolated attempt like the time when a minor officer shot at me, as you'll recall. It's always true of a soldier that when he isn't loyal under every test, he may become a traitor at any time. In this case, it'd be just as well, however——.

COUNSELOR AGUIRRE: That dynamite attempt on my life was, as is well known, of Catholic origin, but as attempts on us presidents can be by the military as well as by religious fanatics, I insist that we find out——.

GENERAL ELOY: I'm probably the only one of us here who has attempted to take his own life. That happened when I was very young. I remember——.

DR. SUÁREZ MEZA: Are you forgetting that attempts to assassinate Indoland's presidents began with me? There was that conspiracy——.

GENERAL PUEBLA: Ah, no, no! That was after the one of General . . . But there's no reason to suspect that the guilty in this present case are Catholics. Yet whoever they are, they must be brought to light and punished.

GÓMEZ URBINA (*in a very smooth voice*): Will you allow me? General Avalos is now taking care of all that and, although I thank you for the interest you show in my health—shall we say?—I want to dismiss all references to my humble person from this meeting. We're only mortal, as the dead colonel has all too truly just shown us, so let's talk of the immortal, gentlemen—of the immortality of Indoland. The situation which the country now faces can be summed up in three words and can also be resolved by them: Pay the debt.

COUNSELOR GERMÁN: You've made a basic error, colleague, perhaps because of your lack of economic experience. By paying the debt you'll annihilate the country's credit. What you should do, therefore, is increase the debt.

GÓMEZ URBINA: I'm fully aware of my inexperience that you've just called attention to. Furthermore, I agree that in a peaceful situation the application of your sophism would not only be possible but ideal. A large loan could always be negotiated with another country to—how shall I put it?—to vary our national debt. Isn't pleasure precisely in variety?

GENERAL ELOY: But bear in mind that inflation is always highly paid for.

COUNSELOR GERMÁN: But as long as others are paying for it——.

GÓMEZ URBINA: Be all that as it may, gentlemen, this isn't a round-table discussion. Our ex-ambassador to Demópolis arrived by plane tonight with more news. As he was leaving the capital, the Congress of Demoland was in session behind closed doors. The impression prevails in that country that if Indoland doesn't liquidate its debt within twenty-four hours, we will be invaded within forty-eight hours by the highly mechanized—don't forget that point— army of the Federated States of Demoland.

COUNSELOR AGUIRRE: That would be a most awful resurrection of what happened here a century ago!

DR. SUÁREZ MEZA: We could never stand up successfully to such a force!

GENERAL PUEBLA: What a tremendous responsibility you've taken on your shoulders, Mr. President!

GÓMEZ URBINA: Right, but a man without responsibilities is nothing more than a walking corpse. Now, but sparing you the details, I must inform you that all measures humanly possible have already been taken for our national defense, as well as for liquidating our debt to Demoland. By tomorrow, the results of the latter measure will, at the maximum, reach only a tenth part of our debt. (*Uncomfortable coughs.*)

COUNSELOR GERMÁN: But with that as a base you can negotiate. The all-important thing is to have a base.

GÓMEZ URBINA: You forget that this is the first time in the diplomatic history of the continent that an ambassador of Demoland has ever received his walking papers from a neighbor . . . and a small one at that.

DR. SUÁREZ MEZA: Perhaps the submission of your resignation to Congress would . . . There're times when one must sacrifice oneself for one's country, as I did.

COUNSELOR AGUIRRE: An ambassador plenipotentiary who's an expert in these chronic financial crises could be appointed immediately. I propose Counselor Germán.

GÓMEZ URBINA: I'm sorry to have expressed myself so poorly to you gentlemen, but will now try to explain myself better. Our relations with Demoland have been broken off. And by me. Demoland, having just fixed a limit of twenty-four hours for payment of our debt will, therefore, collect what we owe her. As you all know, the universally accepted way of shutting up the mouth of a creditor—pardon my vulgar manner of speaking—is to pay him off. In the present case, I'd like, above all, to apply to my country the French proverb which says that he who pays his debts gets rich himself.

GENERAL ELOY: Well, that's not the only way.

GÓMEZ URBINA: In the case of this particular creditor there's the danger of his applying an embargo after twenty-four hours. And the country that's to be embargoed, gentlemen, is yours as much as mine.

COUNSELOR AGUIRRE: This is certainly a matter that none of us can take lightly, colleague.

GÓMEZ URBINA: Right. If by this time tomorrow we haven't liquidated our debt, by this same time day after tomorrow we'll not only be the economic prisoners of Demoland but its virtual slaves.

GENERAL ELOY: Absurd!

GENERAL PUEBLA: Abominable!

DR. SUÁREZ MEZA: Monstrous!

COUNSELOR GERMÁN: The worst possible business.

GÓMEZ URBINA: This is exactly the attitude I was hoping for from you . . . And now, can I count on your help to save the country?

COUNSELOR GERMÁN: Up to what point? I ask.

COUNSELOR AGUIRRE: I'm with you unconditionally . . . in the moral sense.

GENERAL PUEBLA: Have you thought out a way for us to serve you?

GENERAL ELOY: If you have, let's hear about it now.

DR. SUÁREZ MEZA: Agreed. You must be precise——.

GÓMEZ URBINA: It's all very simple, gentlemen. Not for a moment have I doubted that you'd agree to put up the money we're still lacking.

DR. SUÁREZ MEZA: What!

COUNSELOR GERMÁN: Do you mean to say almost two thousand five hundred million?

GÓMEZ URBINA (*pleasantly*): Exactly. The equivalent of the country's money now in circulation.

GENERAL ELOY (*in a determined tone of voice*): To break off relations was insane, but now we're being trapped in a madhouse.

GENERAL PUEBLA: You're placing us in a most painful situation . . . and to no avail.

COUNSELOR AGUIRRE: What you're proposing, Mr. President, isn't a solution, but a . . . a conflagration.

COUNSELOR GERMÁN: More than anything, you've calculated badly.

GÓMEZ URBINA (*very smoothly*): Am I to understand, gentlemen, that you refuse to cooperate in our national crisis?

COUNSELOR GERMÁN: No, sir, of course not. Indoland before everything. Well, let's see, by making a tremendous effort I could subscribe a million. (*All look at him.*) Well, then, let's say two. (GÓMEZ URBINA *looks at him steadily.*) Oh, well, two and a half, then. But that's all.

GÓMEZ URBINA: Two and a half million. Very well. But won't some one put up more?

DR. SUÁREZ MEZA: They slander me when they say that I'm as rich as Croesus, but I can manage two hundred and fifty thousand indos for such a cause as this.

GÓMEZ URBINA: One quarter of a million.

COUNSELOR AGUIRRE: Everyone knows that my business is bad. I've lost almost all of what little money I had, but for the country's sake . . . a hundred thousand indos. I know. I know, a tenth of a million. (GÓMEZ URBINA *smiles.*)

GENERAL ELOY: All I have . . . well, almost all . . . a million.

GENERAL PUEBLA: Another.

GÓMEZ URBINA: So, let's see. Two million and a half, plus two hundred and fifty thousand, plus a hundred thousand, plus two million are four million eight hundred and fifty thousand indos. Thank you very much, gentlemen.

COUNSELOR GERMÁN: But, as you're clearly to understand, Mr. President, this is on condition that you resign immediately from office so we can put the country on its feet again.

GÓMEZ URBINA: All that would appear to be logical, wouldn't it? But I've another proposition for you gentlemen. We're simply going to throw that chicken feed you've offered into the wastebasket and get down to serious figuring. I must have from you five men the twenty-one hundred million that are still lacking . . . the amounts in direct proportion, of course, to each of your fortunes and to those of the persons you're protecting. Anything else would be unfair. A *pause. All look at one another.*

COUNSELOR AGUIRRE: All the unfairness is entirely on your side, colleague. Never in my life have I heard such gross nonsense.

General agreement.

THE EX-PRESIDENTS (*uttering simultaneously negative monosyllables*): Not in . . . There's not . . . No! No!

GÓMEZ URBINA (*with calm authority*): I beg you not to lose control of yourselves. For the country's sake, gentlemen. (*He opens the leather folder on the desk, takes out a sheet of paper, and calmly glances over it as all present watch him.*) I have a list here—I think it's sufficiently accurate and up-to-date—of the various properties and assets, liquid and real, within and outside the country, owned by all of you. (*General movement of protest.*) Although the assessments naturally are fraudulently low, they represent a sum considerably greater than the one we must raise.

COUNSELOR GERMÁN: But this is intolerable. To pry into our private lives, into our——.

GÓMEZ URBINA: The lives of presidents, whether in office or out, are never private, colleague. But just a moment more and I'll finish. Also listed here are all your bank deposits and those of your . . . associates . . . principally in Demoland.

COUNSELOR AGUIRRE: I refuse to hear more. These are calumnies as false as those that besmirched our great late president-general who died in poverty.

GÓMEZ URBINA: Well, supposing they were calumnies, yet if we are to believe Machiavelli there would still be something to them should there remain any evidence in the form of cash or other assets. But just to eliminate any doubts you may have about these figures, I'll tell you that they've all been checked by the Department of Federal Investigation of Demoland. (*General disconcertion.*)

COUNSELOR GERMÁN: Most probably old figures. I don't know . . . a list of unsuccessful, dead investments.

GENERAL ELOY: Or new figures, invented in the light of recent events.

DR. SUÁREZ MEZA: Or figments of the imagination of some busybody ambassador who wants to keep his job.

GÓMEZ URBINA: I'm sorry to disillusion you. These figures were collected during the past three months and were given to me, at my express request and as a proof of good neighborliness, by the general who's now the president of the Federated States of Demoland.

GENERAL PUEBLA: During the past three months? That's to say, since you came into office. This means that you've been preparing——.

COUNSELOR AGUIRRE: And you probably provoked the breach in relations with Demoland with this plot against us in mind.

COUNSELOR GERMÁN: If that's true, then you're certainly deeper than I thought. You could even be from my hometown. At any rate, this is acting like a bad Indolander and you've played a low trick on us.

GÓMEZ URBINA (*with calm authority*): Although all of us here are, or have been, or want to continue to be presidents—apparently that's an incurable disease with us—I urge you to measure your words and to listen to me a moment more. As I see it, there're two ways ahead of us. One is your—shall I call it?—moral enhancement because of your spontaneous sacrifice of your personal fortunes on the altar of the country. This would be your definitive consecration with the people. The other way is the exact opposite. It would lead to your certain downfall and ostracism. The people would have nothing but contempt for you. They'd even spit on you. There'd also be——.

DR. SUÁREZ MEZA: Posterity will do us justice.

COUNSELOR AGUIRRE: Not the least doubt of that.

GÓMEZ URBINA: There'd also be, as I was about to say, forcible restitution.

GENERAL ELOY: That's unconstitutional.

GÓMEZ URBINA: Isn't personal enrichment under the cover of exercising executive power also unconstitutional? Note well that I said res-ti-tu-tion.

COUNSELOR GERMÁN: You're a dreamer. You can try us or even imprison us if you want to, or go so far as to expropriate our real assets which remember, it'd take months to sell and at sacrifice prices to boot. But, just as a simple matter of curiosity, what means would you use to enforce the uh . . . restitution of any funds that might not be in the country?

GÓMEZ URBINA (*in the manner of a professor when answering a question he has been expecting*): Before leaving Demópolis, our ex-ambassador felt out the opinion there in high government spheres. There's general agreement in the sense that in exercising its rights as a creditor, and also at my request, Demoland wouldn't be adverse to freezing first and then seizing all Indolander funds on deposit in private banks there. It wouldn't matter whether those funds were in the form of titles, deeds, cash, or even gold and silver bullion. After all, Demoland is admittedly a commercial country and only wants to collect what is its due. What else would you expect? Now, gentlemen, let's hear what you have to say.

> *No one speaks. Some take out cigarettes and light them. They all look at one another.* COUNSELOR GERMÁN *rises and walks up and down.*

COUNSELOR AGUIRRE (*always the most diplomatic of the group*): As an Indolander I have to admire you, even though you're ruining me.

GENERAL ELOY: And what will we receive in exchange for this unmentionable attack of yours on private property?

GÓMEZ URBINA: That's quite clear: the glory of having spontaneously saved Indoland, to which will be added the unanimous acclaim of the people. Isn't all that a great thing?

GENERAL PUEBLA: It must be admitted that the dilemma——.

COUNSELOR GERMÁN: Just a moment, gentlemen. Let's not be hasty. And let's not forget about the dead colonel. As I pointed out before, it's certain that he wasn't working entirely on his own. How do we know who might not have been backing him and how far this coup might have gone by now?

DR. SUÁREZ MEZA: True. In fact, it's necessary to determine first if——.

COUNSELOR GERMÁN: If you're still president, to put it bluntly.

GÓMEZ URBINA (*smiling*): Right, gentlemen. I'd forgotten that detail.

GENERAL ELOY: In any event, I'm of the opinion that among ourselves we have enough influence to put an end to this absurdity that's being proposed to us.

GÓMEZ URBINA: You've not only influence, General, but you also have the money. Captain?

THE CAPTAIN (*approaching*): Sir?

GÓMEZ URBINA: Call General Avalos on my private line to the capital garrison and ask him in a very plain way if I am or am not still the presi——.

While he is speaking the door downstage right opens and there stands GENERAL AVALOS *who is tired looking but composed and still energetic.*

GENERAL AVALOS: Mr. President, I have the honor to inform you that without any unnecessary bloodshed an end has been put to the subversive movement under way. The ex-candidate General Jaimes with three associates of his party and of his same rank are now prisoners in the capital garrison. Other prisoners there are two leaders of the Conservatives and three of Communist affiliation. The secretary of war voluntarily submitted his resignation to me, and General Meléndez, president of the official party, is under house arrest.

GÓMEZ URBINA (*impassively*): Thank you, General
Avalos. Now have you anything else to add, gentlemen?

COUNSELOR GERMÁN: I must congratulate you on
your victory, Mr. President and colleague. I'm now willing
to take the measures necessary to comply with the request
you've just made of us——.

GÓMEZ URBINA: To save the country, Counselor.

COUNSELOR GERMÁN: But these operations always take time. As soon as I return home——.

DR. SUÁREZ MEZA: Not less than twenty-four
hours will be necessary to——.

GÓMEZ URBINA: Thank you all, gentlemen, in the
name of Indoland which will bless you while you live and
will revere your memory. But I mustn't bother you any
more than necessary. Certain as I was of your patriotic
response, I've had rooms made ready for you here in the
palace. There's even special attendants for you. You also
have at your disposal my private telephone lines and radio
which are all in direct communication with the various
offices you need to contact in Demoland. In this way, all
can be done at once and, thanks to you, Indoland will be
free tomorrow.

> *Discontented and angry, but self-controlled, the five*
> EX-PRESIDENTS *look at one another, then at* GÓMEZ
> URBINA *who smiles broadly at them, and then at* GEN-
> ERAL AVALOS *who also smiles. They next look at one*
> *another again and, headed by* COUNSELOR GERMÁN,
> *file out one by one through the door downstage right.*
> *The* HOME SECRETARY *enters upstage left.* GENERAL
> AVALOS *starts to leave but* GÓMEZ URBINA *goes to him*
> *and shakes his hand.*

GENERAL AVALOS: I don't have to ask if they
came through.

GÓMEZ URBINA: Our history is full of men who've
sacrificed only their lives for their country, but these are the
greatest patriots we've ever had. The home secretary has

taken care of all other necessary measures from my private office. Again, thank you for everything, General.

GENERAL AVALOS: It's an honor to serve Indoland under you. (*He salutes and exits.*)

GÓMEZ URBINA: And now, Mr. Home Secretary, do you think that I've the authority and strength needed to see that justice is done in our other matter?

HOME SECRETARY: I myself should like to know the answer to that, Mr. President. So far, you've only made history, which isn't the same thing. (*He exits downstage right.*)

GÓMEZ URBINA *loosens his shirt collar and tie a bit and begins to walk up and down, oblivious of the* CAPTAIN *who, unable to contain himself any longer, lets out a wolf whistle such as men give in admiration of pretty girls in the street.* GÓMEZ URBINA *turns around in surprise, then laughs. The* CAPTAIN, *convulsed with laughter, looks at him admiringly as the curtain falls.*

CURTAIN

Act 3

Two days later at eleven o'clock on a sunny June morning. In the air is the suggestion of floating banners and flags, together with the gay sound of military music blending with the incessant murmur of a happy and free people. Sound effects in keeping with the above.

As the curtain rises on the conference room it is deserted and the balcony windows are closed. Immediately, offstage is heard the CAPTAIN.

THE VOICE OF THE CAPTAIN: Make way for the president of the Republic. Make way, gentlemen. Make way!

GÓMEZ URBINA *enters. He is simply dressed in black but wears the presidential band of two colors across his chest. His appearance of fatigue, worry, and sadness is in notable contrast to the general atmosphere of happiness and light. He is followed by the* SECRETARY OF STATE *who wears formal morning dress and his many decorations. The* CAPTAIN *enters after them, closes the door, and takes up his position on guard in front of it.*

GÓMEZ URBINA: Did all go well, Mr. Secretary?

SECRETARY OF STATE: So well that one would say you've had much experience in receiving the diplomatic corps. This morning's reception was a complete and unusual success. I congratulate you on it, Mr. President, and I'm also proud to be able to tell you that the favorable opinion of almost every foreign country is on our side.

GÓMEZ URBINA (*absentmindedly*): Well, that's

something. Thank you very much. (*Something on the table has attracted his attention.*)

SECRETARY OF STATE: I asked to see you in private for a moment because—— (*He stops on seeing that* GÓMEZ URBINA, *without listening to him, has gone to the table and taken up an envelope from which he draws a sheet of paper that he seems to read with absorption, at the end the hint of a smile coming to his lips.*)

GÓMEZ URBINA: Captain . . . (*The* CAPTAIN *goes to him.*) Do you know how this comes to be here? (*He hands the empty envelope to the* CAPTAIN *who examines it.*)

THE CAPTAIN (*returning the envelope*): No, sir. Do you want me to ask——?

GÓMEZ URBINA: No, no. It's not important. (*He puts the sheet of paper and envelope in the left pocket of his coat, looks at his wristwatch, compares it with the clock on the wall, then sets the latter, causing it to strike eleven. All these actions are evidently performed for the purpose of giving himself time for a change in attitude. He turns to the* SECRETARY OF STATE.) I'm sorry, Mr. Secretary. You were saying——?

SECRETARY OF STATE: This isn't official, of course, but the ambassador of Britonia has informed me that, in his opinion, Demoland will soon open parleys for the resumption of diplomatic relations with us.

GÓMEZ URBINA: So? Well, I myself don't believe either that neighbors should turn their backs on one another.

SECRETARY OF STATE: It seems that the men who have the say in Demoland have concluded that it's more to their advantage for their nearest neighbors to enjoy full independence and to act freely on their own initiative.

GÓMEZ URBINA: Always slow but sure. Demoland's policy should necessarily differ from that of other great powers. I'm happy that at last they've seen this.

SECRETARY OF STATE: It's the Britonian ambas-

sador's opinion that Demoland's willing to agree to a settle-
ment on condition that you remain as president.

GÓMEZ URBINA: Which pleases me less. They're
really hopeless. The same old stomach pump, only with a
new nozzle, as they say in my hometown. (*He feels the
envelope in his left pocket and turns to the* CAPTAIN.) Captain, see if the home secretary is still in the palace. If he is,
request him to come here at once. It's urgent.

THE CAPTAIN: Yes, sir, but allow me to remind you
that the chief justice is still waiting in the private salon.

GÓMEZ URBINA: Then tell him to come to me
immediately. (*The* CAPTAIN *exits upstage right.*) So you
no longer think me too bad at international politics, my
friend?

SECRETARY OF STATE: I bow before your great
vision, Mr. President. (GÓMEZ URBINA *smiles bitterly.*) Do
you think that I should ask the Britonian ambassador to a
private luncheon so we can talk at greater length about
Demoland and ourselves? I'm certain that his country will
be interested in having him act as intermediary.

GÓMEZ URBINA: Yes, ask him to lunch. (*The* SEC-
RETARY OF STATE *bows and turns to exit downstage right.*)
Mr. Secretary . . . ? (*The* SECRETARY OF STATE *stops and
turns to* GÓMEZ URBINA.) Have you a cigarette? (*The* SEC-
RETARY *goes to him and holds out a cigarette case from
which* GÓMEZ URBINA *takes a cigarette. The* SECRETARY
strikes his lighter.) No, thank you. I'm not going to smoke
this. (*He looks at the cigarette while adding*) I just wanted
to tell it so face to face. (*Looking at the* SECRETARY OF
STATE *again.*) Don't forget that I'll need the presence of
the full Cabinet for the demonstration tonight. See you
later, my friend.(*The* SECRETARY OF STATE *exits.* GÓMEZ
URBINA *walks slowly to the table and there, still with his
air of preoccupation, shreds the cigarette to bits in an ashtray. He then wipes his fingers on the white handkerchief
that he wears in the breast pocket of his coat, after which
he looks at the handkerchief again and gives a deep sigh.*)

The CHIEF JUSTICE *enters upstage right.* GOMEZ URBINA *turns to him slowly.*

CHIEF JUSTICE: You're seeing great days, Mr. President, and it looks as if you had a star of your own. May God keep it bright for you until you reach my age, or even live beyond it.

GÓMEZ URBINA: Are you turning religious, Mr. Chief Justice?

CHIEF JUSTICE: My final escapade, sir. (*He pauses.*)

GÓMEZ URBINA: I want to show you this. Last night I found it pinned to my pillow. (*He takes a folded sheet of paper from the right pocket of his coat and hands it to the* CHIEF JUSTICE.)

CHIEF JUSTICE (*takes out his eyeglasses and holds them up to his eyes without putting them on. Reads*): "If you want to save your life that is so valuable to the country, call an election immediately and forget about the President Matías matter. A loyal citizen." (*He looks up at* GÓMEZ URBINA.) This sounds like a cloak and dagger conspirator of another century. Well?

GÓMEZ URBINA: A few moments ago, on returning to this room, I found this. (*He hands him the note that he put in his left pocket.*)

CHIEF JUSTICE (*as before*): "Your life will be in danger if you don't punish the assassins of Matías and especially so if you call an election. Go on with the first, but not the second. A faithful friend." Umhu, umhu. And——?

GÓMEZ URBINA: That's all. It's typically Indolandish that my life should be in danger in one case or the other, or in both cases, or even in some as yet unstated third. But what do you think will happen if I do both things at the same time, that is: call an election and punish the assassins of Matías?

CHIEF JUSTICE: Anonymous letters are always interesting because often they contain at least a modicum of the truth. May I, in turn, ask just what you have decided to do?

GÓMEZ URBINA: My duty. Get ready to do yours. (*An inquiring look from the* CHIEF JUSTICE). You're to preside over the special tribunal which will try both the intellectual and the actual assassins of President Matías.

CHIEF JUSTICE: A very special tribunal, indeed, and extraordinarily solemn.

GÓMEZ URBINA: The assassination of a president is an extraordinary crime.

CHIEF JUSTICE: I suppose that you already have all the clues in your hands?

GÓMEZ URBINA: All.

CHIEF JUSTICE: Will you allow me a remark?

GÓMEZ URBINA: Of course. Make it, Mr. Chief Justice.

CHIEF JUSTICE: When a man has done as much for his country as you have, he must weigh matters very carefully. There can be acts of a president which seeming to be just and actually being so, can, nevertheless, lead to destruction. My old friend Justice is a blade of many edges. If my inferences are correct, sir, I'm afraid that you won't be able to punish the assassins of Matías unless you remain in the presidency and assume dictatorial power.

GÓMEZ URBINA: Be that as it may, I shan't continue in office very long. I think I've found the formula which will enable me to call the election today, Mr. Chief Justice. (*The* CHIEF JUSTICE *makes a gesture.*) I have it all thought out already.

CHIEF JUSTICE: You're a brave man, too. But have you thought about who can carry on the new policy regarding Demoland as laid down by you? Independence is dangerous when it isn't under the strictest control. It can lead to actions that are irreparable.

GÓMEZ URBINA: I have faith in the destiny of Indoland. Not one of its presidents, however incompetent or corrupt though he might have been, has been able to mar that destiny fundamentally. The people of Indoland move by instinct and inertia, Mr. Chief Justice. Once in a hundred years or so they combine their instinct with faith. I'm trying to adapt myself to the people's rhythm of moving, that's all.

CHIEF JUSTICE: You could do some great things if you'd remain in office as president—with or without seeing justice done to the assassins, and with or without my old friend the Constitution.

GÓMEZ URBINA: I've thought of all that, too. But I'm only an ordinary man and have no desire to be a dictator or tyrant.

CHIEF JUSTICE: Not even to save your country?

GÓMEZ URBINA: Espccially not to wrong it. I come from the people, from nothingness.

CHIEF JUSTICE: That's just where the dictators come from.

GÓMEZ URBINA: But that's not for me. I simply want to go back to where I came from and that's all. It's my way of being free. I've already thought all this out, I tell you. I think it would be abominable to be feared and to know that others would say that I was right only because they were in terror of mc.

CHIEF JUSTICE: Well, be all that as it may, you're a most exemplary man. Even more, a rare specimen of a man. Take care of yourself.

GÓMEZ URBINA: You flatter me. Incidentally, I want you to announce the news of my decision to the president of the official party and to the Speaker of Congress who're waiting outside.

CHIEF JUSTICE: I understand that you've let General Meléndez keep his position as president of the official party.

GÓMEZ URBINA: Such matters must be kept quiet —in the family closet, as it were. The general readily understood that his house arrest was meant only to prevent him from making another mistake—or several. He has apologized to me fully, and now I know that I can count on his life . . . never on his good will.

CHIEF JUSTICE: You're incredible. Yet it was the most sensible thing to do. Anyone else, however——.

The CAPTAIN *enters downstage right.*

THE CAPTAIN: Pardon me, Mr. President. The home secretary had already gone. I telephoned your message to his private secretary, though, who told me that the home secretary had left in answer to some very urgent call and that he didn't know where the secretary was to be found.

GÓMEZ URBINA: Everything's urgent in this country. Thank you, Captain. Can I count on you, then, Mr. Chief Justice?

CHIEF JUSTICE: Without any reservations whatsoever, sir.

GÓMEZ URBINA: Thank you. Now I must go over my speech to the people for tonight, but I'll ask you not to leave the palace, and I don't want your colleagues to either. I'll be needing you all before long.

The CHIEF JUSTICE *bows in silence.* GÓMEZ URBINA *exits upstage left. The* CAPTAIN *stands guard at the door downstage right. The* CHIEF JUSTICE *stops before him.*

CHIEF JUSTICE: Captain——.
THE CAPTAIN: Mr. Chief Justice?
CHIEF JUSTICE: You who read so much will understand better than anyone else what I have to say.

THE CAPTAIN: I'd like to think so, sir, but you're too deep for me.

CHIEF JUSTICE: An extraordinary man, the president . . . and don't forget that I've known more than a dozen of them. It's a pity, though, that he hasn't a wife and children. He needs someone very close to him. I don't know why, but he makes me think of Lincoln and his melancholy after the end of the Civil War in his country and especially just before—— (*He breaks off.*)

THE CAPTAIN: Are you suggesting the possibility of an attempt on the president's life?

CHIEF JUSTICE: My dear boy! On the very day of his apotheosis? You're letting your imagination run away with you, Captain. No, no, it's only that the man is alone too much and loneliness is a bad bedfellow.

THE CAPTAIN: You make me feel easier now.

CHIEF JUSTICE: In any case, it would be better for you not to leave him, not even for a moment, and especially tonight. I don't like the idea of his getting notes here without even knowing who brings them.

THE CAPTAIN: That's worrying me, too. If you know anything, sir, I beg you to——.

CHIEF JUSTICE: All I know is that politics, like everything in this world, is the work of man's own hands, and that men spend their while here in an unstable condition. Their lives are a long oscillation between stupidity and genius, between bravery and cowardice, between criminality and sainthood—and seldom do they become fully one thing or the other. This man, our president, has already shown genius—nothing now stands in the way of his being stupid. There's nothing to keep him from being a coward now that he has been so brave. There remains to him the choice between being a criminal or a saint . . . and I'm afraid that he'll choose sainthood. There're always others, too, who're confronted with the same dilemma, and one doesn't know which side they'll finally fall on. In any event, keep calm, Captain, so that you can be on the alert. (*He exits quickly upstage right.*)

The CAPTAIN *makes as though to follow him for more information, but the ringing of the telephone stops him.*

THE CAPTAIN (*speaking into the telephone*): The president's office. Yes, Captain Peláez. (*Pause.*) Impossible.

The president is very busy. (*Pause.*) Ah, it's you, Mr. Secretary? The president ordered me to locate you as soon as
possible. (*Pause.*) Ah! I understand. You're not in your
office. But he's very anxious to see you. I'll tell him that . . .
(*Pause.*) Very well, if you prefer . . . (*He makes a quick
note.*) I'll repeat your message: He's not to see the ex-
presidents till he has talked with you. Right?

The door downstage right opens and COUNSELORS
GERMÁN *and* AGUIRRE *enter. The* CAPTAIN *looks up.*

THE CAPTAIN (*into the telephone again*): I'm afraid
it's a bit late, sir, but I'll tell him anyhow. (*Pause.*) What's
that? You're coming here at once? I'll tell him that, too.
(*Pause.*) Yes, sir. (*He replaces the receiver, then salutes the
newcomers.*)

COUNSELOR GERMÁN: Good morning, Captain
Peláez. Where's the president?

THE CAPTAIN: In his private office, sir. I'll tell him
that you gentlemen have come. (*He draws himself up, then
goes to the door upstage right and gives it three quiet
knocks. There is no reply. He knocks again. The* EX-PRESI-
DENTS *begin to pay attention to what is happening. The*
CAPTAIN *knocks again.*)

THE VOICE OF GÓMEZ URBINA: Not now.

THE CAPTAIN: Pardon, sir, but Counselors Germán
and Aguirre are here. There's also a very urgent message
from——.

THE VOICE OF GÓMEZ URBINA: Not now.

THE CAPTAIN: But, sir——.

THE VOICE OF GÓMEZ URBINA: Later. Ask them
to wait a moment.

The CAPTAIN *makes a sign of resignation to the others.*

COUNSELOR GERMÁN: Don't take it so much to
heart, Captain. We'll wait. And, by the way, I want to ask
a favor of you.

THE CAPTAIN: At your service, sir.

COUNSELOR GERMÁN: I left a package for the president in my motorcar. Will you be so kind as to get it?

THE CAPTAIN (*disturbed*): Counselor, I beg you to pardon me . . . I'm on guard.

COUNSELOR GERMÁN: I can't trust anyone but you for this. You won't be gone long. (*Resignedly, the* CAPTAIN *bows and starts for the door downstage right.*) And by the way, Captain. (*The* CAPTAIN *turns around.*) My motorcar's in the annex behind the palace. (*The* CAPTAIN *exits.*) I like that chap, colleague. He's a walking model of the new style Indolandish army officer. I'm sorry I didn't have him, or someone like him, when I was here. But I'd rather be without him for a while. (*He laughs.*) He's so absolutely loyal to Gómez Urbina that he makes me nervous. (*Aguirre does not answer.*) You seem to have something on your mind. What's the matter?

COUNSELOR AGUIRRE (*suddenly coming to himself*): I beg your pardon. (*He smiles.*) Oh, nothing, nothing! I was thinking about two things. One of them is: What has he called us here for this time?

COUNSELOR GERMÁN (*laughing*): Not for money again. He knows very well that he can't get any more out of us. The mines themselves have a limit. So that it easy. I myself feel calmer, lighter even than after the . . . our recent contribution.

COUNSELOR AGUIRRE: You're telling me . . . I mean about the limit. But the other matter I was thinking about was those big crowds I met in the streets that're on their way here.

COUNSELOR GERMÁN: The country's demonstration of gratitude is set for midnight, but, characteristically, our Indolanders couldn't resist making a full day of it.

COUNSELOR AGUIRRE: I don't like it at all. (*With a sudden change of subject.*) Do you think he'll really call an election?

COUNSELOR GERMÁN: Do you think we'll have an earthquake today? In Indoland, as well all know, you

can expect anything at any time, including even the opposite of what you're expecting.

COUNSELOR AGUIRRE: If he wants to stay in
office he'll have to amend the Constitution.

COUNSELOR GERMÁN: That old rag?

COUNSELOR AGUIRRE: That relic, colleague!

COUNSELOR GERMÁN: Then that old rag that's a
relic. Yes, true. The poor thing has been patched up more
and is dirtier than a beggar's shirt. But just try to tamper
with that rag to be reelected and there'll be riots and
they'll assassinate you if they can. Don't forget that we
have made a tradition of rags and the worship of empty
words.

COUNSELOR AGUIRRE: But what would you do
if you were in his place?

COUNSELOR GERMÁN: If I'd done what he has,
I'd just sit there in the president's chair for as long as
possible. (*He sits down.*) He's an unusual case, indeed: a
mediocre man with good ideas. Let's see if he really can
carry them out.

The door downstage right opens and GENERAL PUEBLA
enters.

GENERAL PUEBLA: Gentlemen——.

COUNSELOR AGUIRRE: You, too?

GENERAL PUEBLA: The people are delirious! I've
never seen anything like it—not even when the Revolution
broke out, and certainly not in any of the most crucial
moments of our history since then.

COUNSELOR GERMÁN: The counselor and I are
playing a new game, General. It's: What would you do if
you were in *his* place? (*He points toward the door upstage
left.*)

GENERAL PUEBLA: The country's economic independence having been gloriously achieved, I'd retire to my
ranch.

COUNSELOR GERMÁN (*laughing*): But you're forgetting that he hasn't a ranch. Where could he retire to?

The door downstage right opens and DR. SUÁREZ MEZA *enters. While he is exchanging greetings and handshakes with the others,* GENERAL ELOY *enters.*

DR. SUÁREZ MEZA: Good morning, dear friends.

COUNSELOR AGUIRRE: So it's a council of war.

DR. SUÁREZ MEZA: I don't know how I managed to get here. The crowd is unbelievable. I've never seen . . . A most well-earned homage, indeed, but——.

GENERAL ELOY: But much too premature. I don't like it.

COUNSELOR AGUIRRE: I agree with you, General. I don't like it either.

COUNSELOR GERMÁN: Premature? Every Indolander is by nature the early bird of the old saying.

GENERAL ELOY: This is the first time in my political career that I've seen Indolanders enthusiastic about greeting their president. In the past they were only too anxious to get away from him and ran like rabbits.

COUNSELOR AGUIRRE: I'm afraid something's going to happen to him. I've heard rumors——.

GENERAL ELOY: So have I, and I have my fears, too . . . but mine are about the possibility of his extending his term.

COUNSELOR AGUIRRE: Counselor Germán and I were trying to figure out the answers to the latest questions: Why has he called us together again? And what's he going to do next? What would you two do——?

The door downstage right opens again and GENERAL AVALOS *enters followed by the* CAPTAIN *who carries a small package which he gives to* COUNSELOR GERMÁN.

COUNSELOR GERMÁN: Thank you, Captain. (*He rises and places the package on the conference table.*)

COUNSELOR AGUIRRE: What would you do if you were in his place?

GENERAL AVALOS: Call an election immediately.

GENERAL ELOY: I'd extend my time in office. I'm afraid he's going to do just that because it's the most logical thing to do . . . and it's what I'd do myself.

DR. SUÁREZ MEZA: I think we now have a lifetime president, gentlemen. Ah, but if I'd been his age in my time, I'd never have resigned!

COUNSELOR AGUIRRE: Any extension of the presidential term seems to me to be extremely dangerous.

COUNSELOR GERMÁN: You said a lifetime president, Doctor, and why not if he knows how to make the most of his position? Remember that hero of the opposition who when once he sat down in the president's chair wouldn't get up from it till he was forced to?

GENERAL AVALOS: History doesn't repeat itself . . . nor should it. Indoland got rid of that president. We repudiate dictators by natural impulse. They simply don't fit into our climate.

COUNSELOR AGUIRRE: But the times are much more difficult now.

GENERAL ELOY: And how! It's one thing to make a people free, but quite another to govern them in their freedom.

COUNSELOR GERMÁN: A freedom that turned out to be so dear for us!

A bell rings. Every one falls silent. The CAPTAIN *goes to the door upstage left and opens it.* GÓMEZ URBINA *appears.*

THE CAPTAIN: Sir, the home secretary——.

GÓMEZ URBINA (*calmly*): Later, Captain. Good morning, gentlemen, and many thanks to each of you for your advice.

COUNSELOR GERMÁN (*laughing*): Oh, the devil! We forgot about those famous concealed microphones!

(*He takes the package from the table.*) For tonight's ceremony, colleague, I've brought you the presidential band.
made of strands of enameled gold which was presented to
me during my last year in office.

GÓMEZ URBINA (*seriously*): I accept it with thanks
and will send it to the State Museum, colleague. Captain,
please leave us. When I ring the bell, show in the chief
justice, the Speaker of Congress, and the president of the
official party. (*The* CAPTAIN *comes to attention and exits.*)
Sit down, gentlemen, and make yourselves comfortable.
(*All do so, some taking out cigarettes and lighting them.*)
Now this isn't a question of vanity, but I do feel that in
several ways my term is quite different from those of you
gentlemen. And I'm not speaking of the break in relations
with Demoland.

COUNSELOR AGUIRRE: Historical circumstances
are always different, of course.

GENERAL ELOY: The country's no longer what it
was in the happy-go-lucky days of the revolution. Our
people are beginning to think.

DR. SUÁREZ MEZA: I'm of another opinion. The
president's always going to be only one more victim on
the sacrificial stone of the jokes our people just have to
make about their government.

GENERAL PUEBLA: Right. They wouldn't spare
even their own mothers there. But it must be admitted
that the president's opportunity has been splendid, splendid. It's a thing——.

COUNSELOR GERMÁN: Pardon me, but I suggest
that we listen to the president himself who hasn't finished
saying what he wants to.

GÓMEZ URBINA (*smiling*): Thank you, Counselor.
Nothing escapes you. Always the practical man. Well,
then, the difference to which I referred a moment ago in
my term is of a personal nature and a consequence of my
extreme limitations. I accepted office for two reasons: one,
to see justice done to the assassins of my noble friend Presi-

dent Martías and so turn Indoland into a real home for justice because so far the poor thing has only walked the streets here. My second reason for accepting office was to prove to myself that the satisfactions and temptations of power are less lasting than a man's conscience. My experience here has led me to the firm conclusion that justice and democracy must go along together.

COUNSELOR AGUIRRE: I applaud that conclusion without any reservation whatsoever.

COUNSELOR GERMÁN (*raising a finger to his lips and smiling*): Chsst! Chsst! He hasn't finished.

GÓMEZ URBINA: I recognize, however, that I've got into a blind alley and only you can help me. (GERMÁN *makes an instinctive defensive movement.*) That's not necessary, Counselor. This time the problem is moral and political, not economic. (GERMÁN *breathes deeply in relief and smiles.*) Now I want your answers to the following questions. Can I initiate a trial of national importance and at the same time call an election without exposing the country to the danger of anarchy and revolution? Or should I postpone the election and make certain that justice is done, or should I leave the latter task to my successor?

GENERAL AVALOS: In these matters you should follow your own conscience.

GÓMEZ URBINA: My conscience urges me on to both courses. I've called you together to inform you that I now have in my hands all the evidence necessary to punish the intellectual author of the assassination of President Matías. This is, as you all know, what I want to do, but I must think of the country first of all. If I do go through with the trial, I'll have to remain in office instead of calling an election, and will thus expose Indoland to a possible revolution. The people expect an election and there're too many interests involved for a postponement to be considered. But if I do call an election, my government will lose the strength necessary for me to see that justice is done as there'd be danger of a civil war because the intellectual assassin of the incorruptible and great Matías is also a man of national importance, gentlemen.

Expressions of curiosity and astonishment by the EX-PRESIDENTS.

GENERAL ELOY: I think you should be more explicit, Mr. President. We can't risk giving you advice in such a matter without a clearer statement on your part.

DR. SUÁREZ MEZA: Important as the man you refer to may be——.

COUNSELOR GERMÁN: If he exists——.

COUNSELOR AGUIRRE: I agree absolutely with General Eloy.

GENERAL PUEBLA: I, too, think that this whole matter should be made entirely clear to us.

GÓMEZ URBINA (*imitating by a gesture the balancing of scales*): Very well. To put the case briefly: the man who ordered the assassination of President Matías is one of you six gentlemen.

Incredulity and general stupefaction. GERMÁN *is the first to recover his voice, but a second later they all— except for* GENERAL AVALOS—*speak violently.*

COUNSELOR GERMÁN: Are you insane?

COUNSELOR AGUIRRE: This is absolutely intolerable. The most impossible accusation——.

GENERAL ELOY: Aren't you content with having plucked us clean?

DR. SUÁREZ MEZA: Monstrous! Monstrous!

GENERAL PUEBLA: This wounds me deeply in my honor. I can't permit——.

All at the same time

GÓMEZ URBINA (*energetically*): One moment, please. Those who're innocent have nothing to fear. And one moment more, because you must understand that what concerns me most in all this is the fate of our country.

But I've reached the only understanding possible with my own conscience, gentlemen, and so have found two ways out. The first is to ask the guilty one to do away with himself at once. Thus I could, with a clear conscience, call on election and save the country from international disgrace. But if the guilty man I refer to doesn't do as I've suggested, I'll take him with my own two hands to the tribunal itself. The second way out is for me to be eliminated as President Matías was, because only so could I fail to carry out what I know it's my duty to.

COUNSELOR AGUIRRE: That would be the greatest of all mistakes, the——.

GENERAL ELOY: What nonsense! We must be practical——.

DR. SUÁREZ MEZA: Suicide! Or assassination! He's self-destructive. He's——.

COUNSELOR GERMÁN: I repeat what I said before, he's an Indolander in the worst sense of the word.

GENERAL PUEBLA: Where are we anyhow and where's this leading us? I can't conceive——.

All at the same time

A growing roar offstage drowns out the voices. While the above have been speaking, GÓMEZ URBINA, *the first to hear the noise outside, has gone to the central balcony and parted the drapes slightly. He then opens the door downstage right and calls.*

GÓMEZ URBINA: Captain Peláez!

THE CAPTAIN (*appearing in the doorway*): Sir?

GÓMEZ URBINA: What does that crowd in the plaza mean and what are they shouting? Find out at once.

The CAPTAIN *comes to attention and turns to leave but bumps into the* HOME SECRETARY *who rushes in breathless.*

HOME SECRETARY: I can tell you that, Mr. President. (*He looks around.*) But to do so, I must, with these gentlemen's leave, request an immediate private audience with you.

> GÓMEZ URBINA *thinks a moment, then turns to the* EX-PRESIDENTS *who instinctively form a compact group as though of pillars of salt.*

GÓMEZ URBINA: You now know my deepest thoughts, gentlemen, and also the truth. I'm going on to the very end of all this. I beg you—except one—not to leave the palace. I want you with me later on.

THE CAPTAIN: Sir, the president of the official party and the Speaker of Congress——.

GÓMEZ URBINA: Tell them that to wait is to be patriotic now.

> *The* CAPTAIN *exits. The* EX-PRESIDENTS *look at one another, some shrug their shoulders. They leave two by two.* GÓMEZ URBINA *and the* HOME SECRETARY *remain alone.*

HOME SECRETARY: I was afraid this would happen. Just by looking at their faces I could tell that you've already dropped the bomb.

GÓMEZ URBINA: Well, did you want it to explode in my hands?

HOME SECRETARY: And you probably were so outspoken as to give names. That's your business, of course, but I wash my hands of this matter and resign.

GÓMEZ URBINA (*calming himself and smiling*): Again?

HOME SECRETARY: Again and a hundred times more, and at once. I can't and won't serve a dictator.

GÓMEZ URBINA: Are you beside yourself? I, a dictator!

HOME SECRETARY: Even if you don't want to be one, you are.

GÓMEZ URBINA: Explain yourself. I demand it.

HOME SECRETARY: I'm going to explain myself heavy-handedly, Mr. President. The crowd that has gathered out there in the plaza twelve hours ahead of time has come to urge you to perpetuate yourself in office.

GÓMEZ URBINA: I was expecting something like this, but I won't do it.

HOME SECRETARY: But what you don't know is that some John Doe of your hometown or my own, without knowing what he was really doing, started a spontaneous nationwide plebiscite in favor of extending your term in the presidency. All the public offices of the country have been swamped with votes during the past twenty-four hours. A referendum has been taken and it gives you at least seventy-five percent of the valid votes of the country, including those of the women.

GÓMEZ URBINA (*pausing, then cautiously*): I suppose you're certain of all this?

HOME SECRETARY: Against my own heart I am. But the worst of it is you'll have to accept.

GÓMEZ URBINA: I can thank the people and entrust them to the most able man available. Don't you know me yet?

HOME SECRETARY: Precisely because I do know you, I know there's no man more stubborn than you. Your pledge to see justice done obliges you to go along with this new development.

GÓMEZ URBINA: But the matter is already settled. I made it clear to the ex-presidents and, although I didn't mention any names as you suppose, the guilty one knows that I know who he is.

HOME SECRETARY: That's what you think.

GÓMEZ URBINA: But didn't you yourself give me the irrefutable proof?

HOME SECRETARY: This is where the irony comes in. The proof I gave you is all false.

GÓMEZ URBINA (*after an astonished pause*): Have I heard you right?

HOME SECRETARY: False, I say, false as a president's promise. A little more than half an hour ago one of the colonels who was tried for the actual crime of assassinating President Matías hanged himself in the military prison. Before hanging himself he left this written statement. (*He draws it from his pocket, hands it to* GÓMEZ URBINA, *and continues.*) Your courageous attitude in the showdown with Demoland impressed him so forcefully that he felt compelled to reveal the true authors of the plot.

GÓMEZ URBINA (*looking up from the letter*): But this is impossible. Were I to believe it, I'd die!

HOME SECRETARY: When you were on trial and admitted to me that Matías was the man you'd been shielding, I should have suspected the truth. Your absolute faith in him prevented me, however, from letting any doubts develop. But you have to look facts in the face now, sir. President Matías wasn't an incorruptible man. He wasn't even an honorable man. It's evident now that he was killed while about to sign a treaty that would virtually have sold Indoland out to a foreign power. He was also quite prepared to continue the old régime of depredation and abuses, and to sacrifice the only thing we really possess: our national independence.

GÓMEZ URBINA: I don't believe it. (*With energy.*) I don't believe it. The other proof was too logical.

HOME SECRETARY: When confronted with the colonel's confession, all the others who're also being held loosened their tongues, too. The logic you refer to is precisely what took us in from the beginning. It was part of the plan to attribute the assassination to the ex-president against whom all Matías's policies were apparently directed. But the tyrannicide was this man. (*He points energetically to the letter* GÓMEZ URBINA *is still holding.*) I have documentary proof with me. (*He takes more papers from his pocket and gives them to* GÓMEZ URBINA.) Now do you understand why you must accept the dictatorship?

GÓMEZ URBINA (*he looks at his hands, walks back*

and forth a moment, then stops): I still can't believe it.
But if this is true, he'll have gone after what I said in here
a while ago. If for some reason, he's still out there, ask him
in.

HOME SECRETARY (*holding out another sheet*):
Don't forget, Mr. President, that I've resigned. Only by
respecting the will of the people can you finish off this man
and see justice done as you want to.

GÓMEZ URBINA: But, by God, man, do you think
I was born to be a tyrant! Power amuses me because every
one repeats my jokes that in my hometown were scoffed at.
It also amuses me because I've been able to carry out some
national hopes that any drunkard in a barroom on payday
would have jeered at as impossible. And, finally, this power
amuses me because it made it possible for me to smash
some hypocrisy and fraud when I had a pile of rocks at
hand and could make light of the police while I threw
them. Nothing more. I've wanted to serve Indoland. But I
can do so only in my own way.

HOME SECRETARY: As you wish. Your fate is in
your own hands. Decide what you will, and may God help
you.

GÓMEZ URBINA: Does man really decide? Well,
show him in and let's get this over with.

HOME SECRETARY: Before obeying your last
order, I want to remind you of this: the truth is that the
tyrannicide is always at least in part right. The man who
kills a snake in the woods, or a wild beast in the mountains, or a shark in the sea is a hero. Amongst us he is a
hero who kills a cockroach or a spider, or runs down a
pedestrian in the street. Be very careful in what you do.
Remember that Matías passes as a martyr. Don't make
another one now.

GÓMEZ URBINA: Wise advice. Thank you, my
friend. Now ask him in.

The HOME SECRETARY *looks at him steadily a moment,*

nods, and exits downstage right. GÓMEZ URBINA *rubs his hands sadly, lowers his head and walks up and down. The noise of the crowd which is still undefinable increases offstage. Suddenly the door downstage right opens and, headed by* GERMÁN, *the six* EX-PRESIDENTS *return. The* HOME SECRETARY *enters behind them.* GÓMEZ URBINA *is disagreeably surprised.*

GÓMEZ URBINA: What's the meaning of this intrusion, gentlemen?

COUNSELOR GERMÁN: It means, Mr. President, that we've considered your words of a short while ago and that we profoundly resent your accusation. Each of us has served Indoland in his own way and even though some profited in doing so, they profited because they made it possible for the country to profit. But we refuse categorically to permit you to accuse any one of us of doing what you've charged. We're ready to insist upon an investigation by Congress and, if you carry matters any further, you'll have to face a revolution. Don't forget that you yourself made us untouchable and that, thanks to your own idea, we are the saviors of the territorial integrity and the liberty of Indoland.

GÓMEZ URBINA (*cold, calm*): An excellent speech, colleague, but it won't keep me from carrying out what I intend to, although now it's going to hurt me more than before for reasons best known to me.

COUNSELOR AGUIRRE: Then I can see no way other than the one you yourself pointed out: dictatorship, violation of the national Constitution, the——.

GENERAL ELOY: Right. Just what I saw coming.

GENERAL PUEBLA: Before taking such a step, you should consider the fact that we're solidly agreed to deny your accusation.

DR. SUÁREZ MEZA: Our stand is that no man who has been a president of Indoland should be exposed to such disgrace.

GÓMEZ URBINA: Even though he has killed a president?

GENERAL PUEBLA: The Revolution is——.

GÓMEZ URBINA: *Was* the Revolution, General. We can't go on justifying or covering up anything whatsoever in its name. But you're saying nothing, General Avalos.

GENERAL AVALOS: I'm of the opinion that you should be guided by your own conscience and do your duty. Nothing is more important than Indoland.

GÓMEZ URBINA: True, true. As for the rest, I must tell you gentlemen that the situation here has changed very much within the past few minutes. As the home secretary will bear me out, the people, in a spontaneous plebiscite, have elected me as president for an unlimited period. This means that nothing else is necessary. I can, if the well-being of the people so requires, annul the Constitution and promulgate a new one. I can change the system of our government from its roots to the topmost leaves. I can even change the whole political life of the country. This isn't what I want to do, though. I was ready to call an election and make the condition that the intellectual assassin of Matías would eliminate himself or give himself up voluntarily. But your attitude has made me determine to take the bull where he has to be taken: by the horns. This will simply everything: there won't be an election now, and I'll see that justice is done regardless of whatever may be necessary. (*Pause.*) Now have you anything to say?

Astounded, all look at the HOME SECRETARY *who shows them a whole sheaf of telegrams which pass from hand to hand.*

COUNSELOR AGUIRRE: Seventy-five percent of the votes! This changes everything, naturally. The will of the people is sovereign.

GENERAL ELOY: Above all, if the army is with them.

GÓMEZ URBINA: Is it, General Avalos?

GENERAL AVALOS (*firmly*): It is, Mr. President. You have my word for that.

DR. SUÁREZ MEZA: And you have my full admiration and also my envy. You can now make your dreams come true . . . and . . . and count on me in every way.

GENERAL PUEBLA: I congratulate you, really, but I urge you to move with caution, especially in this matter of seeing justice done.

COUNSELOR GERMÁN: If all this is true——.

GÓMEZ URBINA: Do you doubt it? Then go out onto the balcony and look at the people in the plaza.

COUNSELOR GERMÁN (*smiling*): Now it's I who haven't finished. I wanted to tell you that you'll have changed the history of Indoland forever.

GÓMEZ URBINA: Can I count on all of you—in every way?

GENERAL ELOY: Well, frankly, yes. What the devil!

COUNSELOR AGUIRRE: You ask that after this triumph of democracy!

GENERAL PUEBLA: As before and always, Mr. President.

DR. SUÁREZ MEZA: Of course, of course.

COUNSELOR GERMÁN: Even the shade of a doubt is offensive.

Laughter and shaking of hands.

GÓMEZ URBINA (*with a bitter smile*): Thank you, and now that the official family of the Revolution has spoken, I request you to leave me alone. I still have an important matter to attend to. I'll need you later on when I speak to the people.

They begin to exit while speaking ad lib in lowered voices. The HOME SECRETARY *looks significantly at* GÓMEZ URBINA *who nods.*

GÓMEZ URBINA: General Avalos, will you wait a moment?

AVALOS *returns. The* HOME SECRETARY *exits. When*
AVALOS *and* GÓMEZ URBINA *are left alone and the door*
has been shut, GÓMEZ URBINA *walks slowly up and*
down for a moment. AVALOS *waits patiently.*

GÓMEZ URBINA: Have you ever lost faith in a
friend, General?

GENERAL AVALOS: Not only in a friend but in
one who was also my chief. That's even harder.

GÓMEZ URBINA: I remember that, and so believe
what you've said. (*Pause.*) Did you know, General, that
President Matías wasn't really an incorruptible man?

GENERAL AVALOS: I knew that he was a weak
man.

GÓMEZ URBINA: Did you know that he was preparing to support the vested interests of the old régime and
was even willing to go to the extent of helping to destroy
the country's best interests?

GENERAL AVALOS: I was aware that he wasn't a
Indolander.

GÓMEZ URBINA: And did you know that his coming to power was to be the means of delivering Indoland
over economically to a foreign power for fifty years?

GENERAL AVALOS: I knew that, too.

GÓMEZ URBINA: Well, then, only he and his
closest and most secret associates, in addition to his
assassin——.

GENERAL AVALOS: I'd call the last named his
executioner.

GÓMEZ URBINA: It's one and the same thing. But
besides himself and his most secret associates, his . . . executioner, and you are the only ones who knew all this,
General.

GENERAL AVALOS: I think that his executioner—
or assassin, if you prefer—acted for the country's benefit
and wanted only to protect the fundamental idea of the
Revolution.

GÓMEZ URBINA: But that's precisely why I spoke before of a new Constitution, of a new system of justice, of an unprecedented social organization. Up to now almost the only result of the Revolution has been—as someone has said—to make the rich richer and the poor poorer.

GENERAL AVALOS (*shows some warmth for the first time*): And what did you expect? But that means nothing when the idea itself is taken into account. The revolution can't be condemned outright because of some evil or filthy men, or because of some thieves and bandits who took part in it! That would be like condemning a good mother because one of her sons has turned out to be a no good idler or thief.

GÓMEZ URBINA: True, but can we judge the Revolution in the abstract? No. General. No. Men do the work of men. To hold to the opposite would be absurdly ambiguous. It was men, and men alone, who made the Revolution.

GENERAL AVALOS: I'd say instead that it was the Revolution that made the men.

GÓMEZ URBINA: In that case, wouldn't it, then, have cost just the same to have made them all good?

GENERAL AVALOS: Men can be evil and inferior even when the ideas are good. Ideas live longer than men.

GÓMEZ URBINA: I agree with you on that. But, can ideas be good or real without men? Surely you're not going to tell me that your own line of conduct follows the vague outline of a cloud?

GENERAL AVALOS: The people are no more than a cloud that is always changing its shape, Mr. President. They have a fixed form only within some of us. That is to say that the people exist only for those who believe in them —and I believe in them.

GÓMEZ URBINA (*looking carefully at his hands*): Curiously enough, so do I. (*A slight pause.*) General Avalos, I'll never forget that you saved the country again in the recent crisis. But I don't know which pains me more:

Matías's betrayal which seems to follow an ingrained tradition of ours as the stigma of an incurable people; or his assassination which so disheartens me because it has plunged us back into the night of our history, while at the same time making a myth of him. An end must be put to all this. Now you're the head of the army because I made you that. I therefore leave the immediate punishment of the assassin . . . or of the executioner . . . of Matías in your hands. Here you have the confession of one of his actual assassins who has just placed himself beyond the reach of human justice. Justice, General, is the privilege of the people and is to be executed by their government, not by any one man, no matter who he may be. I therefore order you to proceed without any more loss of time. Were I to order this of another, perhaps I wouldn't be obeyed. But I trust you.

> *For a moment, the two measure each other with a look in such a way that it becomes clear that* GÓMEZ URBINA *has pronounced* AVALOS's *death sentence. The latter then draws himself up stiffly.*

GENERAL AVALOS (*inscrutable*): I assure you that your order will be carried out, Mr. President. (*He gives a stiff salute and exits.*)

> GÓMEZ URBINA *reflects a moment, heaves a deep, bitter sigh, and then shrugs his shoulders as one does when having a chill. The noise outside increases. The* CAPTAIN *enters.*

THE CAPTAIN: Sir, the people have already overflowed from the plaza into the palace itself. There's no way of holding them back. The guards wouldn't dare attempt to. You yourself will have to calm them. They must see you.

GÓMEZ URBINA: And why not? This is their hour.

Show in the ex-presidents, the chief justice, the Speaker of Congress, and the president of the official party at once, as well as the Cabinet members who are waiting.

> *The* CAPTAIN *exits.* GÓMEZ URBINA *smiles sadly while he waits. All those he sent for enter, except* GENERAL AVALOS.

SPEAKER OF CONGRESS: Mr. President of the Republic, before announcing this to the people out there who are gathered in the greatest and most solemn demonstration in our history, the Congress of Indoland wishes, through my humble person, to express its profound gratitude to you. This parchment, inscribed in letters of gold, proclaims you to be the Father of the Economic Liberation of our country and decrees that this happy day of the nineteenth of June be designated for coming generations as the Day of Our Economic Independence. (*He extends the parchment to* GÓMEZ URBINA.)

GÓMEZ URBINA: Thank you very much, Mr. Speaker of Congress. (*He takes the parchment.*) Open the balcony windows, Captain.

> *As the general air of expectancy increases, the* CAPTAIN *opens the balcony windows, first on the right, then on the left, and then in the center. The roar of the crowd increases within the room. Fanfares and* vivas *are heard.* GÓMEZ URBINA *walks slowly with a firm step to the center balcony. Just before he reaches it, the* CAPTAIN *goes to him.*

THE CAPTAIN: Mr. President?

GÓMEZ URBINA (*looking at him coolly*): What is it, Captain?

THE CAPTAIN: I know my rank doesn't entitle me to such an honor, but will you permit me to accompany you out there?

GÓMEZ URBINA: If you want to, yes, and thank you. You give me the feeling of having a son.

Both go out onto the balcony. GÓMEZ URBINA *raises his arms to calm the tumult which gradually subsides. Silence, more or less, follows.*

COUNSELOR GERMÁN: *Papa habemus.*

SPEAKER OF CONGRESS: It's the will of the people.

COUNSELOR GERMÁN: Only a passing moment as even were ours. These people are never content.

COUNSELOR AGUIRRE: But if the law is on his side, why not?

CHIEF JUSTICE: So long as the law you refer to isn't the law of the jungle——.

GENERAL PUEBLA: We're living through a great moment.

GENERAL ELOY: Provided he lives through it himself——.

DR. SUÁREZ MEZA: Quiet. He's going to speak. Let's listen to him.

GÓMEZ URBINA: People of Indoland. I revere and respect your sovereign will, but I want to ask you to relieve me of an obligation that is greater than I have strength or capacity for. I beg your permission to call an election so that the most capable, the cleanest, the best, and the most exemplary citizen amongst us may come into office to govern this land that produces the miracle of our daily bread. (*Sounds of protest from the crowd which he quiets.*) This is my way of serving you best: to yield my position to him who can do more for the fatherland. Permit me——.

The crowd does not let him finish. An infernal and glorious tumult breaks out anew. Voices chant rhythmically: No! No! No! Gómez Urbina! Gómez Urbina! Gómez Urbina! *Each phrase is repeated three times.*

Again GÓMEZ URBINA *waves his arms and partial silence is gradually restored.*

GÓMEZ URBINA: Thank you. But how could I ever really thank you? For that I'd need a voice that could reach into the whole country and thousands of hands to shake your hands. But I still have more to tell you. As I've promised, the assassins of President Matías will be punished, but it will be a tremendous shock as well as a much needed lesson for Indoland and her politicians to learn that Matías was no martyr. He was only a trai——.

Above his words the loud sound of a shot rings out. Shouts rise but die down into the absolute silence that follows. Meanwhile, GÓMEZ URBINA *is seen to raise his hand to his chest, totter, and then support himself by holding on to the balcony rail. Ad lib from voices within and without, but before anyone onstage can move,* GÓMEZ URBINA *enters, apparently supporting himself by holding his arm about the* CAPTAIN'S *shoulders, although in reality he is holding the* CAPTAIN *up. When, amidst the general shock and between the two ranks formed by those present,* GÓMEZ URBINA *and the* CAPTAIN *reach centerstage, the* CAPTAIN *slumps down dead. The general stupefaction seems to freeze the silence and preserve it.*

GÓMEZ URBINA (*With a sad smile as he looks at the body of the* CAPTAIN): Poor marksmanship, gentlemen. I hope that his blood will be the last shed in Indoland and that, finally, we'll put an end to our custom of human sacrifice.

During the following simultaneous dialogue, GÓMEZ URBINA *goes to the glass case, takes the national banner from it, and covers the body of the* CAPTAIN *with it.* GENERAL AVALOS *enters while* GÓMEZ URBINA *is doing so.*

CHIEF JUSTICE: After witnessing such an event as this, one must believe in destiny.

GENERAL ELOY: The captain was a hero.

COUNSELOR GERMÁN: His death convinces me. Not another word about an election. Mr. President, you can always count on me.

COUNSELOR AGUIRRE: On all of us!

PRESIDENT OF THE OFFICIAL PARTY: You're our chief forever!

SPEAKER OF CONGRESS: Our guide!

GENERAL PUEBLA: We'll follow you in everything!

DR. SUÁREZ MEZA: And the country will be just what you want it to be.

All at the same time but spoken to GÓMEZ URBINA *so as to be heard individually*

GÓMEZ URBINA (*rises on finishing covering the body of the* CAPTAIN *and finds himself face to face with* AVALOS. *He draws himself up stiffly*): Thank you, gentlemen, but with this young man my own youth has also died. (*A change in manner.*) I thought that I'd given you my last order, General Avalos.

GENERAL AVALOS: Before carrying it out, Mr. President, I request you, for honor's sake, for dignity's sake, to permit me to discover among Matías's friends the author of this attempt on your life which fills me with indignation and sorrow. It was you who was to have been killed. I beg you to believe me.

GÓMEZ URBINA (*looking at him penetratingly*): I believe you, but this doesn't change anything. It's a consequence of the other. Take whatever time you need and then do what I ordered you to.

GENERAL AVALOS: It will be done, Mr. President. You have my word.

GÓMEZ URBINA: And now, gentlemen, we're going to work a transformation in our country. The Constitution, Mr. Chief Justice, will be replaced by another which will foresee . . . (*He stops, smiles and again raises his hands to his chest.*) No . . . no . . . it wasn't so bad after all . . . the marksmanship, I mean. A weak heart doesn't need a bullet through it for it to fail. Captain Peláez . . . (*All look at him in amazement.*) Forgive me, I forgot that you had died for me. In the center drawer of the desk in my private office there's a little, round, black box with some pills which . . . (*He stops, out of breath. The* SECRETARY OF STATE *and the* PRESIDENT OF THE OFFICIAL PARTY *exit hurriedly upstage left and return at once. One has the box of pills and the other a glass of water.* GÓMEZ URBINA *takes two or three pills, then sits down in a chair, center, and smiles.*) Thank you very much, Mr. Secretary. And thank you, Mr. President of the official party. (*For a moment he takes on the look of the* MR. NOBODY *of Act 1.*) This is it . . . a pity . . . too late.

SECRETARY OF COMMUNICATIONS: The president is ill. A——!

SECRETARY OF FINANCE: A doctor! A doctor!

GÓMEZ URBINA: One isn't . . . necessary . . . now. The mainspring has played out and there's no watchmaker who can put a new one in. (*Subdued murmurs and movement.*) Please, I've little time left. No more myths. I'm just one more Indolander who dies while doing his duty. Myths are our greatest enemies. Reality, more reality, like air! As your doctor I order this. (*He pauses for breath.*) General . . . Avalos . . . (AVALOS *draws near.*) You were right . . . The idea . . . save the idea. Amongst our people there should be neither traitors nor tyrants. Take care of them while you live . . . And may you live a long time. (*He smiles.*) Until one of these days, gentlemen . . . (*He closes his eyes and lets his hands fall. The* CHIEF JUSTICE *goes to him and feels his pulse.*)

CHIEF JUSTICE: I'm no doctor, but in my long time I've seen many a person depart from this life. (*He draws himself up solemnly.*) Gentlemen, the president of the Republic is dead.

The curtain falls slowly on the general silence and shock. The solemnity is absolute. The curtain rises immediately on a scene that, unexpectedly, is full of action.

SECRETARY OF WAR: Long live the president of the Republic!

COUNSELOR GERMÁN: Extraordinary to the very end!

SECRETARY OF STATE: Our only statesman!

SECRETARY OF COMMUNICATIONS: A great martyr!

SECRETARY OF PUBLIC EDUCATION: What an example for the coming generations!

COUNSELOR AGUIRRE: A stoic!

SECRETARY OF FINANCE: A Spartan!

SECRETARY OF ECONOMICS: What a loss!

PRESIDENT OF THE OFFICIAL PARTY: The man who was to guide our destinies!

SECRETARY OF AGRICULTURE: The one who had the deepest feeling for the soil of Indoland!

GENERAL AVALOS: Wretched is the country that loses a man like this!

SPEAKER OF CONGRESS: But happy is the country that has won him for its history!

GENERAL ELOY: Gentlemen, come to yourselves. He himself said he didn't want any more myths, didn't he?

CHIEF JUSTICE (*stroking his goatee*): But what can the poor man do about that now?

The curtain falls somewhat more rapidly to rise immediately on the characters who maintain their dema-

*gogic and declamatory postures. The scene imme-
diately fills with action. As each curtain falls and rises,
all the necessary changes of light are to be made.*

SPEAKER OF CONGRESS: With all due respect,
gentlemen, the gravest part of this is that we're back again
where we started. Who's to replace provisionally this great
man?

VOICES (*ad lib*): There's no problem.—None at all.
—The Constitution has provided for this.—We have a
great home secretary.—The home secretary.—Of course,
that's it.—All solved immediately.—And all legal.

HOME SECRETARY: Allow me, gentlemen. Less
than an hour ago I handed in my irrevocable resignation to
President Gómez Urbina. I'm not a politician and I
neither can nor want to launch into politics!

VOICES OF PROTEST (*ad lib*): Ah, no, man!—Come
on!—Don't complicate matters!—This is absurd!—Ridiculous!

HOME SECRETARY: May the idea disturb you at
least somewhat, gentlemen, if it's possible, that amongst
you yourselves you killed this man who had no more
friends here than Captain Peláez and me. I'm leaving and
as I haven't had time to appoint an undersecretary, it's for
you to say whether you're going to put another executive
officer in the president's chair.

*The curtain falls more quickly to rise immediately on
the scene where the action increases rapidly.*

CHIEF JUSTICE: I remind you, gentlemen, that
Congress is now in session. All can, therefore, be carried
out in due order.

SECRETARIES OF WAR, ECONOMICS, FINANCE,
STATE, *and* COMMUNICATIONS, *and* PRESIDENT OF
THE OFFICIAL PARTY (*ad lib*): In that case, I think that
I . . .—By no means, sir, I'm the . . .—That's not so. I . . .
Don't even think of that. I'm the one to carry out his great

program.—Get on with you, man. I, because I . . .—But,
listen to me, all of you.—Why?—Not you, I.—I.—I.—I.—
I.—I.—I.—I.—I.—I.

>The curtain to which has been attached the national
>emblem with the motto. "Indoland Undivided and
>Free," falls quickly on the squabble.